The Rise to Respectability

The Rise to Respectability

Race, Religion, and the
Church of God in Christ

Calvin White Jr.

The University of Arkansas Press
FAYETTEVILLE • 2012

ISBN-10: 1-55728-977-8
ISBN-13: 978-1-55728-977-3

16   15   14   13   12   5   4   3   2   1

Text design by Ellen Beeler

⊗ The paper used in this publication meets the minimum requirements of the American National Standard for Permanence of Paper for Printed Library Materials Z39.48-1984.

Library of Congress Cataloging-in-Publication Data

White, Calvin, 1973–
    The rise to respectability : race, religion, and the Church of God in Christ / Calvin White, Jr.
        p. cm.
    Includes bibliographical references and index.
    ISBN 978-1-55728-977-3 (cloth : alk. paper)
    1. Church of God in Christ—History. 2. Mason, C. H. (Charles Harrison), 1866–1961. 3. African Americans—Religion. 4. United States—Church history. I. Title.
    BX7056.A4W45 2012
    289.9'4--dc23

2012022538

In loving memory of my grandmother, Adeline D. Walker (Big Mama), and my aunt, Emma Stigger, who both lived this and passed it on to me.

They lived their lives by the words in the song below, which they sang to me as a child.

I Am on the Battlefield for My Lord

I am on the battlefield for my Lord.
I'm on the battlefield for my Lord,
and I promised Him that I
would serve Him 'til I die;
I'm on the battlefield for my Lord.

I was alone and idle, I was a sinner too.
I heard a voice from heaven say there is work to do.
I took the Master's hand, and I joined the Christian band;
I'm on the battlefield for my Lord.

I left my friends and kindred bound for the Promised Land,
the grace of God upon me, the Bible in my hands.
In distant lands I trod, crying sinner come to God;
I'm on the battlefield for my Lord.

Now when I met my Savior, I met Him with a smile,
He healed my wounded spirit, and owned me as His child.
Around the throne of grace, He appoints my soul a place;
I'm on the battlefield for my Lord.

I am on the battlefield for my Lord.
I'm on the battlefield for my Lord,
and I promised Him that I
would serve Him 'til I die;
I'm on the battlefield for my Lord

—song written by Sylvana Bell and E. V. Banks

Contents

Preface

In many ways, this research project started years ago when I inadvertently over-heard what black people refer to as "grown folks' conversation" after a friend's mother whispered something about "those sanctified folks." Aware that her comment was not intended to be a compliment, I remained puzzled by what she actually meant as I was one of those sanctified folks and just about everyone who had made any lasting impact upon my life up to that point had also been one of those sanctified folks. As an undergraduate, the meaning of her comment became clearer as I began to see the historical class divisions within the African American community and I slowly came to understand that oftentimes within the black community, religious denominations reflected one's class standing.

With the emerging self-help movement, blacks argued for a more dignified worship experience that reinforced the rising status of the race. In the process, some in the black community deemed "sanctified folks" or followers of Holiness as unsupportive of the efforts of uplift because of their refusal to abandon charismatic worship styles that many educated blacks began to view as neither right nor proper. Pentecostalism remained left out of the conversation and few mentions of how this religious movement shaped its members' worldview exist. During the late nineteenth and early twentieth centuries, as blacks focused on respectability and educating the race, those who joined the Pentecostal move-ment often found that their new religion contained within itself a natural ten-sion between an inward-looking, Holiness-based restorationist vision and the outward-looking progressive, self-help movement. However, through closer examination, I found that Pentecostals in fact supported racial uplift and, although it may have looked differently due to their strict adherence to sanctifi-cation, they offered relief to the poor and subscribed to respectable standards of behavior in much the same manner as their Baptist and Methodist counterparts.

Consequently, this project grew out of my desire to answer the question I had pondered for years, and an attempt to offer a revisionist historical interpre-tation of the denomination led me to the difficult task of writing a book about Charles Harrison Mason and the Church of God in Christ (COGIC). Let me first say with no ambiguity that this work is not an apologetic interpretation of COGIC, nor is it meant to paint its early membership as misunderstood martyrs who were unduly persecuted by the larger black community. Instead, the follow-ing pages reveal that the denomination's members were anything but docile victims. They suffered from all the frailties of humanity as they often sued one another in the court system, projected their righteous indignation upon nonbelievers, and bitterly fought over church property and money. At the same time, the reader will see that as members desperately tried to hold onto their religious beliefs, they also supported racial uplift, helped to shape the American historical narrative, and profoundly influenced African American culture. For instance, one cannot turn on a radio today and not hear COGIC's influence upon popular music, which began with gospel music and figures such as Sister Rosetta Tharpe and Al Green, who rose from COGIC's ranks.[1]

Additionally, this book is not intended to represent the most astute theological interpretation of Pentecostalism; instead, I am a historian and I examine COGIC within a historical lens. The book reveals that the denomination represents a microcosm of the African American experience. Rooted in the hardships of slavery and coming of age during the Jim Crow era, COGIC's story is more than a religious debate between competing progressive and conservative clergymen. Rather, this book sees the history of the church as interwoven with the Great Migration, the struggle of modernity, class tension, and racial animosity—all representative parts of the African American experience in America.

Acknowledgments

Impoverished and often uneducated, COGIC's early membership left little to no official records; however, this makes their story no less worthy of being told. In an effort to author this history, every known small cache of primary source materials has been mined for this book. At times, to capture their story, I had to depend on secondary source materials and previously published works on the denomination. Often frustrated by the lack of primary source materials and a hesitancy to accept only one's memory as confirmation of a story or event, this work was completed with the help of countless people who said, "I think they might have sources," or others who literally shared their materials with me.[1]

Ironically, similar to COGIC members digging out a congregation, some of my research trips took me down dusty roads in Holmes County, Mississippi, in attempts to interview Dovie Marie Johnson, a lady who amazed me with her personal insight to Charles Mason. She told me countless stories (many not used in this book) but only after I ran her errands around the small town of Lexington. Also, Elder William Dean, the pastor of St. Paul Church of God in Christ, gave me personal tours of Lexington and shared sites with me that would have never shown up on maps in the state archives. From Lexington, I traveled north on Interstate 55 to Memphis, Tennessee, where the University of Memphis Special Collections Room, the Memphis Public Library, and the Shelby County Archives provided excellent resources for this project. A very special thanks must be given to the late Oddie Tolbert, an employee of the University of Memphis and COGIC member who had the presence of mind to keep yearbooks and church annuals that form the foundation of the collection housed in the Memphis area archives. Those that Mr. Tolbert did not personally donate, historian Elton Weavers helped to locate and then donated his finds to the local archives. After I completed my research in Memphis, the Gilder Lerhman Institute awarded me a Schomburg Fellowship that allowed me to travel to Harlem, New York, where special collections at the Schomburg Center for Research in Black Culture provided me with valuable early primary source materials including the Sherri Dupree Collection, which makes up one of the largest archival collections of black Pentecostals known to exist. The materials contained sparse copies of the *Truth* and a treasure trove of other sources about COGIC and the black Pentecostal experience.

At the end of the fellowship and when research money became scarce, archivists at the Flowers Pentecostal Heritage Center in Springfield, Missouri, graciously copied every known source they housed on COGIC and mailed the information to me. Included were pictures of Mason and other members of the early church. I must say, to all the archivists, librarians, and county clerks who aided in my research process, thank you. Thank you also to the staff at the University of Mississippi and University of Arkansas interlibrary loan offices for the long hours and assistance, and to the staff at the Arkansas Historical Commission, the Mississippi Historical Commission, and the many others who helped me research this project.

On a more personal note, I would first like to thank my wife, Shatara Porchia-White, for her love, support, and understanding. Without her, this work could not have been completed. I express my gratitude and love to Adeline D. Walker, my grandmother, who deserves all the credit for who I am today. Thanks to Calvin and Dorothy White Sr., my parents, and my siblings, Patricia, Anthony, Janette, Stanley, Rodney, Tawanna, and Anjalenia, who all taught me life lessons in their own way. A special thanks to Joseph Ward, Robert Haws, Theman Taylor, and Harry Readnour, who convinced me to attend the University of Mississippi and to think about life in the long term. My major professor Ted Ownby, the chair of my studies, deserves a great deal of credit for his constant editing, suggestions, and guidance throughout my work on this project. I greatly appreciate the advice of other professors, Nancy Bercaw, Charles Ross, and Ethel Young-Minor, whose suggestions aided in the completion of this research project. Also a very special thanks to Professor Brett Shadle, who traveled with me to Africa and deserves the credit for opening my mind to the global black experience.

I would like to extend a special thanks to Parnell Henderson, a wonderful man and boss, who gave me the opportunity to begin my teaching career under the watchful care of "real teachers." I thank Dr. Winthrop Jordan, the University of Mississippi Graduate School, Mr. and Mrs. J. L. Holloway, Robert C. and Sandra Connor, and the Gilder-Lehrman Institute of American History for their gracious financial support. I have continued to receive the support of my colleagues at the University of Arkansas. I could not have asked for a better person to mentor me as an assistant professor than Elliott West. I have also had the opportunity to work under two great department chairs, Jeannie Whayne and Lynda Coon, and a terrific graduate student, Mary Margaret Hui. Last but certainly not least, I would like to thank the University of Arkansas Press and all the staff members that supported this book and made sure it saw the light of day. Thanks to Larry Malley who first took notice of this project when I was still a graduate student. Additionally, I would like to thank Julie Watkins, Deena Owens, and Melissa King for all their hard work and patience in the production stage of this book. I conclude with a special thanks to my friends Charles Robinson II, Scott Varady, Michael Williams, Jonathan Hutchinson, Emily Machen, Benjamin Purvis, Chris Danielson, Charles "Chuck" Westmorland, Vincent "Vince-a-Rooney" Lowery, Benjamin Grob-Fitzgibbon, and James Gigantino, who read this manuscript and listened to me complain hours upon hours about this project.

The Rise to Respectability

Introduction

The Roots of the Study

During the late nineteenth and early twentieth centuries, heated debates erupted over vestiges of black religious traditions rooted in slavery. A new younger, educated progressive class of clergymen argued for a more dignified religious experience, while black Holiness believers, often composed of uneducated ex-slave preachers, stood in opposition, holding on to rituals such as shouting, dancing, and charismatic preaching, and the church served as their battleground.[1] Followers of Holiness rejected the modernization of black religious practices and as the movement spread, Charles Harrison Mason and Charles Price Jones emerged as its two most significant leaders. In the eyes of progressives, however, Holiness seemed incompatible with the values of the new rising black middle class and emerging self-help movement that stressed a refined rational religious liturgy. Despite disapproval, Holiness persevered and congregations composed of rural uneducated blacks in Arkansas, Mississippi, and Tennessee laid the foundation for what became the largest African American Pentecostal group in the world.[2]

Several scholars contributed to the theoretical framework in which I place Charles Mason and his religious followers. First, Laurie Maffly-Kipp influenced the conceptualization of this project when she argued, "After emancipation, generally, rural blacks tended to cling more tenaciously to older customs and traditional forms of worship, but in southern cities [such as Little Rock and Memphis] with the growing numbers of educated African Americans also grew their interest in a more rationalized uniform religious experience."[3] This meant that by the 1880s, the battle lines over the future of African American religion had been drawn and Evelyn Brooks Higginbotham reinforced my thinking when she stated, "At one extreme existed the ranks of black educators, lawyers, and ministers who had grown conscious of their class status, and culturally alienated from the masses of the less educated."[4]

Theologian David Daniels shows that the framework is not new and had been first invoked around the turn of the twentieth century when he revealed that Carter G. Woodson, the father of African American history, identified a "generational gap that resulted in conflicting concepts of black religion as blacks transitioned from slavery to freedom." Woodson identified the groups as "a conservative majority and a progressive minority within the African American churches," who "fought to control the future of black Christianity." To Woodson, "the progressives advocated for a reshaped and reorganized church designed to increase its usefulness in helping uplift the black masses, while the conservatives acted as perpetuators of the old time slave religion." Woodson also described the progressives as "committed to education, innovation, and worldliness but labeled the conservatives as being bound by ignorance, wild emotion, and dimwittedness."[5]

It would be within this transformative period that Mason, a conservative, came of age and formulated his own ideas about religion, resulting in the formation of the largest black Pentecostal denomination known as the Church of God in Christ. Headquartered in Memphis, Tennessee, COGIC, at the time of Mason's death in 1961, possessed a membership that arguably numbered nearly half a million. Today, the denomination consists of nearly five million members and is debatably the fourth-largest religious organization in the United States. The denomination whose earliest roots lie in the Arkansas-Mississippi Delta also has a thriving presence in Africa, Europe, and the Caribbean. Yet, the scholarly neglect of Mason and COGIC is striking, as no academic work offers a comprehensive history of the Church of God in Christ or details the life of its founder.[6]

With the study of black Pentecostalism emerging as a new field of historiography, scholars have begun to ask new questions and examine the effects of the Holiness-Pentecostal movement upon African American history. Furthermore, they have come to realize that a group as large as COGIC could not have existed for more than a century without affecting the larger African American community. Most books, articles, and dissertations dealing with Pentecostals, however, mention COGIC as a side note or, at best, devote chapter-length attention to the religious organization and its members. For example, Grant Wacker's *Heaven Below: Early Pentecostals and American Culture* and his and James Goff's *Portraits of a Generation: Early Pentecostal Leaders* offer the most astute interpretations of first-generation Pentecostalism written, but both works mention COGIC only occasionally.[7] David Daniels, one of the foremost authorities on African American Pentecostals, in his 1992 dissertation, "The Cultural Renewal of Slave Religion: Charles Price Jones and the Emergence of the Holiness Movement in Mississippi," makes reference to Charles Harrison Mason, but Jones and the Church of God are Daniels's principle focus of study while COGIC remains in the shadows.[8]

In more recent publications, John Giggie's *After Redemption* examines the transformation of African American religion in the Arkansas-Mississippi Delta, while Randall Stephens's *The Fire Spreads* offers a compelling overview of the role of Pentecostalism in America, refuting what he views as an overused argument that Pentecostals were simply a lower-class uneducated group of worshipers. Again, Mason and COGIC are not principle subjects of study. While Anthea Butler's publication *Women in the Church of God in Christ* offers a full-length monograph, her major focus centered on the roles women played and not the denomination as a whole. Therefore, to fill the hole in the current historiography, this book places Mason and COGIC at the center of an academic monograph while also exploring the extent to which class, respectability, and the efforts of racial uplift intersected in the development of African Americans' religious life after emancipation. More important, my aim is to add another layer to the historiographical debate, blending Daniels's work with the more recent scholarship and arguing that Mason and the development of COGIC cannot fully be understood without recognizing its roots in slavery.[9]

However, COGIC's membership did not remain static and the successive chapters detail how the Pentecostal denomination dealt with the tensions of the recovery of African-based religious practice together with the extremely stringent standard of "bourgeois" behavior imposed on churchgoers as they transitioned from the southern rural areas into the urban centers of the South and North. Recognizing this, I incorporate the works of Butler, Giggie, Stephens, and Harvey, highlighting that under the influence of sanctification, COGIC accepted or rejected progressive ideas on its own terms as it grew into a black religious mainstay. This study moves beyond the previous research, providing the first full-length academic-study of COGIC from its inception to the civil rights movement, arguing that the emerging self-help movement within the African American community profoundly affected the development of COGIC.[10]

In chapter 1, I detail the early life of Charles H. Mason and analyze the motivating factors that led Mason to join the Holiness movement. The chapter also examines the lives and contributions of Charles P. Jones and other relatively unknown Holiness leaders in Arkansas and Mississippi who had a profound effect on Mason's life and spiritual development. While two articles have dealt more exclusively with COGIC and Mason as their primary subjects, they produced a limited history of the denomination. The first, Elton Weavers's article "The Metamorphosis of Charles Harrison Mason: The Origins of Black Pentecostal Churches in Tennessee," offers excellent insight into the personal character of COGIC's founder. Weavers theorizes that after Mason's near-death experience during childhood he "metamorphosed" into the man he became.[11] While Mason's brush with death shaped his faith, chapter 1 of this research simply places Mason into the context of the larger struggle occurring between the "progressives" and "conservatives" over the future of black religious traditions.[12]

Weavers's article also largely focuses on the activities of Mason once he settled in Memphis, leaving untold his early activities in Mississippi and Arkansas. Using a recently discovered court case, church yearbooks, and oral interviews, chapter 2 of this monograph will provide an in-depth history of Mason's earlier activities in Arkansas and Mississippi, which contributed to the official formation of the Church of God in Christ. In this chapter I analyze the contentious break between Mason and Jones, revealing much of the resentment and jealously that arose as the friends separated over the issue of glossolalia. In addition, I highlight the public discourse over the issues of right and proper religious practices as local newspapers began reporting on the charismatic worship occurring in Mason's congregation.

In chapter 3 I examine Mason's so-called opposition to World War I and expand upon Theodore Kornweibel's article, "Bishop C. H. Mason and the Church of God in Christ during World War I: The Perils of Conscientious Objection," which details the Federal Bureau of Investigation (FBI) surveillance of Mason during World War I.[13] While Kornweibel produced an excellent article about COGIC's objection to the war, this chapter, through the reevaluation of governmental records and oral interviews, attempts to produce a more detailed narrative of the sequence of events that occurred in Memphis, Tennessee, Lexington, Mississippi, and Paris, Texas, from 1917 to 1918. Kornweibel concluded that COGIC's pacifism remained a part of a much larger movement composed of religious objectors who stood in opposition to the war and that, in reality, the denomination harbored no true objections to the war outside of their religious theology. Although those findings are true, I also argue that due to the interracial nature of Pentecostalism, whites often mistakenly viewed white Holiness-Pentecostal preachers' interactions with black congregations to be subversive, which also helped bring the denomination to the attention of federal authorities.

The international aspect of COGIC remains one of the most woefully understudied facets of the denomination. Walter L. Williams's *Black Americans and the Evangelization of Africa* remains the standard that shaped the historiography on black missionary efforts in Africa, arguing that at the turn of the twentieth century, black Baptists, African Methodist Episcopal Church members, and Presbyterians all took an interest in uplifting blacks not only in America, but also in Africa.[14] Additionally, historian Sylvia M. Jacobs added to the historiography when she authored *Black Americans and the Missionary Movement in Africa*. Jacobs speculated that during the first years of the twentieth century the most important issue facing Americans was human progress and civilization. Most white Americans believed that Anglo-Saxon life and culture represented values of universal application that should be applied to African Americans and the continent of Africa. Jacobs theorized that "blacks in America took the lead using missionary work and the self-help movement to persuade blacks in America and Africa to subscribe to Victorian practices."[15]

Jacobs and Williams both chronicle the missionary efforts of the major black denominations, but their works failed to include the missionary work of any Pentecostal denominations. Today, COGIC has a worldwide presence worthy of study and chapter 4 will focus attention on the denomination's international efforts in West Africa, the Caribbean, and Europe. Moreover, the chapter reveals that COGIC missionaries adopted Victorian principles of respectability and imposed these values under the guise of sanctification throughout their missions. In the same vein as John Giggie's *After Redemption*, the chapter reveals that COGIC abandoned its initial efforts of apostolic purity and embraced many of the values of the denominational churches. More specific than Giggie, I link COGIC's initial push toward social respectability to the denomination's missionary effort in Africa by showing that COGIC's leadership also saw the futility of uplifting the race in America while whites continued to view Africa as a backward heathenish place.

Research revealed that COGIC women led the denomination's missionary efforts in many parts of the world, and consequently, gender became an unexpected subtheme of chapter 4. Anthea Butler, one of the leading authorities on the subject of COGIC women, shows that although COGIC's ordained leadership roles were exclusively male, the denomination's women acted as teachers, enforcers, and modelers of Holiness-Pentecostal beliefs through their organization and participation in what she termed a "sanctified life." Her study views the official role of "Church Mothers" as an un-ordained leadership position that possesses great spiritual power within the congregation. I assert that women also used the Home and Foreign Mission Board as a special domain in which they enforced and spread the standards of respectability under the guise of sanctification throughout COGIC's missionary efforts abroad.[16]

While continuing the march toward respectability, the city of Memphis remained conducive for the growth of the denomination, as chapter 5 reveals. During the years of the Great Migration, Memphis became a popular destination for poor rural Delta blacks, and this ever-increasing population brought Mason a steady flow of converts who transplanted their religious customs and traditions once practiced on plantations into urban Memphis. With the tremendous growth, COGIC quickly became the largest black denomination represented in the city, giving it local respectability among the white population and, in later years, even among the black middle class.

As COGIC's membership advanced educationally, they recognized the profound contradictions of their theology, which taught "of the world but not in the world." When the national civil rights movement began, COGIC found it impossible to maintain a passive stance toward the movement as its members indirectly pulled the denomination into several national civil rights events. For example, Clenora Hudson-Weems's *Emmett Till: The Sacrificial Lamb of the Civil Rights Movement* argued that the lynching of Emmett Till remains one of the most understudied catalysts of the national movement and that the family's decision to hold an open casket viewing forced the United States to confront its problems with race. Although Hudson-Weems acknowledges that the Tills were members of COGIC, the denomination's efforts in the movement are not analyzed and remain absent from the narrative. Therefore, chapter 6 examines COGIC's stance on civil rights issues and how the denomination's educated second-generation membership forced the church to move from reluctant to active participant in the civil rights movement, which stirred an activist spirit within the denomination. Furthermore, I surmise that the lynching of Till overwhelmingly caused blacks to stand up (including COGIC) for their rights as many felt that their perceived silence somehow condoned the act. Moreover, it would be within the context of the coming of the civil rights movement that COGIC took its final step from a backwoods to a mainstream religious denomination.[17]

The Emergence of Holiness

Initially a biracial movement, Holiness emerged in the late eighteenth century as a result of white members' disgust with the Methodist Episcopal Church. According to historian Vinson Synan, "They missed the so-called 'old institutions' such as camp meetings and the emphasis of plainness in dress, as young ministers looked toward innovations such as robed choirs, organs, and seminary-trained ministers." Many feared that "if the practice of camp meetings ceased, then the heroic fire of Methodism would also die and the religious apathy of the times could be remedied with the return to the camp meeting revivalism that preceded the Civil War."[18]

The movement climaxed when, in 1867, ministers who followed Reverend John S. Inskip, pastor of the Green Street Methodist Episcopal Church in New York City, issued a call that started the National Camp Meeting Association for the Promotion of Christian Holiness. The association called, "Come brothers and sisters of the various denominations, and let us, in these forest-meetings, as in other meetings for the promotions of Holiness, furnish an illustration of evangelical union, and make common supplication for the descent of the Spirit upon ourselves, the church, the nation, and the world."[19]

In 1867 the Vineland Camp Meeting Association met in New Jersey for the purpose of promoting a renewed interest in an emotional worship experience.

Many also saw the Holiness revivals as a unifying force that could help reunite Methodism. The Holiness camp meetings provided the opportunity for Methodists of the North and South to come together on a common platform and begin healing the break caused by the Civil War and the question of slavery that had created a divisive regional split within the denomination. Supporters of Holiness often looked beyond race, which allowed them to transcend the racial barriers of post-Reconstruction America. For example, they often worshiped with blacks, as the ideals of Holiness, which placed an emphasis on an intense emotional religious experience, were characteristic of black worship traditions. As the camp meetings spread, black and white Christians met and sang, preached, and testified together in an emotional style reminiscent of earlier religious customs practiced in clandestine slave meetings.[20]

In 1875 controversy arose in the Holiness movement as a radical sect within Holiness in the South began spreading the doctrine of sanctification that stressed personal standards of dress, pure living, and avoiding worldly amusements. Sanctification adherents also condemned the summer resort atmosphere of the camp meetings, and what they believed to be the growing coldness and formality of religious practice, even within the Holiness movement. Loyal Methodists became alarmed over new doctrinal emphases such as sinless perfection, that a believer could live free of sin, as well as strict requirements that truly sanctified believers abstain from such indulgences as coffee, pork, doctor visits, and prescribed medicines. These doctrinal and moral issues embedded themselves in the South, and as a result, the move to curtail and eliminate the new fanaticism became particularly strong in the region.[21]

Traditional Methodist clergy began to resent the Holiness associations specifically; clergy members accused the Holiness associations of teaching "glossolalia," the religious principle of speaking in tongues that Methodists believed to be a heretical doctrine. A turning point occurred in 1894 when the bishops of the Methodist Episcopal Church South ratified a statement opposing the so-called radicals of Holiness. Their announcement proclaimed that "there has sprung up among us a party with holiness as a watchword; they have holiness association, [H]oliness meeting, holiness preacher, holiness evangelist, and holiness property." The administrative council further claimed that they did not "question the sincerity and zeal of these brethren," as they hoped "the church would profit by their earnest preaching and godly example." However, the council "deplored their teaching and methods in so far as they claim a monopoly of the experience, practice, and advocacy of Holiness, and separate themselves from the body of ministers and disciples."[22]

The bishops' message disavowed the new developments within the Holiness movement, enacting legislation that forbade Holiness evangelists and their associations within the Methodist denomination—something that black mainstream religious denominations would also later do. By 1895, mostly in the South and Midwest, approximately twenty Holiness organizations existed among white Protestants. Even among them, bitter controversy arose over various interpretations of sanctification, giving rise to twenty-three new groups between the years of 1893 and 1900. "No other period in religious history witnessed the creation of so many new religious groups centered around a central issue in such a short period of time." Similar schisms also occurred within African American denominations, which led to the birth of the black Holiness movement and, ultimately, the Church of God in Christ.[23]

The immense contributions of COGIC to the black church, the Holiness movement, and Pentecostalism, beyond a shadow of doubt, influenced black religious life. COGIC also did more than simply affect black spirituality; the denomination became a part of the African American historical narrative as small COGIC congregations became active participants in local communities throughout the country, providing more than a worship experience for its members. These churches acted as self-help institutions where many of the poorest segments of the population found spiritual as well as secular relief.

1

In the Beginning, There Stood Two

The Reconstruction of African American Religion and the Birth of the Black Holiness Movement

Charles Harrison Mason: The Charismatic

The specifics of Charles Harrison Mason's birth remain a point of contention among historians.[1] A historical marker located at the corner of 930 Mason Street in Memphis reads that Mason's life began in 1862 on a plantation near Bartlett, Tennessee, while the Arkansas census claims it began on September 8, 1866, the son of former slaves Jeremiah and Eliza Mason.[2] Whatever Mason's date of birth, the Evergreen Plantation, located on the outskirts of Memphis, clearly provided his earliest memories and his most vivid recollections of his mother. Born in Charlotte County, Virginia, in 1824, Eliza Mason became a victim of the domestic slave trade, which at its height during the 1830s relocated thousands of slaves from Virginia and Maryland to the cotton-producing states of the South. Remembered as a devout Christian, she exposed her children to a religious culture composed of emotional prayer, song, dance, and most important of all, clandestine "brush harbor" meetings. As a slave, Eliza almost certainly participated in these religious gatherings where under the cover of darkness and shrouded in secrecy, slaves "stole away" to pray, dance, and sing late into the night. Historian Albert Raboteau summarized, "slaves frequently held their own religious meetings due to the disgust for sermons that taught obedience to their masters." In slave-led gatherings, however, blacks prayed and poured out their needs to God as services usually climaxed when a slave preacher delivered a sermon about the invisible hand of God working to secure their freedom. Peter Randolph, an ex-slave and Baptist minister, offered a firsthand account of these meetings when he reminisced, "Slaves assembled in swamps away from the reach of the patrols," and once everyone arrived, "preaching and singing occurred until people got happy and both men and women fell to the ground under the influence of the [S]pirit."[3] Brush harbors gave blacks religious autonomy and became an important component of slave religious culture, and after emancipation, many, including Eliza, continued to adhere to these practices, which profoundly influenced their children.[4]

With the conclusion of the Civil War, the Masons saw that Republicans advocated for black political and social rights; however, it became evident that southern resistance would not allow them or any other blacks to achieve full equality. Republican efforts to secure blacks' civil rights came to an end in 1877 as a result of the disputed presidential election of 1876. In an attempt to maintain control of the White House, Republicans agreed to conclude Reconstruction and withdraw federal forces from the South. In return, southern Democrats regained control of state governments and implemented a rigid social hierarchical system predicated upon black submissiveness and economic exploitation in the form of sharecropping.[5]

Designed as a system of peonage, sharecropping replaced the plantation system after the Civil War. Although technically free, blacks continued to labor under repressive conditions, experiencing little to no economic independence as planters fixed exorbitant interest rates on crop returns. Many signed or "made their marks" on contracts that literally re-enslaved them. For instance, labor agreements dictated the required daily work hours in the fields, the times a laborer could take breaks, and some even restricted visitations during work hours. If workers broke these rules, planters levied excessive fines that were added to a laborer's bill at the end of harvest. Although both blacks and whites became victims of the system, sharecropping, coupled with Jim Crow, overwhelmingly became the freedmen's economic curse.[6]

Life for blacks in Tennessee grew even worse when, in 1878, a mild winter produced conditions conducive to an outbreak of yellow fever. In July, newspapers first reported the epidemic in the city of New Orleans; consequently, Memphis officials immediately established checkpoints at points of entry into their city. Despite officials' best efforts, by August Memphis reported its first deaths and within weeks, thousands of residents, including the Masons, fled the city.[7] The *Arkansas Gazette* reported on the flight of blacks from Shelby County when the paper indicated that Conway County, Arkansas, had become the new Kansas as one thousand blacks from Tennessee settled in the region.[8] Blacks congregated to the north of the Arkansas River, which ran through the county, in an area known as Howard Township, established in 1862. The constant flooding of the river gave Howard rich soil, making the area suitable for commercial crop production. In typical southern fashion, planters owned much of the land and black migrants supplied the labor force, resulting in a classic southern agricultural culture.[9]

While prompted to move because of the yellow fever epidemic, blacks had also heard of job opportunities, cheap land, and better living conditions in Kansas, and Arkansas, which had attractions of its own, lay along their route. A labor shortage existed in the state and farmers, businessmen, and railroad promoters welcomed black immigrants. Labor agents gave exaggerated descriptions of Arkansas as a new Africa, a "tropical place where plenty of fruit grew" and blacks also viewed the state as a possible safe haven from social and economic oppression. For instance, black steamboat passengers headed west frequently stopped in Helena where they observed a thriving black merchant class. Even Helena's working class seemed to fare better, making their living not as sharecroppers, but on the docks along the Mississippi River.[10]

Similar to hundreds of other families, the Masons settled in Howard, Arkansas. They found none of the economic prosperity they had hoped for, but Mason's parents found employment as sharecroppers and continued the labor practices they had while still enslaved.[11] Educational opportunities also remained poor as county officials provided limited opportunities for blacks. Southern whites frowned upon educating black children, claiming, "Teachers acted more as political emissaries" teaching doctrines of "social equality." Local whites insisted that northern teachers were especially problematic because they "displayed bad character" and made black schools centers of "potential trouble." Such attitudes toward educating blacks forced Mason into the fields, representing a defining moment in his life; without a secular education, his worldview continued to be rooted in slave traditions of the past, which shaped his future religious outlook.[12]

As he grew older, his belief in his slave ancestors' Christian practices of root work, superstition, and visions grew stronger. Evidence of this appeared in the summer of 1880, when at the age of fourteen, Mason contracted a fever.[13] During what has been described as a near-death experience, he believed God revealed to him images of heaven and the horrors of hell in a series of dreams. Spared from death, his fever broke, giving greater strength to his religious convictions.[14] Church historian James Counts recalled the recovery when he wrote, "On the first Sunday morning in September 1880 the glory of God came down upon him in his bed." Mason awakened and "walked out upon the threshold of the door, looking up to heaven" praising God for his recovery. Immediately, Mason dressed himself and began to witness to neighbors as "he went skipping along and rejoicing over the light of salvation that was shining . . . in his soul."[15]

In all probability, the Masons did not escape yellow fever as medical findings reveal that hallucinations occur within the first two to three days of the illness, which offers a rational explanation for the visions.[14] Convinced, nonetheless, that divine intervention saved him from death, Mason dedicated his life to serving God and the following year, Israel S. Nelson, his half-brother, formally baptized him into the Baptist faith. Although the details of the next decade of Mason's life remain obscure, most scholars believe he spent the 1880s working in the fields and helping his brother pastor the Mt. Olive Missionary Baptist Church in Howard.[16]

More important, the 1880s became a critical transformative period that brought both religious and cultural changes for blacks. With the triumph of white supremacy and the codification of Jim Crow laws, the church became the center of blacks' public and private spheres. Many believed it to be a necessity that clergymen now not only looked after the spiritual needs of their congregations, but also stressed the usefulness of the church as a means of challenging segregation.[17] In the opinion of the great intellectual W. E. B. Du Bois, black preachers should serve as "leaders, politicians, and idealists" as they used their pulpits to better the race.[18] In 1891, at the age of twenty-five, Mason formally joined the ranks of the black clergy when he received a ministerial license from the Mt. Gale Missionary Baptist Church in Preston, Arkansas. But despite his ordination and licensure, he delayed dedicating himself fully to the ministry, recalling, "I petitioned God for three things: an education, a wife, and a house paid for," and afterward, he insisted that "my life may be turned over to the ministry."[19] Believing that God heard his prayers, Mason wed Alice Saxton in 1892, but the marriage soon fell into turmoil. Keeping his promise to God, Mason continued to preach, but Alice objected to the lifestyle of a preacher's wife. Constant travels yielding little or no money led to the demise of their marriage and in 1893 the two divorced. Free of marital responsibility, Mason moved to Little Rock in November and enrolled in Arkansas Baptist College.[20]

Deemed the most important aspect of racial uplift, blacks' pursuit of formal education after slavery became their number-one priority. The success of Booker T. Washington served as an example of what could be accomplished with hard work and thrift. Washington's achievements as a student at Hampton Institute and his work in establishing Tuskegee inspired other blacks to duplicate his efforts in helping to educate the black masses. Also recognizing the importance of education, the Colored Baptist Association of Arkansas proposed the establishment of an institute of higher learning at their annual convention in Hot Springs in August 1884. Elias Camp Morris, the president of the association and a man who would rise to a leadership position among black Baptists nationally, argued that black Arkansans needed a better trained clergy to model proper social behaviors while also caring for the spiritual needs of the people.[21]

In spite of his friendship with Booker T. Washington, Morris refused to believe blacks could only prosper in the South through industrial education. He believed that vocational training might suffice in the short term, but true progress for the race would come only with the acquisition of a liberal arts education. Watching blacks "hanging around" and falling victim to black codes such as vagrancy laws that forced them back into the service of planters and former owners disturbed Morris. Additionally, the widely held beliefs among many that they still needed whites for guidance troubled him as well. He believed blacks should open their own businesses, establish banks, and publish periodicals to disseminate what they had learned in the process of becoming business owners.[22]

For Morris, blacks' future in the South rested on continued economic and social improvements and their gradual acceptance by white southerners. With this philosophy of self-help and self-reliance, the Colored Baptist Association of Arkansas founded the Ministers Institute in November 1884 in the basement of Mt. Zion Missionary Baptist Church. Renamed Arkansas Baptist College in September 1885, the institution became the flagship for black Baptist education in the state, attracting men from as far away as Alabama and Georgia.[23]

Mason's studies at Arkansas Baptist lasted only three months; he later reflected on his short-lived stay when he remembered, "I thought education would help me out in my preaching, but it was not God's plan." He believed that God had shown him "that there was no salvation in schools, and colleges, for the way they conducted themselves grieved my soul." In rejecting Arkansas Baptist's educational system, Mason claimed that he had "bade them a final farewell to follow Jesus, with the Bible as my sacred guide."[24] He offered no further specifics about his dissatisfaction with Arkansas Baptist, but his departure might be explained by the college's new interpretation of the scripture.

In the era of post-Reconstruction racial uplift that stressed education, Arkansas Baptist instructed ministers to interpret the Bible using an intellectual lens that emphasized the importance of reason and scholarly criticism and discouraged the use of prophetic prophesies, root work, and over emotionalism, which had once been at the center of slave religion. Rooted in the religious slave tradition of his mother, however, Mason viewed the Bible as the infallible word of God and objected to a curriculum that insisted ministers "master New Testament Greek, theology, and Church history."[25] More important, his decision to leave school placed him among the rank-and-file of a growing group of black clergymen who would become known for their efforts to conserve elements of slave religion. Departing Little Rock in February 1894, Mason returned home where he joined the black Holiness movement, a conservative religious reaction against those who sought to modernize and refine religious traditions as part of the racial uplift movement.[26]

Blacks across the South rejected the modernization efforts for many reasons. A congregation in Savannah, Georgia, for example, "branded a cleric as evil" because he supported "the necessity of an intelligent Christian experience" and rejected the "root work, superstition, and belief in dreams and visions" associated with slave religion. Many blacks believed the surge in denominationalism to be a great source of harm, fearing that it symbolized a growing institutionalization of black religious life. A Baptist missionary in Mississippi recorded his unsuccessful attempt at preaching to a local congregation about involvement in denominational work. Historian Paul Harvey noted, "Upon arriving at the church, the newcomer discovered that the pastor had gotten it into his head that the missionary wanted to reign over him as a king. So, the pastor instructed church officers to shut the doors and refuse the missionary entry."[27]

Exactly how Mason became aware of the Holiness movement may never be known, but source materials suggest two prominent black Holiness members who might have introduced him to the movement. The first, William Christian, an ex-slave and Baptist minister who lived in Wrightsville, Arkansas, and preached throughout the Delta, had grown frustrated with the evolution of black Christianity since emancipation. According to John Giggie, "Christian believed that blacks had grown distant from the simplicity of the early Christian church of their ancestors." In Christian's opinion, "black Baptists and Methodists had exchanged emotional worship for a more reserved style and had come mistakenly to believe that faith meant quiet inward study, padded pews, and an educated minister to uplift the race."[28]

Christian's frustration centered around a growing black middle class that perceived religion in more sophisticated terms. Viewed as a powerful force within the black community, class distinction shaped every aspect of black life, including religion. Scipio A. Jones, a prominent black lawyer in Little Rock, reflected the growing middle-class status of blacks in Arkansas. Known to friends as a "good Methodist," Jones owned several businesses and attended the Bethel AME Church, which possessed the wealthiest black membership in the city.[29] The rural community of Hope, Arkansas, also boasted a small but influential black middle class. Referred to as the "big Nigguhs" of Hazel Street, the community reflected the rising status of the race, and as one resident noted, "They could do and own things that the rest of us could only dream of having." They vacationed, owned homes, and obtained education that changed their outlook on life, including the perception of black church life.[30]

William Christian believed that the contemporary black church required things of followers that the Bible did not prescribe and his disgust may have been generated by the constant bombardment of black newspaper advertisements that read: "your home, your church, your school will be incomplete until supplied with a first class Estey organ."[31] In the opinion of Christian, sinners simply needed to confess their sins to be saved. He defended his position with the biblical reference that when sinners begged for redemption, Peter simply replied repent. Christian theorized, "the Apostle meant that repentance lie in achieving sanctification," grace given to sinners once they experienced their conversion. Christian taught that sanctification or a second blessing consisted of a moment when the Holy Spirit saved sinners as it had on the day of Pentecost. The Spirit released both men and women from the desire to sin and made them holy, a status attested by the power to heal, testify, prophesy, and cast out demons. In return, sanctified Christians lived a holy life on earth by abandoning secular dancing, swearing, and the use of tobacco and alcohol.[32]

Holiness converts also adopted a charismatic liturgy; they yelled, clapped, and cried when they experienced the reception of the Holy Spirit, and these charismatic rituals most likely attracted men such as Christian due to its resemblance to slave religious practices that occurred during clandestine religious gatherings.[33] After his conversion, Christian established a new church based upon the tenets of sanctification. Known as the Church of the Living God, his followers used the Bible as "their guiding light to righteousness" and retuned to what they believed to be the apostolic purity of their ancestors. During Mason's enrollment in Arkansas Baptist College, he likely read Christian's critiques of the Baptists and Methodists expressed in the frequent letters he wrote to the *Arkansas Baptist Vanguard*, the school's newspaper, as Mason's later explanation for his rejection of the school's curriculum strongly resembled those of Christian.[34]

Amanda Smith may have also introduced Mason to Holiness. Smith, an ex-slave and evangelist, also endorsed the principle of sanctification and in *An Autobiography: The Story of the Lord's Dealings with Mrs. Amanda Smith the Colored Evangelist*, Smith alleged that blacks' newfound worship style stifled her spirit. For instance, while attending a Baptist church in New York, church leaders chastised Smith for her inadvertent screaming during worship services. Black religious leaders now believed that such behavior should be put aside, as they found it incompatible with the growing intelligence of the race. In the view of progressives, a charismatic liturgy remained out of step with right and proper liturgy, but Smith found the Holiness movement not far removed from the emotional worship she had experienced as a child. In her autobiography, she echoed William Christian's argument that sanctified Christians lived pure from the corruption of man and free of all intentional sin. As Smith distributed her autobiography throughout the South, Mason might have read it, though no direct evidence of this has been produced.[35]

According to his own account, Mason delivered his first Holiness sermon in 1894 at Mt. Gale Missionary Baptist Church in Preston, Arkansas. Rather uneasy about his recent acceptance of Holiness, Mason prayed for assurance. In the tradition of his slave ancestors, he retreated to the solace of the woods, fell upon his knees, and prayed that God give him evidence of a call to the movement. By the conclusion of the revival, several converts joined the Mt. Gale Baptist Church and Mason took the revival's outcome as a divine sign that God wanted him to continue.[36]

Reasons varied as to why blacks joined the Holiness movement. Many became a part of the association because of what they believed to be a surge in denominationalism, while others sought membership because of the charismatic nature of the movement that reminded them of an emotional liturgy blacks developed while still enslaved. Black churchgoers simply preferred, if not insisted on, a spiritual experience that rational liturgy simply could not provide.[37] Arguably, it would be the latter that attracted Mason to Holiness and evidence of this can be seen with his continued use of brush-harbor gatherings, prophetic prophesy, and emotional charismatic preaching that he used to grow COGIC in its early years.

In the beginning, however, Mason faced opposition from those who knew him best. Upon his return to Conway County, his Holiness lifestyle brought unwanted attention as he now condemned the thriving local juke joint scene and preached the consumption of alcohol and the use of tobacco to be unholy. Any minister who used the products, according to Mason, indulged in a lifestyle that remained incompatible with Christian principles. His preaching also invited family tension. Israel, Mason's brother, disagreed with his condemnation of the Baptist clergy, but Mason remained steadfast in his convictions and continued to preach and conduct Holiness revivals throughout Arkansas. Conversely, as Mason's sermons grew in popularity among the rural poor, they became increasingly unpopular among the black progressives living in Little Rock.[38]

Blacks became aware that cities offered more economic opportunities than rural areas; therefore, many moved into urban centers in search of jobs. Men dreamed of owning their own businesses as blacksmiths and carpenters while women filled positions as domestics, cooks, and laundresses. Free of the exploitative measures of sharecropping, a small black middle class emerged in many cities.[39] Although Little Rock remained small compared to other southern cities in the late nineteenth century, middle-class blacks there owed their class standing to privileges granted while still enslaved. Owners often hired out slaves who possessed labor skills and some whites even allowed their slaves to keep a small portion of their earnings. Many also became trustworthy in the eyes of whites, "which allowed them to assume leadership roles within the black community."[40]

The Rectors and the Andrews families, for instance, boasted a level of wealth that made them the most notable black middle-class families in the city. Chester Ashley, a leading businessman who allowed his slaves to enjoy privileges almost unheard of for any black person during the nineteenth century, had once owned both families. The Ashley slaves acquired education and other skills necessary to assume positions of leadership after emancipation. For example, Charlotte Andrews Stephens, an Ashley slave, attended Oberlin College and became a schoolteacher in Little Rock. She recalled, "class distinction existed among slaves in Little Rock perhaps to a greater extent than among whites" and after emancipation, it would be these members of the black middle class who challenged the tenets of sanctification, which indicated that a holy lifestyle with faith allowed sanctified Christians to live free of sin.[41]

Progressives responded with the biblical argument that all men fell short of God's grace as a result of original sin. J. H. Eason, a national Baptist leader, openly denied the claim of moral purification by sanctified Christians. To Eason, "sanctification never completely purified and was not a single act of faith but a series of progressive acts designed to aid believers in their quest to live a Christ-like life on earth."[42] Elias Morris, as did most of his peers, thought of sanctification as a "call to service, a getting ready for a meeting in which to worship God and a laying aside of secular matters, that for the time, the whole being may be devoted to the service of God, but not human perfection."[43]

Critics argued that cultured ministers would discourage shouting, as it did not conform to the conventional patterns of dignified worship. No one championed this position more than Morris through his insistence that respectable worship rituals highlight the progression of the race since emancipation. "We make no effort to eliminate the Holiness worship from our service," he said, "but we think the right to regulate it, so that it may be more profitable than injurious, should be reserved by the leaders and disseminators of thought who are laboring faithfully to advance the Christian system."[44] In spite of Morris's critiques, Mason, now well entrenched in the Holiness movement, spent 1895 preaching throughout Arkansas and Mississippi before settling in Jackson, Mississippi, in 1896 to work with Charles P. Jones, a fellow Holiness preacher.

Charles Price Jones: The Intellectual

While no direct evidence detailing the first encounter between Mason and Jones exists, it is widely believed that the two met in Little Rock. Jones, similar to Mason, had been called to the ministry in Arkansas but was not a native of the state. Born on December 9, 1865, in Georgia, Jones left his home state at the age of seventeen. After drifting through parts of Mississippi and Tennessee, he eventually settled in Cat Island, Arkansas, where in 1884 he joined the Locust Grove Missionary Baptist Church. Although he began preaching as an itinerant preacher in 1885, he did not receive a ministerial license until 1887. Later that year, he moved to Helena and joined the Centennial Baptist Church where Elias Morris, the president of the Colored Baptist Convention of Arkansas and church pastor, took an interest in Jones and persuaded him to attend college.[45]

In 1888 Jones moved to Little Rock and enrolled at Arkansas Baptist College, but unlike Mason, he flourished in the liberal arts curriculum. Refusing to subscribe to the Washington model of education that mocked blacks for their desperate attempts to master Greek and Latin, Jones learned both languages well enough to secure employment as a schoolteacher in Grant County. As a result of the need for educated ministers, he had additional opportunities and became the senior pastor of Pope Creek Baptist Church. In November 1888, St. Paul Missionary Baptist Church in Little Rock elected him their senior pastor.[46] After three years of service, Jones left Pope Creek in 1891 to accept a call to serve as senior pastor of Bethlehem Baptist Church in Searcy, Arkansas.[47]

Later in the year, he graduated from Arkansas Baptist College and married Fannie Brown of Little Rock. The newlyweds departed Arkansas in August 1892 after Jones accepted the pastorate of the Tabernacle Missionary Baptist Church in Selma, Alabama. While there, he became well liked for his arousing sermons and in his own words, "was very popular as a pastor and evangelist."[48] Despite his popularity, just as Mason had in Arkansas, Jones became troubled with the condition of the Baptist clergy. He believed that they were not "toting fair with Jesus" and he grew tired of a faith that "brought no fruit or fruit of such poor spiritual quality that it produced no real results."[49] While in Alabama, the couple welcomed into the world their daughter Ole Ma, but the child died shortly after birth. Grief stricken and at a spiritual low, Jones found himself dissatisfied with the current state of religion and in need of something more from his faith. He wrote that "this conviction ate me up . . . but it seemed that the 'wee' was upon me and if I withheld from the church I was slighting my obligation to the Spirit."[50]

The same year he moved to Alabama where, according to theologian David Daniels, "he encountered the Holiness movement through Joanna Patterson Moore, a white member of the American Missionary Association, who encouraged him to seek a deeper spiritual quest." Moore had moved south after the Civil War and worked to establish schools for blacks and to organize churches. However, Jones personally attributed his conversion to Holiness to a deep inner reflection caused by spiritual dissatisfaction. "I had no idea at all of taking up holiness as a fad, or a ism, or a creed, or the slogan of a cult. I just wanted to be personally holy." He further stated, "as a Baptist I had doctrinal assurance, but I wanted spiritual assurance, heart peace, rest of soul, the joy of salvation in the understanding of a new heart, a new mind, a new spirit, constantly renewed and comforted by the Holy Ghost." And in late 1893, after three days of fasting and praying, Jones found the answers to his prayers. He claimed that "God sanctified me sweetly in his love and I became a [H]oliness minister."[51]

In much the same fashion as Mason, Jones embraced Holiness and incorporated the theory of sanctification into his daily life but found most of the clergy in Alabama opposed to sanctified living. Frustrations can be seen in his writings when he penned, "Lord give me power to convince my people and my generation of the beauty of holiness and advantages of righteousness." He further stated, "My people love beauty, but the beauty of the flesh is vain and deceiving and soon passes. They want to advance in the world, but worldly advantages prove only a snare for wealth promotes robbery, engenders pride and breeds strife, which to my people was fatal."[52] As a result of mounting disappointments, in February 1895, after refusing two previous offers, Jones accepted leadership of Mt. Helm Missionary Baptist Church in Jackson, Mississippi, and the church would provide both Jones and Mason a foundation from which to launch their first serious public critiques of the Baptist clergy.[53]

Mt. Helm began under the watchful eyes of slave owners who allowed their human property to meet in the basement of their church edifice, the First Baptist Church of Jackson. After the Civil War, the congregation longed for control of their spiritual lives, and the assertion of spiritual independence led congregants of First Baptist to evict their black counterparts from their basement. In response, Thomas and Mary Helm, local white Presbyterians, allowed the displaced congregation to build a temporary church on their fallow land. To express their appreciation, the congregation named the church after the couple. In 1868, the Helms decided to sell the land to the church and the congregation proceeded to fund the construction of a new permanent structure.[54]

The church grew into one of the largest congregations in Jackson, making it both religiously and socially important to the black community. More important, parishioners allowed Holiness preachers to address their church and, as a result, a large number of congregants joined the movement over the years. The congregation often participated in healing services and the ritual of foot washing, which attracted men such as Mason to Jackson to preach. In 1895 when Jones accepted leadership of the church, he tapped into a well-established Holiness tradition that allowed him to intensify his criticisms of the Baptist faith. His condemnations, however, would not go unnoticed, as the General Missionary Baptist Association (GMBA) of Mississippi mounted a fierce rebuttal that signaled a turning point in the history of African American Christianity in the South.[55]

Standing at the Vanguard

The GMBA formed from the efforts of black Baptist congregations in the Midwest and urban North. After the Civil War, they established the North-Western Baptist Missionary Convention for the purpose of organizing Baptist congregations into associations and conventions in the South. In 1865 John F. Boulden, their first missionary, arrived in Natchez, Mississippi, where he led the efforts to organize black Baptist congregations. He relocated to Columbus, Mississippi, in 1867 and with the help of Larry D. McAllister and Allen Henderson, two black ministers, he continued to organize black Baptist congregations in northeastern Mississippi. Through their combined efforts, the men organized congregations and merged them into the first Baptist associations in that section of the state. In the meantime, Marion Dunbar, a former Mississippi slave, worked to organize Baptist congregations in central Mississippi. By 1868, often in the face of danger, Dunbar, alone, had arranged for the establishment of the first permanent black Baptist associations.[56]

White resistance made black missionaries' efforts extremely difficult. As one missionary reported, "bands of armed and masked men prowled around at night whipping and murdering and I have devoted nights to watching for the protection of life and guarding our buildings against fire." State and local governments offered little to no protection, as politicians pandering for votes often threatened missionaries in public.[57] Even in the face of this opposition, in 1872, five Baptist associations in the northern and central sections of the state created the General Missionary Baptist Association.[58] A group of young ministers, all born near the end of slavery, led the new association's central committee and members intended to use the association as a self-help organization to uplift the black masses, making the race more educated, disciplined, and refined. As a means of accomplishing these goals, the committee instituted that formal education become a requirement for the licensing of ministers, along with the recommendation that power to elect pastors be taken away from individual congregations and instead be given to the new central committee, thus setting up a jurisdictional system similar to the African Methodist Episcopal Church. Board members also increased their scrutiny of uneducated slave preachers, requiring them to preach rational and logical sermons, and frowning upon their use of dreams and visions as mediums of divine communication.[59]

As historian Patricia Schecter writes, Ida B. Wells emphasized the problems with the black clergy, claiming that they "proved too often morally unfit and injured the interest of the entire race." Wells argued that "a weak uneducated clergy that lacked the respect of God, self, and community betrayed the principles of truth, honesty, and self-respect." She offered explicit criteria that the black clergy should meet and argued, "men of the cloth should be cultivated in intellect, dignified and earnest in manner, noble of purpose and consecrated to their work." For Wells, "these men had access to the rank and file more than either teachers or journalists; therefore, she insisted that they must be the teachers of proper morals and values in and out of the pulpit." Wells similarly advocated the argument of the GMBA's central committee regarding the proper behavior of preachers. She believed that blacks needed to reform their modes of public worship and condemn what she called black ministers who acted like monkeys in the pulpit or preached merely with the goal of getting people "happy."[60]

In 1897 the GMBA convened its annual meeting at Mt. Helm and focused its agenda on the increased political disfranchisement of blacks in Mississippi. Once southern Democrats returned to power in the South, they undertook a campaign to nullify black political advances, especially the right to suffrage. Across the South, states began to employ methods designed to systemically disenfranchise blacks. Louisiana, for example, bestowed suffrage only upon men whose grandfathers met state voting requirements. Known as the grandfather clause, the statute accomplished precisely what was intended; it disqualified the vast majority of blacks because their grandfathers had been slaves. Whites in Mississippi approved the levying of poll taxes and implemented educational requirements designed to disenfranchise blacks, the so-called Mississippi Plan deprived thousands of the right to vote.[61]

The number of disenfranchised blacks in the state had grown so large that by 1897, the GMBA decided the issue had become a threat to racial advancement. Although not opposed to political participation, Jones and Mason both believed their counterparts placed more emphasis on the social, political, and educational needs of blacks and neglected their spiritual needs. In response to the secular agenda, the two published and sold their first booklet, a treatise on the twelfth chapter of first Corinthians titled *The Work of the Holy Spirit in the Churches*. The pamphlet criticized the growing surge in denominationalism among blacks, which they believed divided Christians into camps assembled in the name of a particular denomination instead of Christ. Jones declared that, "Christians' loyalty belonged to God and not to a particular denomination whose faults they might overlook." He also believed, "the scripture was the infallible word of God and rejected the Baptists' progressive innovations that sought to use the Church as an institution to promote social change, which tailored the biblical message to its own ends, corrupting leadership, and abolishing pure Bible readings."[62] Along the same lines as William Christian, Jones and Mason believed the church needed to return to apostolic purity and reject man-made religious traditions by following the Bible as a sacred guide.

Angered by what they viewed as "heretical doctrine," the GMBA repri-
manded Jones and Mason for their views. With the use of a printing machine
installed in the basement of Mt. Helm, Jones and Mason replied by publishing
a bimonthly periodical titled *Truth*, in which the two continued their critiques
of the GMBA's practices.[63] In addition, they also published an open invitation
welcoming all interested ministers to a Holiness convention at Mt. Helm. For
two weeks the participants studied the Bible and conducted prayer meetings.
The GMBA responded with threats to withdraw the right hand of fellowship
from all ministers in attendance, and some opponents of the convention even
damaged the buggies and saddles of the attendees. Led by Mason and Jones, the
convention highlighted a growing schism within the ranks of the Baptists in
Mississippi.[64]

While little is known about the men who gathered at the convention, all
harbored resentment about the state of the Baptist denomination, but it would
be a mistake to assume that their discontent mirrored one another's. Jones's
reaction to the Baptist clearly stemmed from an intellectual and theological dispute over the surge in denominationalism. Whereas Mason remained more disturbed with the transformation of black religion as it moved from the private
spaces of the slave quarters to church edifices in the public sphere, which now
demanded a refined religious experience. Mason and others like him noticed
that supervisory organizations such as the GMBA were slowly removing congregational power and placing that power within the hands of central committees
all under the auspices of denominationalism. In the process, these committees
denied uneducated preachers access to pulpits because of their refusal to conform to rational liturgy void of emotionalism. Mason and Jones both reacted
negatively to the GMBA but for different reasons, which would later come to a
head as a dispute between the two over the future of Holiness.

Additional controversy arose in Natchez after a fire destroyed a dormitory
at the Colored Baptist College for Girls. The importance of the educational
needs throughout the state prompted black Baptist associations to sponsor a
series of revivals to raise funds for the construction of a new dormitory. In
an attempt to aid in the fundraising, displaced students requested that Jones
conduct a weeklong revival at Asia Missionary Baptist Church in Lexington,
Mississippi, but by week's end, Jones succeeded in alienating the majority of the
congregation. Members opposed the theory of sanctification, and in their anger,
they dismissed the pastor for allowing Jones to conduct what they referred to as
a "Holiness revival." The Mississippi Colored Baptist Association demanded that
Jones return to Lexington to issue a formal apology to the upset congregation.[65]
Unable to return, Jones sent Mason, but annoyed that Jones himself did not
return, the congregation refused to allow Mason to speak. In protest, he began

preaching at the south entrance of the Holmes County Courthouse. After several days of preaching and attracting large crowds of local blacks, the white leaders of Lexington banned him from preaching on the square.[66]

John Lee, a black resident of Lexington and daily attendant of the sermons, allowed Mason to continue preaching at his home but within days the growing number of attendees forced participants to find a larger place of worship. A local planter allowed Mason to continue worship services in an abandoned cotton gin on the outskirts of town.[67] Blacks packed the gin, and whites grew suspicious, disapproving of the loud singing, shouting, and dancing. They remained particularly fearful of black religious gatherings; their worries began while blacks were still enslaved, as whites remained acutely aware that slave conspiracies or rebellions often originated out of unsupervised religious meetings.

Attempting to frighten the attendees, someone fired gunshots into the gin and wounded several parishioners. Instead of discouraging participants, the news and curiosity surrounding the revival drew more people. Mason remembered that "the devil being stirred shot in on us while some were praying and shouting." He claimed that these actions "only served to advertise and add to the success of the meeting," as many believed that "if they held meetings under these conditions, it must be of God."[68] No evidence of the actual proceedings of the nightly meetings exist, yet after closer examination of the descriptions of the services, it becomes clear that Mason's Holiness gatherings very much resembled the "brush harbor" meetings of his slave ancestors, explaining whites' fearful reaction to the all-night meetings.

Southern society treated black Holiness believers with added disdain, and the threat of bodily harm to attendees of all-night worship meetings remained real. In Auburn, Alabama, five men dressed in disguises pulled a black preacher from his home and carried him into the woods and whipped him severely. The crime—upsetting whites by conducting worship meetings that ran late into the night—was that laborers were unable to tend to their duties with due diligence the next morning. Even with the threat of violence, Mason remained undeterred. His message resonated with the poor black population because it freed them from the restrictions of the growing Baptist denomination that now placed an emphasis on a refined liturgy.[69]

For instance, women flocked to Mason's services as they found them more accommodating and less stifling than denominational churches. The charismatic nature of Holiness allowed them to become active participants in religious service as they danced, shouted, and testified about the goodness that Jesus had bestowed upon them through testimonials. Men also found services to be just as welcoming; if called to preach, the uneducated could do so without acquiring a formal education or approval from a local Baptist association. For marginalized illiterate black men, Mason's churches became the only public sphere in which they could exercise authority. Most of all, lack of adequate healthcare attracted both men and women to Mason's services. He promised, with uncompromising faith, the possibility of divine healing, which offered an alternative remedy to healthcare that many could neither access nor afford.

The lack of economic and educational advancement coupled with a marginalized black majority made Holmes County ideal for Mason's success. Land speculators organized the county in February 1833, bringing with them their slaves who constituted the county's first black population. Rich alluvial Delta soil dominates much of the western part of the county, while less fertile red soil and flat land dotted with thick forests make up the eastern half. The rich Delta soil made much of Holmes County suitable for a plantation economy, and the agricultural market's ever-increasing need for labor led to an increase in the black population. When the census bureau made its first nationwide count of blacks in 1870, they outnumbered whites there by three to one. Data revealed that in 1870, the county's population stood at 19,370, of which, census data collectors identified 13,225 as black, thus making the county 68 percent black with a primary occupation as farm laborer. When Mason arrived in 1897, he found an impoverished black population that had grown even larger; 1890 data revealed that the county's population had grown to 36,828, and blacks made up an astounding 28,708 of the total population, making the county 78 percent black with occupations that ranged from farm laborer to washerwoman.[70]

As in many Deep South counties after the Civil War, the lives of Holmes County blacks remained largely unchanged. To maintain the traditional southern social hierarchy over the black majority, the white minority employed violence and brute intimidation. In October 1875, William J. Taylor of Goodman sent a telegram to James Z. George, the powerful Mississippi Democratic Party leader, requesting that the party pay transportation fees to ship a cannon to Lexington.[71] Goodman explained that the local party wanted to display the cannon in front of the Holmes County Courthouse on election day to deter blacks from voting. The members of the local Democratic Party drew a line in the ground to represent a firing line and dared any black person to cross in an attempt to enter the courthouse to vote.[72] To reinforce these tactics, local whites also formed a group called the "red shirts." As one reporter put it, "the Klan terrorized . . . by night but the bolder red shirts kept their colors flying by day."[73] Whites argued that their actions defended the virtue of white society and continued to make the South safe for white women who remained afraid of being sexually ravished by uncontrollable black men.[74]

Education for blacks in the county also remained in a horrific state. The Freedmen's Bureau first organized the Holmes County Public School District, but education did not extend beyond segregated one-room shacks with nearly illiterate teachers. In 1870, the black population stood at 13,225, yet only 221 black children were recorded as attending school, which was accompanied by an illiteracy rate of 41 percent. Conditions had only slightly improved by 1897 as data indicates a black population of 28,708 with an illiteracy rate of 35 percent. The heavy dependence on an agricultural labor force meant that blacks overwhelmingly continued to work in the fields, and as indicated by the census data, the acquisition of education seemed to be a luxury that most blacks simply could not afford.[75]

In the absence of educational or economic progress, blacks in Holmes County continued to labor as sharecroppers and Mason's charismatic preaching, which resembled that of ex-slave preachers, resonated with the black populace. As historian John Blassingame stated, "Slave preachers had special oratorical skills and were masters of the use of vivid phrases and words." Described as displays of "crude eloquence" they crafted sermons to excite churchgoers and work them into a frenzy that usually led to loud screams known as shouts. Sermons delivered in this manner were seen more as performances coupled with groans and moans infused with elements of call and response from the congregants and in Holmes County, these rituals remained popular as many blacks' daily lives continued to center around slave traditions.[76]

At the end of a successful two-week revival, Mason believed it necessary to establish a permanent church in Lexington. With the help of recent converts, he purchased a vacant lot and his male followers constructed the first permanent COGIC structure in Mississippi. Thirty converts stood as charter members and voted to name the structure St. Paul Church of God. The new members chose Mason as their pastor and he carried out his first official duty in that capacity when he baptized Addie Golden Coruthers, Lula McCollough Washington, Blanche C. Copper, and Charles Pleas.[77]

Mason's congregation applied for membership into their local Baptist association, but the organization composed of progressive ministers rejected the request on the basis that he preached the doctrine of sanctification. The association also disapproved of the congregation's emotional worship style that consisted of late-night services accompanied with loud noises that frightened people not affiliated with the movement. The organization viewed Mason as an uneducated religious fanatic who stood in New Testament doctrinal error, and members alleged that only the most uncultured segment of the black population followed the Holiness movement. Even with the association's denial of membership and condemnation, Mason continued to prosper among the rural poor of Holmes County. His congregation grew so large that he decided to relocate permanently from Jackson to Lexington so that he might oversee the congregation full time.[78]

A Movement of Their Own

As the Holiness movement expanded, it encountered problems because of poor organizational structure and oversight. Mason and Jones had to address complaints against younger preachers who used their influence to divide congregations. Grievances stemmed from younger preachers demanding better pay and worshipers who complained that preachers completely "laid down the hoe" when the Holy Spirit called them to preach. Congregants simply saw this as a way for preachers to rid themselves of fieldwork and become economically dependent upon congregations. In January 1904, the Holiness association called together all ministers associated with the organization, which ironically forced Jones and Mason into a denominational structure, something they had openly criticized the Baptists in Mississippi for doing.[79]

On January 14, the first general governance meeting convened in Jackson, Mississippi, with William S. Pleasant, Jones's assistant pastor, serving as president pro-tem and Charles P. Jones as chief of the convention. After committee selections, the general assembly elected Jones, Mason, and John A. Jeter, another Holiness minister who preached throughout Arkansas, as state overseers with administrative control over all black Holiness churches in the tri-state region.[80] Jones received jurisdictional control of Mississippi; Arkansas became Jeter's jurisdiction; and Mason received control of all Holiness congregations in Tennessee. The group designated Jackson, Mississippi, their regional headquarters and in similar fashion as the GMBA, the Holiness general assembly passed a resolution that no church possessed the right to vote on the acceptance of a pastor without the approval of two or more of the overseers. In case of conflict between a pastor and congregation, the board of deacons retained the right to request an investigation from one or two of the state overseers. If the overseer found the pastor at fault, he possessed the authority to dismiss a church's leader. Congregations did retain the power to change a trustee when they found his tenure hostile to their spiritual well-being and peace, but a state overseer could also remove any trustee whose faith became opposed to the tenets of Holiness.[81]

This administrative structure provided the organizational basis for what would become the Church of God in Christ. Unlike their Baptist counterparts, the churches in the Holiness association remained congregational, with appointed trustees holding ownership of all church properties. The assembly allowed for the names Church of Christ, Church of God, or any scriptural name to appear on deeds, but specified that the name "Churches of God in Christ" should be the official name of the Holiness organization. On January 21, 1906, the Holiness assembly convened a ratification meeting to allow all the churches in the tri-state region to review and approve the document. The general assembly reconvened on August 5, 1906, and, after seven days of deliberation, voted to accept the "Rules of Government of the Churches of God in Christ" as its binding charter.[82]

Even with the growing success of the Holiness association, Mason and Jones continued to battle over images of religious respectability. Progressive clergymen believed that acceptance from whites would stem not only from an educated mind but also from a dignified worship experience and they believed Mason and Jones hindered their efforts. However, controversy within the Holiness organization would erupt as factions found themselves in disagreement over the issue of glossolalia, the religious doctrine of speaking in tongues promoted at the Azusa Street revival. The rift caused a permanent split between the Holiness movement trailblazers and became a secular issue of respectability in the civil courts of Tennessee, Arkansas, and Mississippi.

2

We Will Let the Courts Speak for Us

*Controversy within the Holiness Movement and
the Excommunication of a Saint*

In 1905, a group of African Americans sat for a photograph in Niagara Falls, Canada. Poised in front of the waterfall and attired in dark suits, bowties, and hats, these men represented America's finest blacks. Among them sat William E. B. Du Bois, who had, with the acquisition of an education, achieved the ultimate level of respectability. That day, with the flicker of a snapshot, Du Bois witnessed the fulfillment of a dream, the creation of the Niagara Movement. The organization, similar to the General Missionary Baptist Association of Mississippi, dedicated itself to ensuring black equality. Serving as the forerunner of the National Association for the Advancement of Colored People (NAACP), the Niagara Movement quickly became the most prominent black secular organization in support of racial uplift in America.

By 1906, the organization's efforts seemed in jeopardy as the nation's daily headlines informed the country of the Azusa Street revival. Rooted in the tradition of Holiness, the revival threatened the efforts of all black self-help organizations as newspapers spread images of rowdy uncultured blacks who spoke in unknown tongues. Progressives shuddered when newspapers across the country reprinted the *Los Angeles Daily Times* account of the activities at the revival, reporting that "a colored mammy" shouted and ran about swinging her arms in the air as she yelled, "Yoo-oo-oo gou-lou-oo come under the bloo-oo-oo-boo-loo," concluding, "Few of her words are intelligible," but her testimony kept the crowd spellbound as she danced and shouted in the "most outrageous jumble of syllables." Viewed as a colossal embarrassment, the revival became part of the national conversation and of particular importance to blacks as it threatened the efforts of uplift.[1]

The Azusa Street revival began in 1906 in Los Angeles, California, a result of the controversial theory of sanctification. Julia W. Hutchinson, a black member of a local Baptist church, subscribed to the theory and began teaching sanctification as a separate work of grace. Angered by her teaching, Hutchinson's pastor expelled her and eight other members who believed in the theory. Undeterred, Hutchinson, with the help of her sister and brother-in-law Ruth and Richard Asbury, established the Santa Fe Street Church of the Nazarene. Hutchinson agreed to serve as pastor but, in keeping with the gendered roles of the period, thought it best that a man serve as the assistant pastor, which she believed would give the new congregation legitimacy in future business dealings.[2]

Terry Neely, general secretary of the new congregation, recalled that on a recent trip to Houston, Texas, she met William J. Seymour, whom she described as a Baptist minister who left the Baptist church and joined the Holiness movement because of his displeasure with the denomination.[3] Born the son of freedmen in Centerville, Louisiana, Seymour's parents escaped the hardships of sharecropping. His father worked as a brick mason and his mother, through unknown means, acquired land in St. Mary's Parish, Louisiana. Although no evidence exists indicating that Seymour received a formal education, he could read and write, and following his conversion to Holiness, he studied with Charles Fox Parham, a white Holiness minister who embraced the theological theory of speaking in tongues, which Parham believed provided converts evidence of a baptism by the Holy Spirit.[4]

A strict Methodist, Parham was born and raised in Iowa and later attended Southwest College, a Methodist institute in Winfield, Kansas. After several bouts of sickness, Parham, according to historian Randall Stephens, left the Methodist denomination and joined the Holiness movement due to its promise of divine healing.[5] After marriage Parham settled in Topeka, Kansas, and established the Bethel Bible School in 1898 where he began teaching the controversial doctrine of speaking in tongues to students for the first time. In 1905 Parham relocated the school to Houston, Texas, where Seymour enrolled and embraced his teachings. Aware that Seymour's presence broke Jim Crow laws, Parham refused to conform to the racial custom and allowed his first black student to attend. As Parham's wife, Sarah, recalled, "Seymour's intense interest in learning" moved her husband to allow him to become a regular attendant for the Bible lessons as "he was so humble and so deeply interested in the study of the Word that Mr. Parham could not refuse him."[6]

After completing his studies, Seymour departed Texas for Los Angeles and assumed the position of assistant pastor at the Santa Fe Street Church of the Nazarene. Staying true to his teachings, in his first sermon, Seymour preached about the baptism of the Holy Ghost and the necessity of the experience of speaking in tongues. Taking exception to the doctrine of glossolalia, Hutchinson padlocked the doors of the church, as she embraced Holiness and sanctification but refused to accept the belief of a third blessing by the Holy Ghost. Convinced that Seymour preached the truth, the Asburys invited him to continue worship services in their home and on April 9, 1906, while conducting a prayer meeting, Seymour and five other members began to speak in unknown tongues. Taking the event as evidence of the third blessing, Seymour began to spread the news of the event throughout the city.[7]

As the curious and faithful overcrowded the Asburys' home, the meetings moved outside, taking on the characteristics of a tent revival. Aware of the negative images tent revivals conjured among the general public, the Asburys secured the use of a two-story abandoned Methodist church building. Located at 312 Azusa Street, the structure stood in need of serious repair, and even after improvements, conditions remained poor. For instance, wooden produce carts stacked atop one another served as the first pulpit while congregants used the bare floors of the building as pews. Nevertheless, night after night, people packed the building to witness what newspapers described as general chaos and a "weird babel of tongues" that had become the newest religious sect of the city.[8]

As congregants continued to crowd the Azusa Street structure, news of the revival spread throughout the country. Working-class blacks especially enjoyed hearing the news that a black man of their class standing had gained national attention. Moreover, newspapers reported that interracial crowds assembled to hear Seymour, standing in direct contradiction to the Jim Crow laws that blacks despised. During a time when black men possessed little to no authority over whites and the widely held assumption of black inferiority permeated throughout society, no matter how insignificant, Seymour brought hope. As he stood before the interracial crowds and commanded their attention, Seymour channeled the dreams of equality of thousands of blacks.

Blacks throughout the Deep South took pleasure in the news of the large crowds gathering to receive the third blessing at the hands of Seymour and as the religious fervor spread, Charles H. Mason felt "the [S]pirit called him to Los Angeles where the great fire of the latter rain of the Holy Ghost had fallen upon many."[9] However, Dovie Johnson, a lifetime member of St. Paul Church of God in Christ and resident of Lexington, Mississippi, remembered the visit differently. According to Johnson, in December 1906, Charles Simmons, her uncle, first informed Mason of the revival. A member of Mason's Lexington congregation, Simmons worked as a railroad porter and his job afforded him the opportunity to visit many of America's major cities. While in Los Angeles, he attended worship service at Seymour's church. Johnson remembered that after her uncle's usual greeting to Mason, "I see you have not made it to heaven yet," and Mason's reply of, "I see you have not either," Simmons proceeded to inform him of the Azusa Street revival.[10] Hearing the firsthand account, Mason's interest grew until March 1907 when he traveled to Los Angeles accompanied by fellow Holiness preachers John A. Jeter of Little Rock and Dennis Young of Pine Bluff, Arkansas. The trip would mark the turning point in the ministry of Charles H. Mason, his friendship with Charles P. Jones, and the history of African American religion in America.[11]

The Birth of the Pentecostal Movement and the Church of God in Christ

When Mason and his colleagues arrived at the Azusa Street revival they found no choir, hymn books, or order of service, only an around-the-clock meeting where anyone moved by the Spirit could preach, sing, or dance. An upstairs room, referred to as the upper-room, had been set up to allow anxious pilgrims to pray for the Spirit. The first day, Mason remained uneasy about what he saw and heard. Sitting to himself, he pondered the things he encountered, but remembered, "I did not stumble. I began to thank God in my heart for all things, for when I heard someone speak in tongues, I knew it was right, though I did not understand."[12] The second night, Mason found a seat at the altar and began to pray where later in the evening, he received the baptism of the Holy Ghost and spoke in tongues for the first time. Mason later reminisced:

> I heard the groaning of Christ on the cross. All this worked in me until I died out of the old man. I felt something raising me out of my seat without any effort on my own. There came a wave of glory into me and all of my being filled with the glory of the Lord. When I opened my mouth to say glory, a flame touched my tongue which ran down in me. My language changed and no word could I speak in my own tongue. My soul was then satisfied. The Spirit had taken full control of me[;] how to and what to sing all his songs were new. I wanted the church to understand what the Spirit was saying through me. I began to speak in tongues. He gave me the gift of interpretation. I now could interpret sounds, groans, and other spiritual utterances.[13]

Mason remained in Los Angeles for five weeks, after which he returned to Lexington determined to duplicate his California revival experience. Immediately he began to preach the concept of speaking in tongues as a New Testament doctrine with such boldness that people from other denominations began to attend his services. His increasing numbers meant the loss of members in other established denominations and, as a result, opposition soon surfaced. Outraged progressives alleged that Mason fell prey to the heretical doctrine of speaking in tongues because of his lack of a theological education.[14] According to theologian Cheryl Sanders, "Aware that speaking in tongues and the so-called 'commotion' that accompanied it did not fit into Victorian modes of worship, progressive blacks began to worry, as they understood that whites judged their fitness in other arenas based upon their competency in operating their churches." African Methodist Episcopal bishop Daniel Payne registered his disdain for the so-called commotion occurring in these religious services when he remembered that he once "requested a pastor stop his congregants from dancing," and informed the pastor, "to sit down and sing in a rational manner," because the way in which they worshiped "was heathenish and disgraceful to themselves and the race."[15]

Opposition grew so great that Mason began receiving death threats, but he stood bolder and firmer, proclaiming, "if you fight this truth, you will die" because he believed he stood for God and His word.[16] In an attempt to escape the constant harassment, his Lexington congregation began worshiping in a "brush harbor" in the woods. Finding a suitable place in the forest, members cleared an area of brush, tied poles to small trees, and laid brushes and weeds atop the makeshift structure to form a roof. They brought planks to be used for seats or placed sawdust on the ground; nevertheless, as church services began, the loud singing made finding Mason and his congregation easy for his opponents. Congregants became victims of adversaries who threw rotten eggs and who, on occasion, fired gunshots into worship meetings. Even under such conditions, Mason remained undeterred and while leading his Lexington congregation, he expanded his ministry into Memphis, where residents also viewed the concept of speaking in tongues with the same disdain and suspicion.[17]

Changes had occurred in Memphis since the yellow fever epidemic of 1878, which had originally caused Mason and his family to flee. By 1900, blacks constituted a greater percentage of the total population, comprising 84,803 of the city's 153,557 residents. Although blacks made up more than 55 percent of the total population, they still remained at the bottom of the social hierarchy. Plagued by limited educational and employment opportunities, Mason found an impoverished black population in need of relief from poverty-induced social ills. For instance, educational opportunities were poor to inadequate at best, as census data reveal that of the 10,227 students attending schools in 1900, Shelby County recorded only 122 black teachers. Data collectors also recorded that 30 percent of the black population remained illiterate, which forced thousands of unskilled black laborers into the cotton fields of nearby Arkansas and Mississippi where they continued to be exploited for their labor.[18]

Poverty stricken and disenfranchised, black Memphians longed for something more than their daily life provided, which allowed Mason and his Holiness-Pentecostal message to thrive. In particular, Pentecostalism directly addressed issues that plagued the impoverished population, such as divine healing in the absence of adequate healthcare; alcoholism, which Pentecostal theology strictly forbids; and that with faith, God would provide in the face of economic hard times. Adept at addressing the needs of the poor, Mason conducted his first revivals in Memphis on street corners and later in a tent referred to as his tabernacle. As word of the tent services spread throughout Memphis, the number of attendees grew to well over a hundred within two years. The enlarged membership forced the congregants to purchase a lot at 392 Wellington Street where his male followers built a wooden structure and named it Saints Home Church of God.[19] The Wellington Street congregation flourished as the city's black population continued to provide a steady flow of converts whose testimonies attested to the benefits of membership in the denomination.

By late 1907, however, trouble loomed on the horizon as local newspapers reported that Mason began holding all-night meetings that often ran into the early morning. The *Commercial Appeal* published an article titled "Fanatical Worship of Negroes going on in the Holiness Churches" that played up stereotypes held by whites about black religious beliefs. The article read:

> Some time ago Rev. Mason had a "visitation of the Holy Spirit" and began to speak the language used by the Spirit. Then the test was applied to the congregation. If the members of his church could not speak and understand such language they were not sanctified, and could not be saved. This gave rise to one of the most remarkable religious fervors that has ever struck even the superstitious Negro church. The pastor pretended to speak the language of the Spirit and the wise ones of the congregation got on to his curves and began using a strange, idiotic jargon, which was alike meaningless to them and the preacher. As a matter of self-defense both the minister and the "wise ones" of his congregation pretended to understand each other, and the result was the language of the Spirit, which all "understand" and which is "meaningless" to all.
>
> The minister would exclaim, "Hicks, hicks!" and the congregation would answer back, "Sycamore, sycamore, sycamore!" and such insignificant words, which lifted the congregation to the highest point of ecstasy, showing what has been contended for years, that the Negro's religion is sound instead of sense.[20]

The negative press garnered resentment from the educated black populace of Memphis as they remained aware that Mason's antics, no matter how foolish some perceived them, directly affected their standing in the city since whites oftentimes did not make distinctions when viewing the black population, rather choosing to see them as monolithic. Therefore, it can be argued that Mason's services threatened progressives' efforts to gain equality in the eyes of whites as they stressed proper dress, respectable behavior, and a refined liturgy.[21]

George Cashwell, a member of Mason's Wellington Street church, authored a letter to the *Apostolic Faith*, which further revealed the resentment many black Memphians held toward Mason's worship services. Cashwell recalled that he had never been "met with such power of the devil [as in Memphis]." In the letter, he recounted the story of a man who came to Mason's church during a worship service. So enraged by what he witnessed, the man dragged his wife from the altar by force and threatened to kill Cashwell as well as the other members. The author revealed "the Glory to God overpowered the man when his wife began to speak in tongues and the Pentecost adverted [*sic*] tragedy." Cashwell concluded that the man was so touched he became a regular attendee of the services.[22]

While the testimonial provides valuable insight about Mason's services, it also raises questions about gender. Due to the charismatic nature of Pentecostalism, women became active participants in church services. In addition, according to Anthea Butler, women also began to exert influence over key leadership roles that gave them a greater degree of power within congregations than they enjoyed in the public sphere.[23] Although we may never know what actually spurred the husband's anger, transforming gender roles could have certainly been the cause; the fact that the husband dragged his wife from the altar provides some clues.

Accounts reveal that during Mason's services, both males and females often lay together at the altar in search of the Holy Spirit. So the husband's anger could have been generated as the result of his wife lying together with male members that, for the times, would have been deemed improper in all other public spaces. However, the overall use of the altar by women reveals the transformative nature of COGIC as both pulpits and altars were viewed as sacred and holy places only to be occupied by men. The fact that Mason allowed women to access the altar in the very same manner as men reveals that COGIC was ahead of their Baptist and Methodist counterparts in how they viewed women's roles in religious services. Viewed as progressive acts by today's standards, most within the black community would have condemned the actions as scandalous and improper, which further demonized COGIC.

I'se Got Ligon, Boss

The general public's perception of Mason worsened when another sensational headline, "Negro House Boy Makes Funny Talk At Police Station" appeared in the *Commercial Appeal*. The paper reported that police arrested Frank C. Ford, a twenty-two-year-old black man employed as the houseboy of Major Eldridge E. Wright, for "funny talk." Wright reported that Ford stayed away from his living quarters all Sunday night and returned Monday morning around 7:00 and refused to speak. When forced, he expressed himself by uttering, according to the maid, sounds like "O-pala, O-pala," and at the same time he raised his hands high toward the heavens and began to speak in some unknown language. An alarmed Major Wright phoned the police station and upon the arrival of patrolmen, police found Ford in his quarters uttering strange noises like "iggy gik wok, muggy pung chugaloo. Iggy gluk aqua pura dub is ferique uggy blok."[24] Police arrested Ford and took him to the police station where, bewildered by Ford's actions, Chief Tom O'Haver personally questioned him, asking, "[w]hat is the matter with you?" Ford replied, "[d]ey ain't nothing wrong boss; I'se got ligon."[25]

George A. Cook and Larry P. Adams, two white men, appeared and greeted Ford with a hug. Frustrated, Chief O'Haver demanded that someone explain the situation. Adams, a former lawyer, Presbyterian minister, and native of Nashville, Tennessee, explained that they belonged to the Apostolic Faith movement. He told the police that the movement was "based on the powers of the Holy Ghost" and centered on the "gifts infused in Him (Holy Ghost) into the apostles at Pentecost." Adams further explained that God had come down on the apostles' heads "in forms of fiery tongues from heaven and filled them with the Spirit." The apostles then "went forth and preached the gospel to every man in his own tongue," something in which Adams, Ford, and Cook were presently engaged. Adams ended his explanation by arguing, "By laying hands on one's head, we baptize and fill the person with the power to speak unknown tongues."[26]

George Cook, a former printer and native of Durham, North Carolina, also tried to justify Ford's behavior, revealing that he had converted to the Apostolic Faith movement in Los Angeles and the previous week he had arrived in Memphis to conduct a Holiness revival at Mason's church. He stated that on Sunday afternoon, Ford fell into a stupor and lay out in front of the altar where he remained until Monday morning when he awoke with the gift of tongues. Following the explanation, Cook begged for Ford's release and O'Haver agreed, but not before he warned, "Mr. Wright fired you and if you don't stay away from that [Wright's] house we'll land you in the county work house," to which Ford replied, "glory be ter Gawd."[27]

The Ford episode highlighted the broader social implications the Holiness-Pentecostal movement had in Memphis and the potential for whites to see black religion as backward and uncultured. On a more simplistic note, the movement upset the labor norms of the city, as workers worshiped throughout the night, which rendered them unable to perform their duties the next morning. For example, when Frank Ford visited Mason's services, Major Wright most likely remained more disturbed that his "house boy" was unable to perform his duties than by the strange actions of Ford. Even more troubling was the involvement of both Cook and Adams, two white men, who not only understood Ford's odd behavior but also worked to secure his release from jail. Their involvement illustrates how Pentecostalism threatened Jim Crow segregation as the event clearly revealed that under the guise of Pentecostalism, both whites and blacks not only worshiped together, but also shared the same religious liturgy.

In June 1907, D. J. Young of Pine Bluff described similar events occurring in Little Rock in a letter to the *Apostolic Faith* when he stated, "I thank God that I am able to report victory through Jesus Christ our Lord. We are in the midst of a great revival here and 'the fire is falling and the people are getting the baptismal.'" Young believed that the Holy Ghost was working as never before and "the Lord has made it known to us that the speaking in tongues is the Bible's evidence of the baptism by the Holy Ghost." He concluded by saying that "the Holy Ghost pray much that we may get out of the way, so that He (Holy Ghost) can run things to suit Himself."[28]

Controversy within the Ranks of Holiness

The concept of speaking in tongues also caused serious controversy within the Holiness movement. After attending the Azusa Street revival, Mason became convinced that glossolalia provided theological proof of divine healing, exorcism of demons, and prophecies, which, in essence, gave him the ability to bridge elements of slave religion with contemporary religious practices. Charles P. Jones, co-founder of the Holiness association, refused to accept speaking in tongues as a New Testament doctrine. Historian Elton Weavers writes, he, instead, regarded the doctrine as a delusion and misinterpretation of the scriptures concerning the day of Pentecost. Jones felt that Pentecost occurred once and modern Christians need not bother looking for a third blessing in the form of baptism by the Spirit accompanied with speaking in tongues.[29]

In an effort to resolve their differences, a Holiness general assembly convened in Jackson, Mississippi, in August 1907. Jones served as the presiding general overseer, and after three days of intense debate, the convention excommunicated Mason, claiming he "has imbibed and now preaches and propagates a dangerous and delusive heresy . . . contrary to the teachings of either Christ or the Apostle." Even after being warned many times by the assembly, Mason had "persistently shown a determination to adhere to and teach this heresy," which caused them to believe that the founder was "possessed with a spirit of deep delusion, which was dangerous and dooming." Unless Mason publicly renounced "the seducing spirit and delusive doctrine that he now holds," the assembly saw no alternative other than to no longer regard him "as in fellowship with us."[30]

Not only did the statement of excommunication apply to Mason but to all others who joined him in the propagation of the doctrine of speaking in tongues. The council specifically singled out Edward H. Driver of Memphis because of his passionate defense of Mason during the convention. They alleged that, "he clearly proved himself and spirit favorable to him [Mason] and the doctrine . . . and we warned all other churches to close their pulpits to the great delusion undertaken by Mason and his followers."[31] After the ruling, Mason returned to Memphis and called together his followers. While standing before the congregation, he asked all in favor of his leadership to stand and instructed those who remained seated to leave.[32]

In November 1907, Mason extended an open invitation to all Holiness ministers who believed in speaking in tongues to convene at a meeting in Memphis. Thirteen men responded to the invitation: Edward Driver, John Bowe, Richard R. Booker, William M. Roberts, Richard E. Hart, William Welch, Allen A. Blackwell, Edger M. Page, Richard H. Clark, Daniel J. Young, James Brewer, Daniel Spearman, and John H. Boone. All in attendance agreed to sever ties to Jones and establish a new Holiness-Pentecostal association with the hope of spreading Pentecostalism throughout the tri-state region of Arkansas, Mississippi, and Tennessee. The officiating body elected Mason as their chief apostle and voted to accept the name General Assembly of the Churches of God in Christ. They also adopted the doctrinal statement that the Churches of God in Christ believed in a baptism by the Holy Ghost accompanied by speaking in tongues.[33]

The delegation also raised money to publish its own bimonthly periodical titled the *Whole Truth*, deriving its name from Jones's periodical the *Truth*. In Mason's opinion, since Jones rejected the doctrine of speaking in tongues, he refused to preach the entire truth of the gospel, while the gift of speaking in tongues allowed him to preach the whole truth. The periodical became instrumental in helping to institutionalize the denomination, as the newspaper became a common sight in the homes of members. The paper allowed church leaders to disseminate their message of sanctification to a wider audience and also enabled members to offer their testimonies to the entire membership of the denomination. The periodical would eventually give the national leadership access to an eager pool of adherents from which they could raise money and distribute information.

The delegation set dates for an annual meeting named the Holy Convocation, a twenty-two-day meeting from November 23 through December 14. The dates were of extreme importance, as they corresponded with the end of the harvest season in the tri-state area of Mississippi, Tennessee, and Arkansas, during which planters released sharecroppers who made up the bulk of Mason's followers from labor obligations.[34] Mason's consideration of the natural rhythmic patterns of the agricultural sector in which his followers lived and worked signified COGIC's awareness of the socioeconomic position of its members, who were primarily rural and poor. As Eugene McCoy remembered, "The early membership consisted of uneducated people from families that typically consisted of nine to fourteen children living off the most meager means as they worked on Mr. Charlie's plantation chopping cotton or harvesting other crops."[35]

Phillips County, located across the Mississippi River in neighboring eastern Arkansas, serves as a model Delta county from which Mason attracted large numbers of congregants. Similar to Holmes County, Mississippi, Phillips County's population consisted of a black majority. In 1880, for instance, the black population stood at 74 percent, but by 1900 the total percentage had grown to 79 percent, making the population three-quarters black. Census files also revealed that in 1870 the illiteracy rate among blacks over the age of ten was 39 percent and by 1900, the rate still stood at 33 percent. Data indicates that blacks in the county had not made many strides in the economic or educational realms as the white minority owned the majority of the land and blacks' primary occupation remained that of farm laborer, thus making the population ripe for conversion to Mason's Holiness-Pentecostal association.[36]

We Will Let the Courts Speak in Plain English

The break between Mason and Jones proved to be less than amicable as dissenting members in Mason's congregations, with the help of Jones, petitioned the courts to issue a series of injunctions in an attempt to force him from his churches. What began as a disagreement over theology quickly became an issue of respectability in the courts and a bitter fight for control of church property. In 1907, congregants in Mason's Conway, Arkansas, church who opposed the doctrine of speaking in tongues petitioned the Faulkner County Chancery Court to issue an injunction forbidding him from promoting the controversial doctrine. The court decided that it possessed no jurisdiction in what it deemed a purely ecclesiastical matter and refused to grant the injunction. Instead, authorities ordered that the membership vote on the direction and leadership of the congregation, which led members to dismiss Mason as pastor and take spiritual direction from Jones and the tribunal in Jackson. Hoping to duplicate the success of the Conway congregation, Jones urged dissenting members in Lexington and Memphis to follow suit.

In October 1908, Henry Scott, Frank Avant, and Sydney Reaves, acting on behalf of the dissenting members of the Wellington Street congregation in Memphis, filed a lawsuit against Mason in the Shelby County Chancery Court. The dissenters alleged that before Mason visited Los Angeles, their congregation's worship style, with few exceptions, resembled that of the Baptist tradition, including rituals such as baptism, the Lord's Supper, praying, and the preaching of the gospel making up the core of their worship services. Unlike the Baptists, the congregation also believed in divine healing and performed the ritual of foot washing, thus making them part of the Holiness movement. The complainants claimed that once Mason returned, he changed the order and form of worship by introducing the practice of speaking in tongues, which did not adhere to the tenants of Holiness.[37]

Agreeing with the complainants, assistant pastor Henry Scott stated that prior to Mason traveling to California he administered the Lord's Supper, sang from hymnals, and preached in plain English but once Mason returned he instructed the congregation to put down the hymnals because they taught them to sing lies. Mason also stopped using the Bible to lead the congregation, substituting preaching in an unknown tongue and urging members to submit to the Holy Spirit so they might receive the blessing of speaking in tongues. In response, a small "ignorant" segment of the congregation began lying at the altar on pallets in an attempt to receive the Holy Spirit.[38] Scott charged that after the introduction of speaking in tongues, worship services regressed into what he referred to as "a ridiculous, farcical sideshow" as people flocked into the church to hear the strange speaking of tongues and to witness people jumping around in strange convulsions. The congregation had been turned into the laughing stock of Memphis because of Mason's diverting of the church property from its original use and implementing new rituals.[39]

In a formal deposition, fifty-two-year-old dissenting member Frank Avant echoed Scott's allegations that before Mason's trip, the congregation sang from hymnals, practiced foot washing, and received the gospel of the Bible in "plain English." Upon Mason's return, he refused to administer the original tenets of the faith. Instead, candidates began to be called to the altar to receive the baptism of the Holy Spirit, which resulted in "people lying out on the floor slobbering until late into the night waiting for the baptism of the Holy Ghost."[40] In response to the commotion, Ed Mosby, a dissenting member, fell to his knees in an act of defiance, and began praying out loud asking that the Lord deliver the congregation from the evildoing of not Mason, but the devil, whom he thought possessed the pastor. Angered, Mason stopped the service and pronounced a curse on Mosby, which frightened a large segment of the congregation to the point of their refusal to attend worship services.[41]

Thomas J. Searcy, a Baptist minister and resident of Memphis, offered an outsider's perspective on the situation. Searcy admitted that he often preached at the Wellington Street church and had become well acquainted with Mason. Under oath, he swore that prior to Mason's visit to Los Angeles nothing out of the ordinary occurred in the worship services and when asked if Mason preached in any unknown languages, Searcy replied, "he [Mason] preached with as good of English as he could but he was not a scholar."[42] Searcy explained that Mason abandoned several canons of the Baptist faith after returning from Los Angeles, and that on a recent visit to the church, he witnessed Mason speak in English and then in an unknown tongue that caused the service to descend into "general confusion and great commotion as other members began shouting, jumping, and yelling in unknown tongues" that Searcy referred to as "jabber" that no one understood.[43]

The actions of Mason and the reaction of his congregants illustrate the growing tension black religion created as progressives, such as Elias Camp Morris and Ida B. Wells, looked for a more refined religious experience. Progressives failed to realize that blacks' worship services had always been more emotional in nature and prior to the twentieth century, emotionalism transcended denominational lines. Historian Vernon Lane Wharton highlighted this when he described black Baptist religious gatherings in Mississippi that lasted well into the night in the 1800s. Women would "go into a frenzy of excitement and roll on the floor for hours together, screaming and crying." Men on the other hand, "walked on their hands and knees" while they "shout(ed) . . . as they swayed their bodies to the time of the music" and clapped "in the most frantic way." Wharton's description indicates that Mason's worship style had not deviated much from the traditional modes of blacks' worship, but what had changed was the social climate that demanded conformity if blacks were ever to meet whites' expectations of religious respectability.[44]

In court, Mason's accusers based their complaint on the diversion of church property from its original intended use. Additionally, detractors argued that Mason did not represent sole authority over the congregation as they received direction and supervisory oversight from a tribunal in Jackson, Mississippi, revealing that although fighting over proper theological protocol, Mason and Jones recognized the monetary value of the properties, which neither wanted to lose. Mason believed that church property should remain congregational, while Jones believed that control of all properties rested within a larger committee structure that members of the association, which included Mason, had

established. To prove this, Jones argued that in 1906, their Holiness congregations in Tennessee, Arkansas, and Mississippi sent delegates to Jackson to set
up a permanent supervisory board and Mason attended the convention as
the Wellington Street congregation's representative.[45] As a participant, Mason
assisted in establishing the bylaws of the tribunal, and delegates elected him to
serve as one of three overseers of the Holiness organization. By accepting the
position, the Wellington Street church, as well as Mason, submitted to the tribunal's disciplinary oversight.[46]

Jones reiterated the argument of the dissenting members, claiming that the
Holiness organization became annoyed with what he referred to as "false ministers" who disrupted congregations. In an attempt to address the issue, he
invited representatives to Jackson to establish ministerial and governmental standards. At the convention, ministers represented their congregations and the
assembly voted to accept apostolic overseers. The new administrators' jobs consisted of overseeing churches and ministers, but all agreed not to interfere with
the day-to-day governance of the local churches except when the harmony and
survival of the congregation demanded oversight by an administrator.[47]

Local congregations agreed to relinquish congregational oversight and
heretical doctrine and unclean ministers who departed from New Testament
teachings became subject to discipline by the tribunal instead of the congregation. The convention also granted the tribunal authority to excommunicate anyone deemed to be a heretical minister. Acting as an overseer himself, Mason
excommunicated William Cartwright, the pastor of the Macedonia Church of
God in Greenwood, Mississippi, after his congregation reported him for conduct
unbecoming a Holiness minister. Using the Cartwright incident as precedence,
Jones argued that when the tribunal excommunicated Mason it acted within its
established rules and regulations.[48]

Tribunal members concluded that Mason's actions had disrupted the harmony of his congregations and, more important, his acceptance of speaking in
tongues marked a clear departure from the faith of the organization. The committee acknowledged scriptural existence of tongue speaking in the twelfth chapter of Corinthians that lists the gift of tongues as one of seven gifts of the Spirit,
but regarded the doctrine as heretical because it created discord among church
members. The association instructed its ministers to treat tongue speaking as a
historical rather than theological doctrine, similar to the concept of the raising
of the dead; but even after the tribunal excommunicated Mason, he refused to
relinquish control of the church property. He argued that his congregations
retained the right of congregational governance; therefore, the tribunal did not
have the authority to excommunicate him or any other member who believed
in speaking in tongues.

Standing in opposition to the introduction of the doctrine, Richard Davis, Lula Washington, Annie Neal, Maud Washington, Edmond Mosby, Gilbert Turner, Jerry Phipps, Samuel Davis Jr., Richard Miller, Lula Haskins, Clara Rady, William Randoph, Ethel Neal, Martha Johnson, Annie Woods, and Peter Jones met in Henry Scott's home and formed their own church. The dissenters elected Scott, Avant, and Reaves as trustees of the new congregation and chose Isaac L. Jordan to serve as pastor. Jordan, a minister since 1895, joined the Wellington Street church in 1900 and helped build the first worship structure. Jordan described Mason's preaching as erratic and juvenile and recounted that while Mason preached he jumped up and down and rolled his eyes up to the top of the building as though he talked to God. He recalled that the congregation remained quiet, except for those who also believed in the tongues. As members jumped, shouted, and yelled in the unknown tongue, Jordan alleged that Mason worked them into a frenzy and when he laid hands on them they fell out on the floor where they sometimes remained all night. Jordan claimed that he agreed to serve as the church's pastor because Mason had brought back from Los Angeles "the tongue language . . . that we couldn't understand." Like many of Mason's disgruntled congregants, Jordan alleged that Mason's speaking in tongues caused him to abandon "the song books," which led "a great many of the members" to not be able to "get along with [Mason's] kind of jabber." In reaction to the events, Jordan agreed to lead the new church in an attempt to allow those members who "prayed in English" to worship peacefully. These members attempted to hold worship service in the building on Wellington Street, arguing that because they contributed money and helped to build the initial structure, they were entitled to some use of the property. Mason refused to allow the nonconformists entry and demanded the return of all keys in their possession. Left without access to the church, the dissenting congregation decided to sue.[49]

Acting on the congregation's behalf, trustees Scott, Avant, and Reaves agreed to serve as primary plaintiffs. Aware of the need to play up the issue of respectability in the courts, the trustees hired Robert H. Booth, a well-respected white attorney, to represent them. After hearing their complaints, Booth filed the suit based on two issues. First, he argued that with the introduction of the concept of speaking in tongues, Mason diverted the use of the property from its originally acquired purpose.[50] Second, Booth believed that since the highest church authority excommunicated Mason, the members of the congregation who continued to adhere to the original faith and order of the church should retain ownership of the church property. He filed the initial lawsuit in October 1907, in which he claimed Mason's dangerous and boisterous followers frightened his law-abiding clients away from worship services. Booth requested that the Shelby County Chancery Court issue an injunction to prohibit Mason and "each and every one" of his followers from trespassing or going upon the church property while the lawsuit was pending. The injunction also requested that the defendants turn over all keys to the sheriff of Shelby County. Chancery Court judge Lamar Heiskell granted Booth the injunction and ordered the sheriff to serve Charles H. Mason, Billy Frayser, Allie Frayser, Sam Jones, Eddie Rodgers, Charlie Wheeler, George Sparks, Willie Roberts, and General Lowery with an injunction stating the aforementioned restrictions.[51]

Mason secured the help of Harry R. Saddler, a local white attorney, who, in his first act as the defendants' attorney, asked Judge Heiskell to dismiss the case. Saddler argued that the suit clearly involved an ecclesiastical controversy concerning matters of church doctrine, discipline, and governance and remained out of the jurisdiction of the civil courts of the county and state. He also petitioned the court to dissolve the injunction.[52] In February 1907, Judge Heiskell agreed to consider his petition and after one day of testimony ruled that the injunction against the defendants should remain in place, but, in addition, the plaintiffs also could not use the property until the courts issued a ruling.[53]

While preparing for litigation, Mason and his followers submitted to the court formal responses to the accusations made by the plaintiffs. In answering the charges, he explained that the congregation possessed no written creed or book of regulations; rather, they believed in the Old and New Testaments. Mason further argued that the original tenets of the church remained intact and the congregation continued to follow the Bible as the infallible word of God. In his opinion, the concept of speaking in tongues represented a higher development of the gospel among his congregation and not a departure from the original tenets of the faith. He justified the introduction of the doctrine with Mark 16:15, which stated:

> Go ye into all the world, preach the gospel to every creature. He that believeth and is baptized shall be saved. And he that believeth not shall be damned. And these signs shall follow them that believe in my name: They shall cast out devils; they shall speak with new tongues; they shall take up serpents and if they eat any deadly thing it shall not hurt them; they shall lay their hands on the sick and they shall recover.[54]

In response to the claim that he turned the congregation into a laughing stock, Mason alleged that black churchgoers always demonstrated great enthusiasm during worship services and prior to introducing the doctrine of speaking in tongues, all his members clapped their hands, ran over the floor, and, at times, even crawled when they fell under the power of the Lord. Arguing that this was not unique to his congregation, Mason stated that even in the black Baptist and

Methodist churches some members "laid out" day and night and that after the introduction of the doctrine of speaking in tongues, his services operated in an orderly manner. He said that his members used to be so happy that they ran, yelled, and clapped as they rejoiced in the Lord, but since his return the members seemed to have calmed down because people now wanted to surrender to the Holy Spirit so that they might receive the gift of tongues. This resulted in more people remaining in their seats, which made for more orderly services than before the introduction of glossolalia.[55]

In addressing his excommunication, Mason emphatically denied that the tribunal in Jackson controlled the churches of the Holiness association, claiming that the congregations in Mississippi, Arkansas, and Tennessee remained independent of the supervisory board. Edward Driver, a fellow Holiness minister and follower of Mason, echoed this sentiment. Driver arrived in Memphis in 1891 and joined the Wellington Street church the same year. As a result of Mason's spiritual tutelage, he became the head pastor of the Hazlehurst Church of God in West Point, Mississippi, and served as their delegate at the January and August 1906 conventions held in Jackson. As Driver remembered, the meetings did not establish legislative powers over the Memphis congregation or any other church in the tri-state region. Driver referred to the gathering as a meeting of elders commonly called a "Holiness Meeting," that convened twice a year. To prove his point, Driver produced an invitation published in the August 1906 edition of the *Truth* that invited ministers to the nonsectarian Holiness convention. The invitation claimed that the convention was "an effort to get all who love the Lord together in the Holy Spirit," but did not mention elected delegates, the question of government, or who possessed ultimate authority over the congregation.[56]

Instead, delegates studied the Bible by day and conducted a revival by night and the Wellington Street congregation relinquished no legislative power to any tribunal. Each church remained independent of the others and their governmental structure remained congregational. If any questions arose over the religion, property, or conduct of a member, the final decision of that matter rested with each church and not the advisory board. Under these rules the general convention in Jackson possessed no authority to excommunicate Mason.[57]

Mason alleged that the general convention in Jackson gathered together for the purpose of conducting their annual revival. Only after the meeting adjourned did some attendants gather for the consideration of creating a supervisory council. The committee would oversee the building of schools, conduct mission work, and purchase a new press. Mason argued that the committee never discussed formulating a governmental body to oversee the churches and the general convention never asked the Holiness congregations to send delegates; rather, he attended the conference as a free and independent minister.[58] Mason insisted that the members of the board possessed no governmental authority to prescribe any doctrine or matter of faith. He added that the Holiness congregations in Rollinson, Arkansas, and the Tennessee municipalities of Bell, Murray City, Dyersburg, Trenton, Milan, and New Hope never sent delegates to the conventions.[59]

As to the question of Mason's legitimacy to lead the congregation, all involved agreed they had never formally elected Mason as pastor. The reason being, when Mason arrived in Memphis in 1897, he preached on the streets and held tent revivals in several outlying suburbs. Only after gaining a reputation as a popular street preacher did his congregation grow. In need of space, members contributed money to build the church on Wellington Street. Mason argued that once the congregation moved into the building, no one questioned his authority to lead.[60]

In addition to defending his record, Mason called into question the authority of Scott, Avant, and Reaves to file the lawsuit. The original congregation never elected the men as trustees and only one of the three served in a leadership position. As proof, he presented the court with the original bill of sale for the land that proved that Ed Loveless, Charles Liddell, David Smith, and Jim Murphy served as original trustees of the church. Mason explained that of the four original trustees, only two remained active in the church and the other two had been replaced. Charles Liddell left Memphis in 1900 and the congregation elected Charles Wheeler to serve out Liddell's term. After the death of Ed Loveless in 1905, his position was taken over by William Frayser. William Roberts had also been named to the position of trustee, bringing the total number to five.[61]

Mason further argued that prior to the allegations, Scott, Avant, and Reaves were not in good standing with the church. Scott had been removed from the position of assistant pastor for "undue intimacy" with another man's wife and, as for Avant, he left the congregation two years prior to the lawsuit and no longer held membership at the Wellington Street church.[62] Mason questioned the other plaintiffs whose names appeared on the bill of complaint, stating that six months prior to the allegations the congregation expelled Jerry Phipps for drunkenness and general immorality and later permanently withdrew the right hand of fellowship from him for his continued immoral behavior. As for Sidney Reaves, Robert Jones, and Samuel Davis Jr., Mason claimed these men never attended the church on a regular basis and the members of the congregation barely knew their names. Furthermore, the number of names on the plaintiffs' bill of complaint only represented twenty-one out of one hundred and fifty members, leaving him with the support of the majority.[63]

Descriptions such as "undue intimacy" with another man's wife, drunkenness, and general immorality offer insight into how the general public viewed the denomination. Black progressives of the time would have certainly made the connection between the congregants' behaviors and how those actions seemed to reinforce age-old stereotypes about blacks' sexuality and their lack of morality. Blacks, themselves, looked toward their preachers as the models of proper behavior and black clergymen's integrity was to be beyond reproach. Whites also viewed black preachers as the standard-bearers for the race and when the black clergy fell short of living up to these standards, the black masses were indicted. The fact that court depositions show that Mason's leadership might not have been the most upstanding citizens and may have struggled with extramarital affairs and drunkenness reveal why the public acted so negatively toward the denomination. To many, COGIC remained an embarrassment and the pending court case threatened to make public the denomination's behavior, which undoubtedly would impact all black Memphians.

In April 1908, Judge Heiskell agreed to hear the case. Mason's attorney wanted to prove that the majority of the Wellington Street congregation supported the doctrine of speaking in tongues, and he presented the court with a list of one hundred and thirty signed names of individuals as proof of support.[64] Mason's legal defense also secured the testimony of Larry P. Adams, a white Church of Christ minister, to defend that his introduction of the doctrine of speaking in tongues did not represent a departure from the basic tenants of Holiness. Similar to Mason, Adams arrived in Memphis in 1895 and began preaching in a tent on a street corner where he and thirty white followers formed a Holiness congregation.[65] Adams claimed that his congregants also lived "sanctified lives" and believed in the doctrine of speaking in tongues as a tenet of Holiness. Adams revealed that he knew of Mason's preaching but never attended his services before 1907 and only recently became intrigued because of the *Commercial Appeal*'s published descriptions of Mason's worship style. Prompted by the series of articles, he attended the Wellington Street church for the first time and heard Mason speak in tongues. Instead of experiencing bewilderment, Adams became convinced that the Holy Spirit dwelled within Mason and in fact his worship service did not deviate much from his own.[66]

According to Adams, the original tenets of Holiness remained intact and Mason preached the same doctrine as before, but now he did so with a better understanding of the entire gospel. Many congregations display a lack of understanding when tongues are first introduced and Mason's congregation to Adams seemed no different. When asked whether it was normal for everyone in the congregation to understand the tongues, he explained that one might get the gift of tongues but not be able to interpret it, while others might get the gift of interpretation and not the gift of tongues.[67] For example, Adams told the court of a twelve-year-old girl who spoke in three languages. One of the languages turned out to be Spanish, which another member interpreted as, "oh, Lamb of God, help me pray, Satan got me bound."[68] Adams claimed that he had heard people speak in Italian and African languages. For instance, during a visit by Samuel J. Mead, a white missionary who lived in Africa for twenty years, Adams witnessed a young woman speak in tongues during worship service. To the amazement of everyone, Mead translated the woman's words and informed the congregation that she had spoken in an African language.[69]

Members of Adams's congregation also lay out on the floor in search of the Holy Spirit and as proof, he described an episode of a young white woman whom he believed to be possessed by demons. The woman's bad disposition caused her to become frustrated and violent over small things, which led the congregation to conclude that demons possessed her body. One night she lay out on the floor for hours as the members prayed for her and after submitting to the Holy Spirit, her disposition changed and she became as peaceful as the ocean when Jesus calmed it.[70] The congregants took the marked change as a sign that the Holy Spirit filled her and cast the demons out and the young lady became a fine model of womanhood for the rest of the congregation to follow.

Gender again came to the forefront of the dispute when Adams provided the court with descriptions of the Holy Spirit speaking through women. The ability of women to receive the gift of tongues in the same manner as men distinguished Pentecostalism from other mainstream denominations that theologically restricted women based upon their gender. The ability of a twelve-year-old girl to speak in tongues destroyed any doubt that the Holy Spirit could communicate through anyone, even a female child. The second example highlights that women could also receive the gift of redemption and grace at the hands of the Holy Spirit. Although the woman never openly spoke in tongues, members concluded that her "changed disposition" and calmness meant that the Spirit had saved her. More important, the woman's actions even lie outside the normal gendered behavior prescribed for white women, which meant black progressives viewed the similar actions displayed by Mason's female congregants in the same manner.

Adams also provided theological evidence that justified Mason's belief in the doctrine of speaking in tongues when he described the day Jesus left Bethlehem for Jerusalem. As Jesus departed the city, he prayed and placed hands on sinners promising that God would bless their souls. During his journey, he continued to lay hands upon people; after arriving in Jerusalem followers continued to praise God in the temples and when the day of Pentecost came, the Holy Spirit found them all together and filled each of them with the Holy Ghost and they began to speak in tongues. Adams also used Acts 10:45–46 to show evidence of speaking in tongues in the Bible. Citing the example of Cornelius, a

Roman centurion who possessed faith in God and was filled with the Holy Ghost and began speaking in tongues, led everyone present to praise the Holy Spirit for the gift. Adams concluded his testimony by explaining that even the apostle Paul laid hands on believers and the Holy Ghost came upon them and they spoke in tongues.[71]

The Ruling That Everyone Understood

Although the defendants produced a credible witness, Judge Heiskell ruled in favor of the plaintiffs, basing his decision on the principle of the original faith. In Heiskell's opinion, when Mason introduced the doctrine of speaking in tongues, he departed from the original tenets of the faith. Avant and the other plaintiffs who continued to adhere to the original doctrine of the faith were entitled to the use and enjoyment of the church property. In conclusion, Heiskell warned Mason that any attempt in the future to preach or hold worship services at the church constituted trespassing. The ruling marked the second time Mason had lost church property due to the controversy caused by speaking in tongues, but he vowed to appeal the court's decision.[72]

Attempting to regain control of the lost property, Mason fired his attorney and hired Robert E. Hart, a black attorney and AME minister. Although a member of the Methodist denomination, which remained one of Mason's most outspoken critics, Hart presented the case before the Western District of the Tennessee Supreme Court in April 1908. In a narrow victory, the supreme court reversed the decision of the lower court. In the opinion of the district court, the Wellington Street congregation did join the association of churches under the control of the tribunal in Jackson; however, evidence failed to convince the court that the tribunal possessed legislative powers over the individual churches. In the opinion of the court, the tribunal acted only in an advisory role to the churches. Even though Mason attended both the meetings, no proof indicated that the Wellington Street congregation elected him to represent them.[73] The court agreed that in 1906 some Holiness preachers undertook the effort to organize and appoint the three men who took the position of overseers but failed to find sufficient evidence that any congregation conferred upon the three men the power to oversee or excommunicate any members. The overwhelming weight of the evidence proved that the defendants' church belonged to the congregational order and that the congregation never submitted to the powers of the tribunal in Jackson.[74]

As to the issue of whether Mason departed from the original doctrine of the church, the court found that the congregation followed no written creed and local minister-led congregations maintained ultimate authority. The continued practice of the ordinances of baptism, the Lord's Supper, and foot washing adhered to the theological theory of sanctification and the defendants only added to the faith by introducing the doctrine of speaking in tongues. As a civil entity, the court acknowledged that it possessed no jurisdiction to rule on the correctness of the defendants' interpretation of the scriptures, but Mason had presented biblical evidence for the proposition that the power to speak in tongues will be given to Christians. The court dismissed allegations of scandalous behavior among Mason's followers due to the lack of evidence reflecting the morality or immorality of the defendants. If the practice of such immorality did exist, the actions remained a matter for church discipline or police intervention, not an affair for the civil court.[75]

In closing, the court restated that no ecclesiastical body existed which possessed the right to decide the correctness of the doctrine preached in Mason's Wellington Street church. Likewise, the court believed that the congregation held no creed outside the Bible and in such a case the majority of the congregation must control its affairs. In the Tennessee Supreme Court's opinion, the chancery court acted incorrectly by awarding the church to Jordan and the other dissenting members. The new ruling indicated that Mason's faction held a majority and decreed a reversal of the lower court's judgment. The defendants retained the right to take possession of all church property.

When Mason and his followers reclaimed ownership of the building they found the structure in a dilapidated condition and unsafe for worship.[76] The sixteen-month injunction had kept the plaintiffs and defendants out of the building, during which time, the general condition of the structure deteriorated. A leak in the roof damaged the floors, causing them to rot. In several places the wooden planks underneath the ruined carpet had swollen, causing the floor to burst. Consequently, before the congregation could retake possession of the property, a new roof, floor, and carpet would have to be installed for the building to be used for worship.[77]

Mason pointed out that the injunction caused the congregation to lose revenue needed for the repairs as parishioners usually donated $180 to $190 a month in offerings before the lawsuit, but due to the injunction, people stopped attending and collections dropped. The collection averaged less than half the normal amount as before and out of fear of losing the entire membership, Mason purchased an auditorium-sized tent for $128.00 and worshiped there until a windstorm tore it to pieces.[78]

To recoup the money lost on repairs, offerings, and sixteen months of mortgage payments, Mason countersued Avant, Scott, and Reaves for damages. In November 1909, Hart argued the case before the Shelby County Chancery Court, calling a series of witnesses with the hope of determining the value of the building and estimating the cost of repairs. William A. Turner, Hart's first witness, stated that he inspected the building on Wellington Street and found the floors rotten and in need of serious repair and while not a contractor, he estimated the cost of replacing the floor at fifty dollars.[79] Henry Turner, a real estate agent who specialized in rental property in Memphis, also inspected the building, placing the property's value at close to $4,000 and citing that the owners could rent the structure for forty or fifty dollars a month.[80]

I. L. Jordan took the stand for the defense and swore that no member of his congregation damaged any church property and the structure was in the same condition before the filing of the initial lawsuit. He stated that because of the lack of funds in the beginning, the congregation had decided on a cheap rubber roof and it began to leak three years ago. Even before the litigation, Jordan argued, they tried unsuccessfully to patch the roof. He also questioned the building's estimated value of $4,000, pointing out that the initial structure cost only $700 to build in 1900 and doubted that the price more than quadrupled in nine years.[81]

On February 3, 1910, chancery court judge Lamar Heiskell ruled that Mason could recover damages. He awarded sixteen months of church rental at thirty dollars a month, which totaled $480 but ruled that the complainants were entitled to equal rights in terms of property use. Therefore, he only awarded half of the amount, totaling $240, to Mason. In addition, Mason recouped $128 for the money spent on the tent. As to the actual building repairs, the court awarded $120 for the replacement of the roof but disallowed the $150 for the replacement of the ceiling and floors. In the end, the court dismissed Mason's efforts to recoup lost offerings during the sixteen-month injunction.

The series of events centered around the lawsuit in Memphis repeated itself in Mason's Lexington congregation when, on October 26, 1908, John A. Lee, a trustee of the St. Paul congregation and a dissenting member who opposed the doctrine of speaking in tongues, filed a lawsuit against Mason in Holmes County in an attempt to gain control over church property. In October, Lee and his faction successfully petitioned Holmes County chancery court judge James P. McCool to issue an injunction that forbade Mason and his followers from trespassing on church property. Mason hired Allen Peppers, a white Lexington attorney, to represent him in court and Judge McCool agreed to hear the case in May 1909 after Peppers failed to get the injunction dismissed.

McCool rendered his decision in July 1909 after two months of arguments and deliberation. Ruling in favor of Lee, the judge decided that since the majority of the "original" congregation opposed the introduction of the doctrine of speaking in tongues, they were entitled to exclusive ownership of the church property.[82] Mason appealed the decision to the Mississippi State Supreme Court, and on September 9, 1909, the state supreme court requested that the court file be transferred to Jackson. The actual court case and ruling of the Mississippi Supreme Court could not be found, but Mason's continued control of church property and leadership of the Lexington congregation indicates a ruling in his favor.

In 1907 Mason found himself in the midst of a theological controversy that became a matter of church governance between him and Jones and a secular issue of respectability in the civil courts of Arkansas, Mississippi, and Tennessee. Although he and his supporters succeeded in winning two of the three cases, they failed to win the support of the general public. Negative media coverage reinforced stereotypes that only the ignorant and buffoonish followed Mason and even Jones, the one-time close friend of Mason, regarded the doctrine of speaking in tongues as an uncultured delusion. More important, middle-class blacks continued to view Mason and his followers as unsupportive of the efforts of racial uplift, which further marginalized COGIC within the African American community. Although unpopular, the denomination continued to grow and Mason's influence among blacks in the Arkansas and Mississippi Delta would eventually bring him to the attention of the federal government during World War I.

3

Mason Told Us Not to Fight

Religion, Respectability, and Conscientious Objectorship

Black progressives believed their participation in World War I would aid in the fight against segregation and therefore viewed the world conflict as an opportunity for racial advancement. Emmett J. Scott served as a source of pride when in October 1917 President Wilson appointed him special assistant to the secretary of war. Scott, the protégé of Booker T. Washington, used his position to advocate for the advancement of the race in the form of integrated training camps and the commissioning of black officers. In a letter penned to the provost marshal general, Scott's advocacy can be seen when he argued, "The attitude of the Negro was one of complete acceptance of the draft . . . and that there was deep resentment in many quarters that he [African Americans] was not permitted to volunteer in connection with the National Guard units."[1] Scott also agreed with W. E. B. Du Bois when he called for the race to close ranks and "Let us, while this war lasts, forget our special grievances and close our ranks stand shoulder to shoulder with our fellow white citizens and the allied nations that are fighting for democracy."[2]

America conveyed that the best way to demonstrate patriotism rested in the purchasing of Liberty Bonds, and African Americans, eager to show their loyalty in return for social advancement, bought more than $25 million worth of war bonds. Black insurance agencies and fraternal organizations acquired large quantities. For example, in Little Rock, Arkansas, Scipio A. Jones, a prominent black lawyer, presented U.S. secretary of the treasury William Gibbs McAdoo with a check worth $50,000 in payment for Liberty Bonds purchased by the

Mosaic Templar chapter of which Jones was a member. In all, before the end of the war, Jones's work in the black community helped to raise over $125,000.[3] The Greenwood, Mississippi, newspaper the *Commonwealth* described a similar event in April 1917 when it highlighted a meeting between local black leaders who pledged their loyalty to the country and the war effort. The article ended by stating that white county officials praised the group for their loyalty but warned against listening to unpatriotic rhetoric that could harm the government or the local community.[4]

Even impoverished blacks did their part to support the war. For instance, in north Memphis on June 23, 1918, Charles Mason delivered a sermon titled "The Kaiser in the Light of the Scriptures" in which he called for unyielding support of the Allied powers. In front of what many referred to as a multitude, he persuaded blacks to purchase Liberty Bonds by depicting the "German leader as the Beast or Antichrist, the man of warfare, pillage, and suffering. Christ, on the other hand, represented peace and the war effort of the allies."[5] Mason defended his request for the purchasing of Liberty Bonds by using Matthew 5:42 when he argued:

> Is it right to buy Liberty Bonds? Yes! Yes!
> What does it mean to buy Liberty Bonds?
> It means to lend your country a certain amount of money. What says the scripture? Matt. 5:42, "Give to him that asketh thee, and from them that borrow of thee turn not away." Brethren, we are living by every word of God—Matt. 4.[6]

Mason ended the sermon by stating, "Our government is asking us for a loan, and we are in no violation of God's words in granting it, and not only to loan, but to loan hoping for nothing to gain." He used himself as an example when he claimed he had personally "loaned" the government more than $3,000 for the purchasing of Liberty Bonds and as far as he was concerned, "the spiritual injunction stands as I have loaned, hoping for nothing in return."[7] In conclusion, he prayed that the time would come when the "German hordes" would be driven back across the Rhine, the independence of Belgium restored, and "for the coming of the Prince of Peace, the day when men will beat their swords no more."[8]

Nevertheless, due to the interracial nature of Pentecostalism, whites became especially suspicious of Mason, as strange white men gathered at his churches and held services that ran late into the night. Whites mistakenly took these activities as pro-German, Socialist, and subversive in nature. Additionally, COGIC members' strict adherence to sanctification, which required congregants to separate themselves from secular activities, allowed the larger black community to assume that the denomination did not support the war nor subscribe to the efforts to use the conflict to pursue racial advancement. As blacks purchased Liberty Bonds and advocated for the drafting of black troops, COGIC's actions often placed the denomination in direct opposition to the black community's war effort, which singled out Mason and COGIC for their perceived lack of support. Yet, the allegation, when examined from a religious perspective, renders a different outcome.

World War I had been underway in Europe for three years when on April 16, 1917, Congress issued a declaration of war. Wilson would endorse the congressional declaration entering the United States into the conflict under the banner of a promise "to make the world safe for Democracy." Days later, he issued an executive order that established the Committee on Public Information and appointed muckraker George Creel to head the new agency. Creel convinced Wilson that the best approach to influencing public opinion about the war included expressions of patriotism and due to large numbers of first- or second-generation German immigrants living in America, unwavering persecution of dissenters.[9]

Despite the government's best efforts, significant antiwar sentiment soon arose among many working-class blacks who felt apathy toward the country because of their lack of social and political rights under Jim Crow segregation.[10] To discourage dissent, Congress passed the Alien, Espionage and Sedition Acts making it unlawful to criticize governmental leaders and war policies and measures. The legislation also set penalties of up to $10,000 and twenty years in prison for those who refused duty in the armed services, incited insubordination, or circulated false reports and statements with the intent to disrupt the war effort.[11] The wartime measures still did not hinder a black Mississippian when he published an anonymous antiwar circular signed "Negro Educator," which urged black men and boys to avoid military service and condemned what he referred to as "well educated Negroes who urged young black men to be killed like sheep, for nothing."[12] The *Washington Bee* also highlighted the division within the black community in an editorial published in April 1917, when an anonymous author wrote that "the self styled spokesman of the black people had no right to offer the services of blacks to the government." The unknown author further stated that "those bootlickers who accepted disenfranchisement and segregation could volunteer their own services for the fighting."[13]

In addition to those who opposed the war on the grounds of segregation, conscientious religious objectors also refused to support the war. In the past, America had relied on volunteer armies, and the country had seldom been forced to confront conscientious religious objectors' stance toward serving in the military. Only with the coming of the Civil War did Americans experience military conscription for the first time and with it came the creation of a system in both the North and South that "provided means by which those with conscientious scruples against war could avoid military service." Draftees could choose noncombatant positions, or in more extreme situations, pay someone to take their place.[14] Passed by Congress in 1903, however, the Universal Military Service Act required "all male citizens between the ages of eighteen and forty-five to be subject to military service, but the legislation supposedly exempted members of religious organizations opposed to war."[15]

As it became clear that America's policy of neutrality would not keep the country out of World War I, conscientious objectors' interpretation of the Universal Military Service Act placed many religious denominations, both black and white, on a collision course with federal authorities.[16] Secretary of War Newton Baker argued that although the country possessed the power to draft male citizens, conscription might not be necessary. Only after top military officials advised that conscription would aid the military's war efforts did Secretary Baker and President Wilson agree to implement the draft. In the South, however, both black and white religious objectors refused to register with local draft boards and consequently the federal government targeted them during World War I because of their pacifist stance.[17]

Historian Theodore Kornweibel summarized the mood of America when he argued, neither the public nor the government displayed tolerance for those who believed that God forbade them to render military service to their country.[18] For example, Kansas Mennonites, with their doctrine of nonresistance and German heritage, drew the attention of government officials when Mennonite men refused to betray their pacifist religious theology and report for induction to the armed services. Blacks also opposed the war as a result of religious beliefs. For instance, in 1917, authorities arrested Robert Russell, an African American and self-described "Holy Roller," for his refusal to support the war. Russell supported his opposition by referencing the biblical mandate of "Thou shalt not kill," which he theorized made him responsible to the word of God and not the secular laws of man.[19]

Despite the patriotic assurances of Mason, suspicions surfaced in Holmes County, Mississippi, that he also opposed the war. Claims that he encouraged his male parishioners to seek conscientious objector status came to light, and to many, this made him guilty of violating the Espionage and Sedition Acts. More important, as Jeanette Keith argued, the poor white population accounted for the majority of the selective service conscription numbers in southern states such as Mississippi and whites were now eager to share the burden with the black population. Local draft board members selected to serve in their counties exercised great authority when deciding who would be drafted and who would receive deferments. Mason's spiritual influence over the black majority, however, challenged their control when he told members to seek religious objector status, thus making it harder for conscription boards to manage the war.[20]

Trouble on the Home Front

Mason's immediate troubles began in early 1917 when word spread that a large spider in Kansas City, Missouri, had spun in its web, "Millions for War." People, including Mason, wanting to witness the phenomenon, traveled from across the country to Kansas City. While viewing the web, Mason allegedly prophesied that the United States would enter the war and many men would travel to Europe to fight, never to return. As a result of his prophesy, when the United States entered World War I, Mason supposedly instructed his male parishioners not to fight.[21]

Federal authorities, however, did not direct their attention toward Mason until August 1917 when Jack Wright, a black resident of Lexington, Mississippi, refused to report for induction to the armed forces. Wright fled Lexington, but federal authorities arrested him in Jackson later the same month. During his interrogation, Wright claimed membership in Mason's congregation and when pressured, he informed authorities that the religious leader instructed his male parishioners not to fight in the war. With the information obtained from the interrogation, the newly created Bureau of Investigations (BOI) opened a file on Mason and instructed agents in Mississippi to compile a detailed report of his activities in Holmes County. In addition, the bureau alerted the Military Intelligence Division (MID) of the War Department and both agencies began collecting information on Mason and his alleged opposition to World War I.[22]

The government's overall scrutiny of religious objectors increased in the first months of America's involvement in the war, and Pentecostal groups ranked high on the list. Organizations such as the Church of God (Cleveland) and the Assemblies of God became outspoken opponents of America's wartime measures. The Church of God, for instance, publicly denounced the war and issued decrees stating that members should not support or make themselves available for military service.[23] The Assemblies of God, however, tempered their pacifist stance, arguing that "the organization officially denounced the taking of human life," but urged their male members "to comply with the law and register for the draft." They also instructed members "to seek legal exemption," when they, in good faith, "could not engage in the taking of human life."[24]

The government would also aggressively investigate alleged black religious objectorship, which explains their investigation of COGIC. In response to Wright's accusation, M. M. Schaumbuger, a special agent with the Bureau of Investigations, traveled to Lexington to further investigate. Upon arrival, Schaumbuger met with county officials who offered incriminating evidence. Chancery County clerk John Fugus explained that John Hart, a black preacher and member of Mason's congregation, revealed that Mason had advised blacks throughout the county not to register with local conscription boards. Hart also informed officials that at a recent baptizing, he had informed Mason that, "unless he stopped speaking against the government and the war, he planned to leave the church."[25] Upon further questioning, the agent learned of four black residents, all members of Troop E, a black cavalry unit stationed in Jackson, who attended the worship services at Mason's church in Lexington. Schaumbuger telephoned the assistant U.S. attorney in Jackson and informed him of his intentions to interview the four soldiers.[26]

On September 27, 1917, Agent Schaumbuger interviewed Jim Beville, Charles Gibson, Arch Moore, and Ben Stigler in the office of the assistant U.S. attorney in Jackson. All four denied attending Mason's church and when pressed to explain why people identified them as members of the congregation, the men explained that on a recent leave of absence, they gathered at the church after a member of the congregation killed a young girl during worship services. The soldiers speculated that as the sheriff responded to the incident, he noticed their uniforms and may have thought they were regular parishioners. The servicemen also denied ever hearing Mason preach against the war or serving in the military but did state that most people in the county viewed the preacher as a menace. The four agreed to act as informants when on leave in Lexington and to report any suspicious activities to their commanders in Jackson. Despite the lack of concrete evidence, Schaumbuger recommended that the file on Mason and the Church of God in Christ remain open for the purpose of general surveillance.[27]

With the federal government on a heightened state of alert, the Bureau of Investigation's decision to conduct further surveillance on Mason as a possible dissenter and cause of local draft boards to miss their conscription numbers should come as no surprise. Whites in Lexington welcomed the attention of federal authorities, as they remained aware that their county's population consisted of a black majority and as rumors of German sympathizers sowing discontent among the black population increased, whites became extremely paranoid. Even more alarming was America's need for manpower, resulting in the increased presence of black men in military uniforms throughout the South, which caused whites to fear a possible challenge to the racial order. No matter how foolish, whites' nervousness about a possible violent black uprising with the help of pro-German or Socialist agents dominated their thoughts, and the August 1917 Green Corn Rebellion where five hundred farmers rebelled against their county conscription board in eastern Oklahoma reminded them of the threat. Led by

Socialists, blacks participated in the movement and successfully ambushed a deputy sheriff. Although officials put down the uprising immediately, fears of blacks conspiring with the Socialist Party spread rapidly throughout the country. Harboring these anxieties, whites in Holmes County would vigorously investigate any rumors of black opposition and welcome the prosecution of any dissenter thought to be causing trouble.[28]

In early 1918, county draft boards throughout the Delta again failed to meet conscription numbers. The Greenwood, Mississippi, *Commonwealth* highlighted the problem in a headline that read "Leflore Will Fall Short on New Registration." In Greenwood, only twenty white youths and eighty-six blacks had registered with the Leflore County draft board by April 1918. The draft board wanted 350, expected 200, but only got 106 new registrants for the county. Officials also noticed high numbers of black men seeking conscientious objector status for religious reasons, and although the Universal Military Service Act clearly provided for the exemption from service due to religious beliefs, it became clear that the War Department intended to convert all able-bodied men into soldiers.[29]

In orders issued on October 10, 1917, the War Department stated that if military officials "handled" conscientious objectors correctly, most would renounce their religious convictions for patriotism. The War Department suggested that officials simply ignore the requests of objectors for exemption from service as one way of prompting their conversion. After reporting to camp, if a draftee continued to object to the war, superiors were to order the continued practice of drilling until his case could be heard. If the recruit refused to obey orders, "he was to be segregated from the rest of the unit in order to keep his ideas from infecting others. Once segregated, all efforts should be made to convert the draftee."[30]

Military officials also used chaplains in their quest to convert draftees to the war effort. Familiar with the Bible, chaplains questioned the validity of the draftees' religious objections to war with the use of biblical references that justified violence. Jesus' use of violence to cleanse the temple of moneychangers served as a prime example that nonresistance remained inconsistent to God's will. Chaplains asked, "If your mother was about to be attacked by an intruder, would you use force to protect her?" If the objector answered yes, then his belief in nonresistance became questionable and he could be possibly converted. If all else failed, the draftee's loyalty to the country was questioned. Chaplains argued that "if a man loved his country, he should be willing to fight for it." They pointed out that "America was fighting to not only save democracy, but also Christianity, and if the United States was defeated, these two institutions would be endangered."[31]

Even with the efforts of the military to convert religious objectors, local draft boards in black belt regions of the South continued experiencing problems meeting their required quotas. Frank E. Ethridge, the inspector of the draft boards in Mississippi, complained in a letter to the sheriff of Holmes County, George Bell, about the county's poor performance. On February 23, 1918, the local board issued a call for one hundred thirty-five blacks, out of which ninety-three would be sent to Camp Pike, Arkansas, for military service. Of the number ordered to duty, only thirty-five reported for induction. On March 13, 1918, the board ordered sixty-five blacks to report, out of which fifty-seven would be inducted. Again, the board fell short of its required numbers and only thirty-four reported for induction. The breaking point occurred three days later when the board called for forty-two blacks to report and of this number only thirteen appeared before the local draft board. The sheriff suggested to Ethridge that the failure in meeting the numbers might be the result of the poorly kept roads throughout the county.[32]

Feeling pressure from state superiors, Ethridge decided to visit Holmes County and found the records of the local board in poor condition and, after a general investigation, concluded the overall performance of the board to be ineffective. Subsequent to dismissing several members, Ethridge interviewed two men the sheriff had arrested for failure to report and their stories placed blame on more than just the failures of the Holmes County draft board. After speaking with the prisoners, Ethridge became convinced that Charles Mason shouldered some of the blame for the draft board's recent problems and once the Bureau of Investigations received word of the agent's suspicions, the agency dispatched Special Agent Harry Gully from their New Orleans office to investigate the matter.[33]

Upon arriving in Lexington, Gully found whites eager to report the strange occurrences happening in the town. The special agent first interviewed the owner of the local boardinghouse who told him that from March 9 through the 16 a white foreigner by the name of Johnson occupied a room at her boarding house. The owner explained that Johnson slept all day and wandered amongst the black residents at night. The innkeeper noticed that the stranger never talked to any of the white residents, but openly conversed with the blacks and preached at Mason's church during the nights of March 9 through the 15 to well after midnight. The woman stated that the stranger left her boardinghouse on the night of March 16 with Mason and the two headed to Durant, Mississippi.[34]

The innkeeper's statement again revealed whites' suspicion of unknown pro-German sympathizers or Socialists stirring up trouble among the black population. For example, rumors surrounded James Vardaman, U.S. senator and former governor of Mississippi. Vardaman voted against the United States entering into the war and opposed the draft and the Alien, Espionage and Sedition Acts. In 1918 Vardaman faced opposition in the Democratic primary from a young congressman who publicly labeled support for Vardaman as an act of treason. As the campaign dragged on, crowds regularly heckled the senator and referred to him as "Kaiser von Vardaman."[35]

Agent Gully found blacks eager to talk about Mason's activities. George Bacon, a member and deacon of Mason's Lexington congregation, when questioned about his preacher's possible antiwar stance, presented Gully with an edited doctrinal statement that read:

> We believe that the governments are God given institutions for the benefit of mankind. He admonished and exhorts our members to honor magistrates and powers that be. To respect, obey, and love the law. We hereby and herewith declare our loyalty to the President and to the Constitution of the United States, and pledge fidelity to the flag which the republic stands. But as a God fearing peace loving, and law abiding people, we only claim or [not a legible word] as American citizens, namely to worship God according to the dictates of our own conscience. We believe the shedding of human blood or taking of human life to be contrary to the teaching of our Lord and Savior, and as a body we are averse to war in all its various forms. We herewith offer ourselves to the President for any service that will not conflict with our conscientious scruples in this report, with love to all, with malice toward none and with due respect to all who differ from us in our interpretation of the scriptures.[36]

Bacon also gave Gully a petition printed in 1918 and signed by Mason that detailed numerous reasons why members of COGIC should be exempt from the war. He stated he did not know who printed the petition but knew they circulated throughout the different "sanctified churches" in the county. Bacon provided more information about the white foreigner, revealing that during personal conversations Johnson informed him that he had originally come from England about twenty months before and traveled the country as an evangelist. At the request of Mason, Johnson left Memphis at the conclusion of a revival and traveled to Lexington to conduct another one among the parishioners in Holmes County. The revival ended in a great success, but Bacon admitted that he never heard Mason or Johnson openly preach against the war.[37]

George Brooks, a black resident who claimed to know Mason and most of his followers in Lexington, did, however, offer incriminating evidence when he informed the agent that he observed the preacher telling blacks that "if they joined his church they would not have to go to war." Brooks also alleged that his wife heard Mason, in one of his sermons, say that "the Negroes did not have to go to war, and they were fools if they wanted to go, because from 1861 to 1866 the Germans came over here and fought to help free blacks."[38] According to Brooks, Mason also led a secret organization that met in the basement of the church, which kept sentries and only those who knew the proper word gained entry to the meetings. Members gathered in the late evenings after the "white folks" had gone to bed, and in these meetings members discussed anti-draft propaganda, which had persuaded a great number of blacks throughout the county to not report for military service.[39]

William Thurman also presented damaging evidence against Mason. A local black resident that records described as a very intelligent "Negro" with good character, Thurman explained that he joined Mason's congregation at an early age and that he and Mason were once close friends until he found the preacher to be a hypocrite. Thurman claimed that prior to August 1917, the church possessed no position with reference to preventing the members from participating in the war and he believed that Mason inserted the new doctrinal statement for the sole purpose of gaining new members and he specifically knew of two Holmes County sharecroppers who joined Mason's congregation with the hope of avoiding the draft. Based on the interviews, Gully concluded that Mason had persuaded blacks in Holmes County not to report for induction to the military and should face charges of obstructing the draft. The agent mailed his report, along with the doctrinal statement, to the Jackson bureau office and ordered the Memphis Bureau of Investigations office to open a formal investigation of Mason's activities and to obtain a search warrant for his Memphis residence.[40]

Once news of the investigations leaked to the press, violence erupted as newspapers in both Mississippi and Tennessee ran sensational stories about the problems occurring in Lexington. In Arkansas, violence occurred when news of Mason's alleged pro-German sentiment spread. The Memphis *Commercial Appeal*, which was widely read in eastern Arkansas, reported that Reverend Jesse Payne, a Church of God in Christ pastor in Blytheville, escaped with his life on April 18, 1918, after whites tarred and feathered the preacher. The article explained that the pastor of the black "Holy Roller" church in the southeast suburbs of the city received such treatment as a result of alleged seditious remarks concerning the president and the war. While speaking to an interracial crowd, Payne, by all accounts, commented that "the Kaiser did not require his people to buy bonds, which made him a better man than President Wilson." Angered by his remarks, audience members threw objects, knocking the preacher from the makeshift stage. After a failed attempt to flee, angry whites tarred and feathered the COGIC preacher.[41]

Highlighting blacks' intentions to use the war to show their loyalty, many viewed Payne's actions as an embarrassment. The article indicated that the

COGIC preacher's congregation had shown little to no interest in purchasing Liberty Bonds, while other local black Methodist and Baptist churches raised more than $2,000 for their purchase. Payne's actions marked a dramatic departure from the efforts of other blacks across the country. As a whole, black clergymen instructed their congregations to support the war at all cost and even the National Association for the Advancement of Colored People advocated that blacks should support the war as a way of showing their patriotism and loyalty. If Payne's remarks were to be taken as a representation of COGIC's leadership, it would place the congregation in direct opposition to the black community over the issue of supporting the war. Furthermore, black Baptists and Methodists, who served at the forefront of the racial-uplift efforts, also remained critical of Payne's antiwar stance, which made it easier for the mainstream denominations to denounce COGIC as an unworthy religious movement.

Due to the violence and negative press, Mason feared for his life, which led him to contact the Bureau of Investigations office in Memphis. Reports show he telephoned the agency in April 1918 wanting to present answers to the accusations against him that the newspapers had recently published. Mason explained that he and his parishioners did, in fact, oppose the war because of their religious beliefs but claimed that since the passage of the Draft Act in 1917, he never advised anyone to join his churches as a way to avoid military service. Shortly after the passage of the act, he, along with other members of the faith, prepared a telegram to President Wilson detailing their religious faith and why they objected to the war. In reply, Mason claimed the president requested that the church doctrine be set forth in the form of a letter, which he and his followers immediately wrote. After some time the denomination received a response advising members to the rules of conscientious religious objectors' status. Mason also swore that neither he nor his church members ever violated the rule set forth and if anyone used his faith as a medium to spread German propaganda, it occurred without his knowledge or consent. In addition, he advised recent converts to the faith that under law, they were not entitled to exemptions and that anyone who joined after the passage of the Draft Act should report for military service if needed.[42]

As to the accusation that his denomination did not support the purchasing of Liberty Bonds, Mason emphatically argued that he had, at times, used scriptural justification to persuade members to purchase the bonds. As to the mysterious white foreigner known as Johnson, he confirmed that Johnson had traveled from England three years earlier and joined the Apostolic Faith movement, but when pressed about personal information regarding Johnson, Mason informed the agent that he knew little about the man, except that he met him through his ministerial work and that Johnson had conducted revivals at both his Memphis and Lexington churches and was no German agent.[43]

Mason did persuade agents in Memphis that he was telling the truth. Reports revealed that the denomination did apply for conscientious objector status and that Mason had first come to the attention of the Memphis office after the ruling on the status of COGIC's national application. Agents' notes also indicated that before the published newspaper articles, contacts within the city regarded Mason as an honest man of deep religious convictions, and although he exercised a great deal of authority over the black population, he never agitated or used his influence in a threatening manner toward local whites. Hence Memphis agents concluded that the government should place Mason and the Church of God in Christ in the same general class of religious objectors.[44]

Eugene Palmer, the special agent in charge of the investigation in Lexington, did not share the Memphis agents' sympathies toward Mason. When Palmer arrived in Lexington in June 1918, he found local whites enraged at what they believed to be treasonable acts. Residents informed the agent that in May 1918, blacks from as far away as Yazoo County had traveled into Lexington to hear Mason preach. To gather information, Sheriff Bell placed an informant in the crowd who later reported that while holding service, Mason excited the crowd by making nasal sounds and speaking in tongues and treated the crowd to prophecies, which he illustrated by calling attention to oddly shaped roots that he claimed foretold the end of time. By the end of the sermon Mason held the audience captive and capable of acting on any suggestion he made. Capitalizing on this, Mason told the crowd that "if you want to stay out of this war you must get right with God, and join my church." Mason argued that "there is no reason for the Negroes to go to war" and that Germany not only would beat the United States for the "mistreatment of Negroes" but that Germans were blacks' "best friends." Mason supposedly ended by saying that Woodrow Wilson had radically changed his stance on the war, originally proclaiming peace but now advocating for this rich man's war that had little to do with African Americans.[45]

After hearing the account of the event, Bell notified the Department of Justice in Jackson of Mason's alleged activities. Feeling they had enough evidence, the Holmes County judge issued an arrest warrant charging Mason with obstructing the draft. Meanwhile, an angry white mob had assembled and threatened to hang the pastor if they caught him before his formal arrest, but the sheriff apprehended Mason before the mob could act.[46] Even in jail, Mason's life remained in danger as lynching became a common mode of punishment for any black that upset racial customs. Mobs, often with the aid of local authorities, removed prisoners from jails and lynched them before large jeering crowds of whites in a carnival-like atmosphere.

When arrested, Mason possessed a bag of unusual objects and incriminating evidence. The bag contained memorandum books with addresses of people and letters stating that writers were sending money to the church and for Mason's personal use. Some letters included personal requests for a piece of an anointed cloth.[47] Bell and Palmer also found small bottles of Hoyte German cologne, which they thought Mason used for anointing the pieces of cloth, but in a time of such heightened alert, anything German equated disloyalty. The bag also contained oddly shaped roots resembling shriveled potatoes, freakish photographs, and clippings of unusual happenings. One of the clippings claimed that a strangely shaped egg foretold the end of time that would be in the year 1918. The two most incriminating pieces of evidence were newspaper clippings regarding references by religious objectors to antiwar scriptures and the federal forms to be used by registrants in obtaining conscientious objector status.[48]

Bell revealed to Agent Palmer that the situation did not look good; he had pacified the lynch mob by telling them the matter would be thoroughly investigated by the Department of Justice but did not think he would be able to keep down trouble or violence if Mason remained in town. In an effort to restore calm, Bell called Jack Gwinn, a well-respected businessman and town leader, and asked what he thought of the situation. Gwinn reiterated Bell's position by stating that he did not think it wise to allow Mason to remain in Lexington any longer. Following their advice, Palmer took Mason out of jail and Sheriff Bell drove the men to nearby Durant, Mississippi, to catch the train to Jackson.[49]

Oral accounts of Mason's arrest vary from those reported in the file of the Bureau of Investigations. Jessie Fields, a lifelong resident of Lexington, recalled that his grandmother told him a different story. Fields stated that after the sheriff arrested Mason, he sent word for the congregation to "do what they could to secure his release." According to Fields, Sheriff Bell took Mason out of his jail cell and placed him in a small room in the basement of the courthouse for his own protection.[50] During conversation, William Dean, the head pastor of St. Paul, said that authorities in Lexington lit a potbelly stove in the room with Mason, making him sweat profusely.[51] In the meantime, deacons of Mason's local congregation traveled to Jackson and secured the services of Perry Howard, a white attorney.[52] Fields said Mason's attorney telephoned the sheriff in Lexington and requested that he relocate his client from Lexington to the federal jail in Jackson. Bell, acting on the advice, took Mason to Durant to catch the train, but as Fields remembered, "the sheriff quickly put Mason on the train in Durant and instructed the conductor to release him in the next county after advising the prisoner never to step foot in Lexington again."[53]

Bureau of Investigations files show that authorities did move Mason, but instead of being freed in Durant, Special Agent Palmer traveled with Mason from Durant to Jackson and turned him over to the U.S. marshal. Upon arrival, authorities drew up a federal warrant against the preacher indicting him on the charge of obstructing the draft. During questioning, Mason made it known that he had churches in several states but mostly in Tennessee and Arkansas, and in recent years his denomination had grown in Texas, California, and Arizona. He went on to say that all churches and preachers in charge reported directly to him as the supervising power. COGIC also contained some white congregations and pastors. Mason mentioned that William B. Holt, a white minister of the faith who lived in Los Angeles, California, oversaw the missionary efforts in the south-west among Spanish-speaking residents.[54] After questioning, Mason was arraigned before U.S. commissioner R. B. Ricketts. He pleaded not guilty to the charge of obstructing the draft and waived a hearing. The commissioner set his bond at two thousand dollars and instructed the preacher to appear before the federal court in Jackson during the November session. Palmer concluded his report by asking the Los Angeles office to investigate William B. Holt, whom Palmer referred to as one of Mason's top lieutenants.[55]

Upon the request of the Jackson office, the Los Angeles office of the Bureau of Investigations began looking into the activities of Mason and Holt in California, which led to the interview of Robert E. Driver, the overseer of the Church of God in Christ in the state. A native southerner, Driver had lived in Memphis where he practiced law and worked as a teacher. He had also been ordained as a COGIC minister and because of his education, Mason appointed him the overseer of California.[56] Driver explained that he first met Mason in 1898 and was immediately impressed with his level of religious knowledge but offered that Mason lacked a formal education and the ability to properly express himself, which led people to misunderstand him on occasion. He also stated that he had witnessed every sermon Mason delivered in Los Angeles, and had never heard him make any statements criticizing the government or its war aims and to the best of his knowledge, Mason never advised anyone to avoid the draft; rather, he requested that they report to duty and seek noncombat positions. As to Mason's general leadership of the churches in California, Driver showed the agents the general statement the churches adopted as to how they felt about Mason's leadership. The testimonial read:

> Just as surly [*sic*] as God called Abraham out of Ur, of the Chaldes, to be the father of the faithful, and Moses from the throne of Egypt to lead his people out of bondage; just as true as God called and anointed Prophets of the Old Testament and the Apostles of the New, to be his messengers to his people, he called this humble, self-sacrificing man, and anointed him with the Holy Ghost and filled him with the wisdom of the Christ, to be a leader of his people. In this dispensation of the

fullness of time, and also had proved himself by a holy, humble life and a manifestation of the spirit of Jesus.[57]

When asked about his relationship with William Holt, Driver informed agents that Holt had joined the church several years earlier and now served as an elder, the private secretary to Mason, and general overseer of the Spanish and Mexican missions. Most recently he joined Mason on a tour throughout the South, conducting revival meetings and had last heard from Holt when he received a postcard dated June 4, 1918. He showed agents the message bearing a postmark from Washington, D.C., which read:

> My dear Brother Driver, I arrived in Washington from New York this morning, I had a good meeting in Boston. I leave here tonight by boat for Norfolk, Va. I am glad to hear you had a good convocation. Give my love to all the Saints. I mean to go through with the Lord. May God bless you all in Jesus name. Pray for me. Your Brother in Christ Wm. B. Holt.[58]

Driver also shared with agents that they could locate a pamphlet concerning a brief history and doctrinal statement of the Churches of God in Christ at Penn Printing, a printing shop located at 1084 South Spring Street in Los Angeles. Prepared by Holt, the pamphlets contained a brief biography of all the elders of the denomination, including Mason, Holt, himself, and others.[59]

Securing a copy, agents gathered the most accurate biographical information about Holt. Holt was born on April 15, 1880, in Fort Worth, Texas, and in 1901, he enrolled in a Baptist college in Redlane, California. While studying, he joined the Holiness movement during a camp meeting in Downey, California, and in 1908 joined the Nazarene Bible College as a divinity student. After graduation, he joined the Church of God in Christ, and in 1916 Mason appointed him to the position of overseer of the Spanish missions. Due to the interracial nature of Pentecostalism at the time, Holt's affiliation with the black denomination raised suspicions and conjured thoughts of pro-German conspiracies. But as the biographical sketch showed, Holt was an American, COGIC preacher, and although he may not have been in complete support of the war, no evidence corroborates that he was either a German conspirator or a member of the Socialist Party.[60]

Driver related that in regard to his personal duty and loyalty to the country, a number of members in his congregation inquired whether or not they should purchase Liberty Bonds and to answer the question, he printed several thousand copies of a brief circular titled "Is It Right to Buy Liberty Bonds?" which read:

> What does it mean to buy Liberty Bonds?
> It means to lend to your government a certain amount of money that say the scripture Jesus said in Matthew 5:42 "give to him that asketh thee, and from all that would borrow of them turn not away." We are to live by every word of God and the Government asking for a loan we are in no violation.[61]

He alleged that he owned Liberty Bonds and encouraged all the men in his congregation to purchase the bonds and at all times remain loyal to the country and obey the laws. When asked whether his members remained satisfied with the government drafting their young men for limited service, Driver stated that it bothered him that his young male members in military service engaged in activities that assisted soldiers in taking human life and placed the responsibility for the participation in the war upon the government and felt that God absolved COGIC or any other religious organization of any wrongdoing.[62]

Special agents spent a considerable amount of time with Driver discussing the organizational structure and beliefs of the denomination, but in the end, he failed to quiet their suspicions. During their conversation, Driver received a telephone call, which his son requested that he take. Agents witnessed that Driver turned and rudely snapped at his son that "he was very busy in secret conference and that he could not be interrupted and whoever wanted to speak with him must call him later."[63] As a result of viewing this event, the agents reported that Driver expressed his true nature and disposition; they believed him to be extremely demanding, dictatorial, and his general personality very repugnant. Agents concluded that in their assessment, the members of the congregation were not German sympathizers but were evading military service because of religious convictions. In an effort to confirm any connections between Driver, COGIC, and German supporters, the Military Intelligence Division (MID) tapped his telephone. Agents also suggested that the church's draft classification status be changed to keep their members from receiving noncombat positions based on false religious beliefs.[64]

In the meantime, Mason traveled from Memphis to Paris, Texas, where a COGIC congregation had been in existence since 1913. Records indicate a worship gathering of some sort took place nightly as Holiness preachers from all over the country conducted revival services. Agents learned that Mason communicated to parishioners that he had been arrested in Mississippi and charged with circulating seditious literature and conspiring against the government. He had been released on a $2,000 bond and was expected to report back to Jackson to stand trial in November and to help defray the cost of his legal defense, he wanted each congregation to raise $1,000.[65]

Agents' notes revealed that the Paris congregation immediately began making the contributions in the form of twenty-five cents, but problems occurred when Henry Kirvin, their pastor, criticized members who donated to the Red Cross instead of Mason's defense fund. In an effort to persuade his congregants, Kirvin began informing them that by paying the twenty-five cents, they not only contributed to Mason's defense fund, but the contribution also allowed for their name to be placed on a registry that would exempt them from military service.[66]

Not all the congregants and preachers agreed with the fundraising attempts. While conducting a weeklong revival in Paris, William C. Thompson, a black Holiness preacher from Chicago, disagreed with Mason's alleged opposition to the war. Thompson preached that the actions of Mason proved to be disloyal and Kirvin's efforts to raise money at the expense of the local congregation placed an undue burden on the membership. After Thompson's sermon, Kirvin vowed to keep him from preaching again, but Thompson refused to leave. To settle the dispute, the congregation sent for Larry P. Adams, a white Holiness preacher, and with his help, forced Thompson out of the Paris church, which resulted in the expelled preacher's willingness to speak with Texas agents.[67]

Thompson let it be known that he opposed the antiwar efforts of Mason and Kirvin, explaining that not only did the congregants give twenty-five cents a month to keep their name on a list but that Kirvin also forced them to buy a pamphlet for fifteen cents a copy. Agents learned from Thompson that Kirvin told his congregation that with the pamphlet, "if an officer approaches you regarding the draft all you have to do is show this to him and he will pass you up."[68] In response to the accusations, the division superintendent C. E. (name not legible) ordered Special Agents Claude McCaleb and John P. Buddleston from the Austin, Texas, office to investigate the matter and make regular reports to U.S. attorney Clarence Morritt. Upon arriving in Paris, the agents secured the help of Texas Ranger Wade Robertson and arranged interviews with local black residents and members of the church.[69]

James Ellis, a thirty-year-old church member and COGIC preacher, provided damaging evidence against Mason and Kirvin when he confessed that he had not registered with his local draft board because leaders of the church told him that as a member of COGIC and a preacher, he should not be involved in taking lives. The frightened preacher also stated, "Our pastor [Kirvin] instructed us not to buy bonds or help the Red Cross because the organization bore the emblem of the beast."[70] Kirvin had traveled to Washington, D.C., to speak to President Wilson and get the Church of God in Christ put on record as conscientious objectors like other churches, so its members, and especially the preachers, would not have to go to war.[71] In reality, the odds that the president granted Kirvin or any other black man a meeting seem highly unlikely, as Wilson's attitude toward race and his feelings toward religious objectors are well documented. Wilson despised conscientious objectors, claiming that he opposed "not the feelings of the pacifists but their stupidity . . . I want peace, but I know how to get it and they do not."[72]

However, when Kirvin returned from Washington, he reported that members would have to place their name on a church register and pay a quarter to have their names sent to Washington. Paying the money meant that they would not have to go to war, but no name would be placed on the list unless the money was paid. Kirvin also returned with little books, which he instructed members to purchase to show as proof that they remained in good standing with the denomination. Ellis presented the special agents the booklet he had purchased and on the last page of the eight-page pamphlet with the title "Doctrinal Statement and Rules of the Church of God in Christ" was the official statement: "We believe that all shedding of human blood or the taking of human life to be contrary to the teachings of our Lord and Savior, and as a body we are averse to war in all its various forms."[73] When agents interviewed Morris Gray, another member of the congregation, he repeated alleged criticisms Kirvin made about the Red Cross. According to Gray, Kirvin told his congregation that they could contribute to the Red Cross if they wanted, but he refused to donate to the organization because it helped keep soldiers on the front lines fighting the Germans. Kirvin also broadcast that he refused to contribute to the organization and to wear what he called the "blood of the beast" because his religion taught him not to kill and they should not either.[74]

In all actuality, the probability that COGIC's leadership preached against the American Red Cross remains extremely likely, as other religious organizations, such as the Mennonites, also had problems supporting the organization. Mennonite sects disagreed about whether or not it was consistent with their nonresistant doctrine to give financial support to the organization. Other sects argued that the Red Cross "was too involved in the war," while some objected not only because of the organization's close ties to the war but also because it was not a Christian organization. Many Mennonites contributed to the Red Cross not out of a sense of patriotism, but out of fear of punishment and ridicule. Therefore, COGIC's behavior would be consistent with other religious organizations that remained uneasy about supporting the Red Cross. When viewed through this lens, Kirvin's criticism of the organization cannot be seen as an isolated event and the fact that such ideas about the Red Cross were floating throughout America's religious communities lends credence that Kirvin actually made the remarks and that COGIC as a whole did not support the organization.[75]

Of greater importance, if Kirvin actually made comments against donating to the Red Cross, he did, in fact, violate the Espionage and Sedition Acts, which made criticizing the federal government or hampering the recruitment of soldiers or hindering fundraising efforts through speech or other printed materials illegal. What Kirvin most likely failed to realize is that the federal legislation also extended protection to the American Red Cross due to the agency's national efforts to raise funds in aid of American soldiers.[76]

John Pierson, another member of the local congregation, echoed Thompson, Ellis, and Gray's versions in greater detail when he told agents that Kirvin preached to his flock that the button worn by the Red Cross subscribers resembled that of the "cross of the beast" and instructed his congregants not to wear it. Pierson revealed that on a visit in 1917, Mason reminded the congregation that God frowned upon war and told them that the members of COGIC must all pay a quarter to have their names put on the church register to exempt them from the conflict. Mason informed the congregation that all whose names were on the church's register and who had paid the quarter would not have to participate in the war but that all those who refused to pay would be cut off from the church and left with no protection. The congregation was also told that their names would be sent to the president so that he could tell who the "Saints" of the church were. When questioned about the money, Mason announced that their quarters would go into the church treasury because "the government could call on them at anytime for money and they would have the needed funds on hand."[77]

Pierson communicated to the agents that Kirvin stood before the congregation and read a letter from Mason in which President Wilson requested that Mason travel to Washington. Kirvin stressed that Mason wanted his help in exempting the church from war service and informed the parishioners that it would take $150 to pay for his expense, therefore asking each member of the church to pay a dollar to a dollar and a half to defray his cost.[78] When the two returned from Washington, they reported to the congregation that they did not get an audience with President Wilson. Kirvin did claim that he and Mason talked to other authorities and the Church of God in Christ "stood well with the government," and that the congregation should "now live a Christ-like life, and if they did not, they would be subject to be jerked up and sent to the war."[79]

After Kirvin returned from the convocation in Memphis in December 1917, he brought back with him little books that he sold to the congregation for fifteen cents each. Kirvin addressed the membership informing them that everyone who purchased a book and kept it on their person at all times proved that they were saints of the church and remained exempt from serving in the war.[80] The congregation also donated money to several "free-will" collections and offerings to lend to the government, but doubted Kirvin ever donated it to the government's war effort.[81]

Women also made the twenty-five cents contribution. Julia Ford, a member of the congregation, revealed that Kirvin preached that "If you women refuse to pay the quarter to put your name on the church register, then you could also be jerked up and put in the Red Cross."[82] Kirvin left the impression that females were just as vulnerable as the men if they refused to pay. Katie Graves, an ex-member of the congregation, reported to agents that she refused to donate and was "turned out" of the church.[83] Nellie Black, the congregation's secretary, said that she paid for herself and her husband, informing agents that most young women in the congregation seemed worried about being taken away from their children; therefore, most gladly paid the money to keep their name on the list.[84]

If true, these allegations reveal that COGIC's female membership's stance toward the war represented a clear departure from other female Pentecostals. Aimee McPherson, the famous Pentecostal missionary, for instance, used the war to help in her evangelizing efforts as she delivered sermons in which she praised the American Red Cross and advocated that every able-bodied citizen should purchase Liberty Bonds. Further highlighting her support, she often prayed for the comfort of the women who had sons or husbands fighting in the war.[85] Even within the black community, the National Association of Colored Women made their support for the war known as they raised thousands of dollars for the purchase of Liberty Bonds. However, before condemnation can be levied upon COGIC's female membership for their perceived lack of enthusiasm for the war, one must consider their class standing. Working as domestics and sharecroppers, COGIC women's socioeconomic status severely impacted their level of support. Many simply could not afford to support the Liberty Bond drives and the fear of being separated from their children explains their payment to have their name placed on Kirvin's list.

Still, on July 16, 1918, federal authorities arrested Mason, Holt, and Kirvin. Law enforcement officials charged them with "violating sections thirty-two and thirty-seven of the U.S. penal code, which prohibited impersonation of a federal officer and conspiring to commit offenses against the government."[86] After arraignment, Mason and Kirvin were released on their own recognizance, but authorities held Holt on a five-thousand-dollar bond and an October trial date gave federal prosecutors time to build a solid case.[87] Since much of the evidence gathered by the Bureau of Investigations consisted of hearsay, substantiating suspicions through the testimony of church insiders remained important. The government's case overwhelmingly rested on the testimony of Reverend Thompson, the Chicago preacher who had given damaging statements to special agents in Texas after a dispute with Kirvin. However, as Theodore Kornweibel writes, to the surprise of federal authorities, when agents interviewed Thompson in Chicago, he defended Mason and Kirvin by saying that "he believed the two to be patriotic and doing good work."[88] With Thompson's reluctance to offer testimony against Mason, the government's case became weak and hard to prove in court.

The prosecution suffered a second setback when Dewitt Winn, the special agent in charge of the investigation, died as a result of the Spanish flu epidemic. Winn's death handicapped the bureau's case and without the testimony of Thompson, the case rested on no solid evidence.[89] In October 1918, when a Paris grand jury of the U.S. district court examined the evidence, the war was in its last phase and with America's eagerness to return to normalcy, the grand jury refused to indict any of the suspects. In the end, neither Mason nor any of his congregants faced prosecution, but other questions remained unanswered. First, what happened to the money congregants in Texas raised? Did the money go toward Mason's legal defense? Or was it really used for the purpose of compiling a list of names for the purpose of religious objectorship?[90]

Although the government failed to successfully prosecute Mason, enough evidence raised suspicions that COGIC's leadership did not enthusiastically support America's war, and at times, the denomination's criticism of the Red Cross did, in fact, violate the Espionage and Sedition Acts. However, it does seem that Mason's opposition to participating in the war was religiously motivated and can be attributed to his understanding of Pentecostalism. The interracial nature of the movement complicated Mason's problems as whites throughout the South remained suspicious and often mistakenly viewed interracial worship services as pro-German, Socialist, and subversive in nature.

Additionally, COGIC's members' strict adherence to sanctification, which required congregants to separate themselves from secular activities, allowed the larger black community to assume that the denomination did not support the war nor subscribe to the efforts to use the conflict to pursue racial advancement, which singled out Mason and COGIC for their perceived lack of support. Yet, the allegation, when examined from a religious perspective, renders a different outcome. COGIC's Pentecostal-Holiness beliefs required that members take a pacifist stance toward the war that often resulted in low county conscription numbers in areas with large numbers of the denomination's membership. As to Mason's preaching against the conflict, source materials suggest that he and large numbers of COGIC ministers did, in fact, preach against elements of the war. However, Mason and his cohorts' actions would remain consistent with other known Pentecostal-Holiness ministers, both black and white, who opposed America's involvement because of its perceived contradiction with their religious beliefs. Source materials suggest that Mason, prior to his arrest, did encourage his members to purchase Liberty Bonds, but as the war effort became a national crusade, COGIC members began to see the contradictions between their inward-looking restorationist Pentecostal beliefs and the progressive secular activities of the war. Overall, COGIC did support elements of the war that they believed were not inconsistent with Pentecostalism, which would show support for blacks' efforts for social advancement—something COGIC in the successive decades proved to be committed to both in the United States and abroad.

4

Come Over to Macedonia and Help

Sanctification Disguised as Racial Uplift

As the late nineteenth and early twentieth centuries became an era of self-help and self-reliance, black progressives quickly recognized they had a duty to uplift the race in both the United States and Africa[1]; in similar fashion as their white religious counterparts, black denominations became especially interested in uplifting the race at home and abroad.[2] The African Methodist Episcopal Church (AME) and the National Baptist Convention (NBC) established religious missions and schools throughout West Africa and the Caribbean, spreading their religious message as well as what they believed to be proper modes of social grace and behavior. American board volunteer Samuel Miller's statement reflected their efforts when he stated that he "not only wanted to go to Africa because of his Christian commitment to spread the faith, but also out of a sense of duty to do all that he could for his black brothers."[3] Although at odds with other black denominations, COGIC also involved itself in missionary work. Often led by women, the church taught its converts the standards of respectability under the guise of sanctification. However, while working in Africa, COGIC missionaries unknowingly duplicated middle-class values and Western standards of behavior while displaying negative attitudes toward native African cultures, which paralleled the criticism they received from the Baptists and Methodists at home.

Black progressives believed that missionary work would build stronger denominations as well as elevate their religious institutions to the level of white spiritual organizations. The historian Walter Williams emphasized this point when he wrote, "AME Bishop Henry M. Turner criticized his church for not doing as much in Africa as white churches and a church without missions was not worthy of respect, and could not be counted among the great churches of the world." Not only would a strong mission encourage pride of accomplishment, but Turner theorized, "Its absence would lower the reputation of the whole black race."[4]

The appeal to compete with white denominations became an effective way in which church leaders challenged America's racial order that rendered them second-class citizens. Although the AME Church, the oldest black denomination, organized a Home and Foreign Missionary Society as early as 1844, the denomination did not appoint its first missionary secretary, James Townsend, until 1878. Upon taking the position, Townsend "predicted the AME Church would become the Continental Church of Africa while uplifting the denomination's African brothers." Townsend brought executive skills to the office and a vision of missionary work that rested upon middle-class values of respectability. He disliked the American Colonization Society's emigration schemes to Africa but, rather, committed himself to African missions and worked to centralize fundraising efforts for African Americans who wanted to work in Africa as missionaries as an extension of the black self-help movement.[5] With the renewed interest generated by Townsend, the AME General Conference, by 1900, viewed "Africa as the largest and most important field" claiming, "the relationship that exists between our race and the inhabitants of the Dark Continent remains so powerful that Africans are bone and flesh of our flesh" and to them, African Americans were the best suited to uplift Africa.[6]

Reformers recognized that much of the prejudice against blacks in America was due to whites' image of African "savagery" and pointed out the futility of uplifting the race in the United States while in the minds of whites, Africa remained a backward heathenish place. H. B. Parks, an AME mission secretary, emphasized how the self-help aspect of uplifting Africa would help African Americans when he pondered:

> Can you see the immense credit that will reflect upon the American Negro when the world is forced to recognize the success of the Movement? Such recognition would do more to improve the conditions here at home than years of legislations . . . Do you see that this is the road through which God would have the race ascend to its proper place of greatness? Is the race spirit strong enough in you to see it?[7]

Witnessing the success of the AME Church, the Baptists also joined in attempting to use the African mission movement as a method of racial uplift.

The black Baptist Church formed in 1805 when northern congregations joined the first independent black Baptist congregation to form conventions, giving a supervisory structure to the denomination in the region. After the Civil War, black Baptists worked tirelessly to form conventions throughout the South, "which registered the largest growth rate in American churches in the late nineteenth century." By 1894, their membership had grown to three times the size of the AME Church, and although relatively new, they offered themselves for mission work when delegates from several states met in Montgomery, Alabama, in 1880 to form the Baptist Foreign Mission Convention (BFMC).[8] The organization sponsored six missionaries who became the first black Baptists to serve in Africa. Concentrating their efforts in Liberia, they experienced little success due to inadequate financial support from their national denomination.[9]

A second attempt came in 1895 when various black Baptist groups created the National Baptist Convention, which appointed Lewis Jordan, a native of Mississippi, to head their newly created Baptist Foreign Mission Board (BFMB). Jordan, known as the father of black Baptist missionary efforts, threw himself into his work, scheduling speaking tours, establishing an efficient fundraising organization, and creating the denominational magazine *Mission Herald*.[10] Fundraising, however, became Jordan's primary goal, as most blacks in the early twentieth century probably first heard of the efforts to uplift Africa when a minister or missionary appealed for funds to support their missions. To maximize donations, missionaries told astounding stories designed to grab the attention of their audiences, as well as their purses. For example, John Coles, a Baptist missionary, argued before potential donors that "Africa must be redeemed from ignorance, superstition, nakedness, domestic slavery, human sacrifice, idols, cannibalism and a million other vices which prey upon our heathen brothers." Coles pleaded for money, asking his audience to "hold the rope while he went down the well of heathen idolatry and spiritual death to bring up our brothers."[11] AME bishop Daniel Payne did the same when he portrayed blacks as "savages," who were "calling upon Christendom to rescue them from the pit of idolatry into which they have fallen."[12] Sensational stories such as these prompted blacks to donate money, as well as sway some to serve in Africa as missionaries.

African American missionaries tended to be individuals who possessed a sense of obligation to the race and almost all came from the black middle class. Most had earned a college education, and for many, it was their school experience that inspired them to become missionaries.[13] For example, Henrietta Bailey received her inspiration at Fisk University, but her family did not support her career choice to work in Africa. Even though she "tried to banish the idea," she could not, "for it was brought up to my mind at every Fisk missionary meeting."[14] Philander Smith College, a Methodist-based institution in Little Rock, Arkansas, sent graduates to Liberia in 1898 as missionaries and while composing letters of recommendation, an instructor penned that one of his student's "intelligence and businesslike demeanor would serve him well as he now turned his attention toward Africa."[15] As students graduated from colleges and employment opportunities remained grim due to their race, missionary work in Africa became an acceptable occupation. With encouragement from their teachers, they entered the field with hope of contributing to the race at home and abroad.

Self-interest also played a role in influencing the commitments black missionaries made to work in Africa. After the death of her husband, Methodist Amanda Smith improved her life through missionary work. Smith experienced economic hardships that forced her into poverty; she worked as a domestic, but rejected the lifestyle of servitude and subsequently became a missionary in both India and Africa. Reflecting upon the time she endured as a domestic, Smith considered herself blessed to be working among her brothers and sisters in Africa instead of living a life of domestic servitude.[16]

William Sheppard echoed Smith's story. A Presbyterian minister, Sheppard became interested in Africa after the codification of American segregation and entrenchment of Jim Crow. Instead of accepting second-class citizenry in America, he opted for missionary work in Africa and enjoyed "considerable influence over the Methodist Mission Board, earned a salary equal to that of white missionaries, and was addressed as 'Mr.' or 'Reverend' in an age when blacks in the American South were given few titles of respect." Missionary work offered Sheppard the status he longed for, all under the auspice of racial uplift. Whatever the motivation of black missionaries, mission work in Africa offered the opportunity to gain self-respect and the chance to assert Victorian principles of social behavior while they helped Africans achieve civilization.[17]

The Church of God in Christ also involved itself in mission work when, in 1926, Elizabeth Robinson, COGIC national mother, argued for the creation of a Home and Foreign Mission Board. Arguably, Robinson's interest might have stemmed from the work of the black Baptists and Methodists in her home state of Arkansas. In June 1892, "the Arkansas Baptist State Sunday School Convention met in Texarkana to recommend that Sunday Schools throughout the state raise funds for mission work in Africa."[18] Later in the year, the Arkansas Conference of AME Churches also involved itself in missionary efforts. At the denomination's yearly conference, delegates approved a resolution to set up missions to be staffed by black Arkansans. To fund the work, the committee recommended that Methodist congregations donate money to support missionary efforts. Throughout the remainder of the 1890s, the Baptists and Methodists of Arkansas continued to raise funds at their annual meetings.[19]

Men such as Reverend Joseph C. Sherrill answered the missionary call. After graduating from Philander Smith College, he worked as a minister in central

Arkansas Methodist congregations. In 1897, Sherrill decided to extend his work to Africa and recruited students from Philander Smith College to aid him in Liberia. The group arrived in Monrovia on January 28, 1899, but for unknown reasons, they eventually settled in the small costal community of Cape Palmas, establishing a mission, school, and church. In letters home, Sherrill boasted that he had the largest mission school in the region and had saved countless souls.[20]

Sherrill's missionary efforts affected COGIC members like Elizabeth Robinson, who had come of age during the height of the African mission movement in Arkansas and most likely knew of Sherrill as a result of reading the *Christian Index*, a Methodist bimonthly periodical published throughout the South. Born a slave in Phillips County, Arkansas, in April 1860, Elizabeth Robinson's future, at first glance, looked bleak but with the coming of the Civil War, her life changed. Although Elizabeth, her mother, and siblings received their freedom as a result of the war, Robinson lost her father as a causality of the conflict. Impoverished and alone, the family refused to become victims of their circumstance. Robinson's mother must have stressed the importance of education because Elizabeth later fondly remembered reading the Bible as a child to adults in her community. In 1875, Robinson experienced another tragedy when, at the age of fifteen, her mother died, leaving five children as orphans.[21]

Although not much is known about Robinson's adolescence, historians can glean a great deal about the time period. In 1875, upon the death of her mother, the country was still in the midst of Reconstruction and most blacks had come to realize that their lives would consist of sharecropping and domestic servitude. Even in the face of such conditions, blacks would never stop trying to improve their lot, and many became a part of the burgeoning self-help movement that stressed respectability and self-reliance. This environment helped Robinson develop her understanding of the world and her place in it. Joanna P. Moore, according to Anthea Butler, first introduced Robinson to the self-help movement and when she later joined the Church of God in Christ it would be the principles learned from Moore that would help her rise in the ranks of COGIC.[22]

By 1925, Robinson had risen to the position of COGIC national mother and hoped to duplicate the efforts of the Methodists and Baptists in mission work for her denomination. While at an evangelistic meeting in Portland, Oregon, Robinson met Ed Searcy, a member of the House of Prayer International Home and Foreign Mission Board, and because of her interest in his work with foreign missions, she invited him to speak at the 1926 convocation in Memphis. After Searcy's presentation, Robinson recommended that the elders organize a Home and Foreign Mission Board for COGIC. In 1927, COGIC leaders appointed Elder C. G. Brown the first secretary of the newly created organization and adopted this mission statement:

The purpose of the organization shall be the winning of lost souls to Christ and to establish the work of Grace in the hearts of believers; to encourage a holy life and the Baptism of the Holy Ghost and Fire among all the nations of the earth, to make ready the people of Africa for the soon coming of the Lord Jesus Christ and the glorious majesty of His Kingdom, to win souls to Christ in love and unity of spirit and faith, by clean, holy people who are walking in the light, with the fellowship of Saints, cleansed through the blood of Jesus by the washing of water by the world, who are under guidance, leading and teaching and the healing of the Holy Ghost.[23]

Robinson's efforts to persuade COGIC elders may have been made easier as a result of interest in mission work displayed by Mason. The founder's family migrated to Arkansas in 1878, and despite optimism for a better life, conditions remained bleak for blacks. Consequently, many looked toward Liberia as a possible safe haven, and in the county where the Masons settled, blacks established a branch of the Liberian Exodus Association that helped to relocate those who desired to leave. Mason's interest in Africa might have stemmed from his early childhood, as his mother's name appeared on the local association's rolls. Although she never left Arkansas, her interest in the movement lends credence to the theory that Mason had knowledge of Liberia and might have even known families that migrated there in the late 1800s, thus also explaining the denomination's missionary interest in the country and Mason's approval for the denomination to involve itself in the work.

COGIC had a readily available pool from which to draw missionaries. Similar to Baptists in Arkansas who drew from their student population at Arkansas Baptist College and the Methodists who did the same at Philander Smith College, COGIC officially opened Saints Industrial College for Negro Boys and Girls in Lexington, Mississippi, in 1917. Early accounts of the school's history vary, but one revealed that on a cold day Mason observed Miss Pinkie Duncan, a resident of Lexington, teaching children in an unheated home. Concerned for their well-being in the extreme temperatures, he invited Duncan to relocate the class to the basement of St. Paul and as the class grew in size, the congregation raised money to hire James Counts, a member of the St. Paul congregation, to serve as headmaster.[24]

Counts led fundraising drives throughout Mississippi and his efforts allowed the denomination to purchase twenty-eight acres and begin the construction of the institution's first buildings. The school served as the educational arm of COGIC, educating children under the auspices of sanctification. By the 1920s, the institute had grown to such importance that delegates at the National

Convocation in Memphis voted to make it a national institution. Saints Industrial College would provide the denomination with an eager pool of adherents ready to conduct missionary work at home and abroad.[25]

COGIC Women Led the Way

Although men received the initial leadership appointments, Robinson retained the authority to recommend, appoint, and confirm COGIC missionaries. Under the guise of sanctification, she would implement her own brand of respectability that COGIC missionaries would spread throughout Africa and the West Indies. The Home and Foreign Mission Board survived with money raised by the Women's Department and its auxiliaries, and COGIC's missionary efforts in Africa cannot be fully appreciated nor understood without an evaluation of the denomination's women. Although at times criticized for their class standing, COGIC women joined their Baptist and Methodist counterparts in the efforts to elevate the poorest segments of the black population, at home and abroad.[26]

The Church of God in Christ experienced rapid growth during the first half of the twentieth century, and black women constituted the greatest percentage of this new expansion. To better accommodate the growth, Robinson created auxiliaries designed to assist women in meeting their spiritual as well as practical needs. Bible Bands, one of COGIC's earliest women's auxiliaries, helped to lay a foundation that would allow women to uplift in their local communities as well as support the denomination's foreign mission work. Eugene B. McCoy, author of the 1922 volume *Yes Lord*, described the Bible Bands as a "group of women who met every Monday from one o'clock until six o'clock to study the Bible. Many in attendance worked as domestics and rather than take off for Sunday service, most women asked to be off on Mondays in order to attend the Bible Band meetings where they could learn to read." McCoy recounted that Mason often attended the classes and taught from the Bible as he rocked in a chair, and when he could not attend, literate women led the group.[27]

Although the Prayer and Bible Bands' primary goal remained the study of scriptures, the meetings also served as literacy classes where leaders used the Bible to teach participants to read using scriptures, therefore, making the new auxiliary a component of the larger black self-help movement. Due to their economic status, domestics in attendance might not have otherwise learned the skill of literacy, and meeting under the premise of a prayer group negated the worries of employers who might have grown angry because of their housekeepers' desire to learn to read.

Under the guise of sanctification, Sewing Circles, another early auxiliary, developed COGIC women's sense of respectability. The sewing auxiliary also gave the women of the denomination an alternative view of their womanhood, which they would later spread throughout their foreign missions. In an effort to utilize skills women had developed from their occupations, COGIC designed sewing circles to help their congregations and the larger community. For instance, local Sewing Circles donated clothing but also trained women to sew and the use of advanced needlework. By teaching women the skills, COGIC gave female members the ability to provide clean and untattered clothing for their children. As Charles Pleas stated, the clubs were similar to the work of Dorcas, the woman from the Bible who "was full of good work and alms" when she provided "coats and garments for the needy."[28]

Club members also subscribed to the concept of respectability by sewing clothing that allowed members to properly dress, while also helping black women to fight the sexual harassment they often endured in public.[29] In her autobiography, Mary Church Terrell, a leading black feminist, vividly depicted the sexual peril black women faced when she remembered how she encountered an aggressive white man whom she believed was about to rape her, while alone at night in a railcar. "I was terror stricken and started to the door when the train slowed to a stop. He seized me and threw me into a seat and then left the car."[30]

COGIC sewing club members helped to establish a formal dress code for the denomination. Profoundly influenced by their understanding of sanctification, women developed a standard of conservative dress designed to demonstrate their holiness lifestyle. Cheryl Townsend Gilkes explained that "COGIC women wore a simple uniform-like dress in the colors of black or white. Older women also adopted a headdress referred to as a Saint, which they wore on trains while en-route to the national convocation or regional meetings."[31] The dress code illustrated COGIC women's commitment to fighting against negative images and placed them among the ranks of their Baptist and Methodist counterparts in the fight to reform stereotypes of black female sexuality. For instance, Benjamin T. Moore, a COGIC member and writer, argued that women of the denomination should cover parts of the body that cultural and religious norms dictated and that clothing revealed who they were publicly; for instance, "street women attempted to attract as much attention to their bodies as possible," but COGIC women "should let their outer apparel reflect the inner person."[32] His statement reiterated the argument of the historian Darlene Clark Hine when she contested that "if popular notions of lewd, lascivious '[N]egroes' justified ritualized rape, then black women would assume control over the situations by controlling their sexuality."[33] As a result, COGIC women developed their own version of a culture of dissemblance, which they used in an effort to change societal views about their sexuality. Sewing Circles gave COGIC women the ability to adopt a strategy of dissemblance, making public travel more tolerable and employment as domestics in white households endurable. Like their Baptist and Methodist counterparts, they took it upon themselves to create an alternative self-image that countered the negative stereotypes about their sexuality.

COGIC's Sunshine Bands and Purity Classes were the last of the women's auxiliaries to impact COGIC women's sense of respectability. As Anthea Butler highlighted, the Sunshine Band targeted the youth by teaching Bible verses, children hymns, and most important, a good healthy dose of Holiness living practices that reinforced morally respectable behavior.[34] Classes taught young girls proper dress and domestic skills that would allow them to clean their homes, which they were instructed to pass on to their family members. Butler further points out, "COGIC women also created purity classes designed to teach rigid morality to young men and women between the ages of twelve and fifteen. In these classes students learned the basics of a sanctified life, which consisted of modest dress, abstinence from sex and alcohol, and to use pure speech."[35]

COGIC women's auxiliaries such as the Prayer and Bible Bands, Sewing Circles, Sunshine Bands and Purity Classes all helped to institutionalize the denomination. Additionally, like other nonreligious women's groups, COGIC female auxiliaries offered members and potential converts tangible skills, which they could apply to their everyday lives. Aware of the needs of the black population, Robinson organized the auxiliaries to act as self-help agencies for the black community, but more important, the organizations created a readymade network that allowed COGIC to raise money for the denomination.

With Mason's authorization, the Home and Foreign Mission Board's national treasury was supported by a system of home and foreign mission bands organized in local congregations throughout the country and women provided the work necessary to raise the money for the denomination's foreign missions. Women cooked and sold dinners, led fundraising drives in their local communities, and unselfishly donated money. At the end of every month, congregations sent all the money raised to the national office for building the treasury that would allow the denomination to support their missionaries abroad.[36]

Not only did women fund the foreign mission work, but they also set the rules and training standard to which COGIC missionaries abided. Rigid in nature and steeped in sanctified living traditions, the rules highlight the moral and respectable conduct missionaries were expected to live by and teach in their mission schools, both at home and abroad:

> Members and missionaries must attend Prayer and Bible Band, Home
> and Foreign Mission Bands and be active in all Women's Auxiliaries

in the Church and governed by the work and obey them that have rule over them. Hebrews 13:17; St. Luke 6:46

They must themselves be commendable and be recommended by their Prayer and Bible Band leaders, Home Foreign Mission leaders and Pastors, as faithful workers. Romans 16:12

All missionaries are requested to pay tithes and offerings according to the scriptures. Malachi 3:8–10, Nehemiah 13:12, Matthew 23:23, St. Luke 11:42. They must attend service in their own church.

All members and missionaries must not wear hats with flowers or feathers nor Short Dresses, Split Skirts or Short Sleeves. Young missionaries who have a desire or gift to do missionary work should go to the aged or more experienced women.

All missionaries must dress in modest apparel as becometh [H]oliness, professing Godliness with good work.

That no young missionary to go here or there with any Elder, or Brother to do missionary work without the consent of their state mother and her Pastor.

Any sister applying for license to do missionary work, having left her home church and is worshipping in another, should get a letter of recommendation from her Pastor at home to the Church in which she worships.

All missionaries holding Meetings must first consult the Pastor and they will not be permitted to teach if it be found out that she talks with weak ones of the church who fight the Pastor.

No sister that has two or three husbands unlawfully according to the doctrine of the Church of God in Christ can be a missionary.

Workers requesting some sister to work, send your request to your Pastor or State Mother.

All sisters applying for license to do missionary work must come before the State Mother's Board, with recommendation from their Pastors.

These rules are to be read in the Bible Band Meetings.[37]

The standards set forth reveal that COGIC women had, by 1926, adopted Victorian principles of behavior, moral conduct, and dress. For example, their policies that regulated dress, although influenced by sanctification, aligned with secular women's organizations as they also attempted to teach proper dress. The rules highlight that COGIC had involved itself in the same racial uplift work as the larger black community; however, their work remained religiously motivated. More important, COGIC missionaries would impose their brand of sanctification as respectability on the masses in Africa and the West Indies.

Progressive Norms Employed Abroad

Although men comprised the majority of the black missionaries in Africa, COGIC women answered the call in large numbers and female missionaries such as Elizabeth White made significant impacts upon the lives of Africans. In 1927, White, who had recently completed three years of service at Cape Palmas, Liberia, under the direction of another denomination, returned to the United States and, acting upon an invitation to attend COGIC's national convocation, she later volunteered to continue her service in Cape Palmas under the direction of COGIC. In 1930, with the financial support of the Home and Foreign Mission Board, White traveled back to Africa, marking the arrival of the first COGIC missionary to the continent, where she established the denomination's first mission composed of huts with thatched roofs in the "bush," which would become known as the Bonika Station. White also began to teach the denomination's doctrine of sanctification but received a cold reception from native Africans. Traditional healers or what she referred to as "juj-juj" men viewed her as a threat to their control, and both men and women fought against her Christian teachings that indirectly attacked their culture. White remembered:

> The ignorance, superstition, evil practice, and spiritual darkness of those in the jungle of Africa revealed more than a need for the preaching of the Gospel. The Gospel itself was not sufficient enough to turn the people in the bush from their heathen practices. Something had to be done in demonstration of what was told them about God. The sick had to be ministered to and healed, wounds needed to be treated properly, and expectant mothers had to be properly taught how to deliver and care for their babies. They also had to be made to realize that marriage of tiny tots to grown men, both young and old, was wrong and ungodly.[38]

White unknowingly employed the same notions of Africa as whites. For example, her use of words such as ignorance, superstition, and evil practice support the notion that the COGIC missionary viewed native Africans in a similar manner as many African Americans saw COGIC members. In essence, COGIC, to a large degree, had adopted the values of as well as religious standards of Western behavior. Although this represented a significant step in the evolution of the denomination, COGIC leaders would not notice the change in the states until years later. Consequently, their initial step toward respectability did not cause the denomination to reconfigure its public image. Although locked in a bitter debate with the progressives over issues of respectability, COGIC, at least in its missionary efforts, differed very little from the Baptists and Methodists.[39]

After two years of work, White successfully converted a small group of Africans to Christianity by traveling to nearby villages and teaching religious lessons to small groups. Eventually, she won the friendship of the locals, particularly the children, and this enabled her to establish the first COGIC congregation in Africa. Similar to black female reformers in the United States, White believed that her major duty in Africa was to improve the lives of women and children who could, in return, spread the teachings to their entire families. Using the model of the Sunshine Bands and Purity Classes, she taught children Bible verses, Western forms of dress, and Holiness living. Going one step further, White rationalized that the best way to make such improvements was to take children under the mission's care, keeping them separated for a period of time in order to teach them Western forms of respectable behavior. In arguing for the necessity of mission or quasi-boarding schools, ironically, her actions were similar to those of the Spelman College founders (the embodiment of respectability) who viewed the homes of its black students in the American South as counterproductive to the morals they were teaching. School officials, therefore, thought separating students from their homes would help to instill in their pupils refined manners, correct Baptist doctrine, and proper religious and social development.[40]

White's responsibilities increased as the number of converts grew at the Bonika Station mission. In 1933, she sent a letter to Memphis urgently requesting that a second missionary be sent to join her, and near the same time, Mrs. Willis C. Ragland of Columbus, Georgia, made application to serve in Africa as a COGIC missionary. Ragland arrived in Africa in 1933, after Robinson confirmed her as a missionary. With funds provided by the church, White and Ragland supervised the building of a stucco worship structure, which, according to White, "was a testimony to our untiring efforts to establish a proper house of worship among the heathens" that she believed would help to raise Africans from their low degraded lifestyles.[41] Again, the words of White sounded similar to those of progressives who, during Reconstruction, felt they had embarked upon foreign missionary work and equated the heathenism among blacks in Atlanta to that in Africa, demonstrating that COGIC missionaries' stances had not remained static and many had adopted Victorian attitudes toward worshiping and social behavior.

White seemed indifferent to other aspects of native African culture such as traditional dancing, which had also become a topic of respectability among blacks in America. In the 1910s, female reformers "singled out African American dance as the most egregious activity contributing to the moral decay of blacks at the time."[42] They believed that secular dance challenged Western conceptions of proper body etiquette because blacks' dance generally "exploded outward from the hips and was performed from a crouching position with the knees flexed and the body bent at the waist, which allowed a fluidity of movement in propulsive rhythmic fashion" and it was these characteristics that reformers argued threatened Anglo-Saxon civilization.[43]

Black missionaries transplanted their disdain of dance from America to Africa, arguing that native African dance also took on a sexual connotation. However, as Leonard Lovett has shown, "African dance expressed in various forms celebrated such aspects of life as victory in warfare, thanks for a good harvest, the birth or death of a family member, puberty rites, marriage, and honoring ancestors." Also, some African dances contained powerful theological implications and remained sacred among Africans. "Spirit possession was the ultimate religious experience that occurred as a result of African dance; African gods possessed participants and spoke through them, all while the person danced in joy."[44]

Rooted in the black Holiness-Pentecostal worldview, COGIC's celebration of dance contained similar connotations. As a result of White's association with the denomination, she would have made distinctions between proper and improper modes of dance among Africans. Even COGIC's founder defended dancing in an article entitled "Is It Right for the Saints of God to Dance?" Mason articulated that,

> Dancing shows that we have victory. Dancing of the people of God is to be in the Spirit of Jesus only, for as in Jesus only can we rejoice and praise God. The people of God do not dance as the world dances, but are moved by the Spirit of God. So you can see that it is all in the Spirit of God and the glory of God. It is not to satisfy the lust of the flesh, or the carnal appetite [referring to the black elites' criticisms of dance] as the world dances, but only to glorify God and satisfy the soul. The world dances of the world, about the world and to the world. The children of God dance of God, for God and to the praise and glory of His name. They have the joy of the Spirit of the Lord in them. They are joyful in their King—Christ.[45]

According to her own view of respectable or sanctified dance, White would have allowed African converts to continue the practice of dancing, but only as a sign of the reception of the Holy Spirit. Her strict adherence to Pentecostalism would have allowed White to make a distinction between secular nonrespectable dance and dance in accordance with the Holy Spirit, which she would have deemed right and proper.

Spending four years in Africa, White, in 1935, decided to return to the United States for a much-needed respite. While home, she searched for new missionaries who could help COGIC's efforts in Africa, specifically "someone with a consecrated heart and a consecrated life who was ready and willing to answer the call to come over to Macedonia and help us."[46] In Dallas, she met Beatrice Lott, who agreed to work with her, and in 1937 the two returned to Africa and established COGIC's second mission at Tubake, Liberia. Before the completion of the second mission, the threat of danger caused by the eruption of World War II forced all three to return home.[47]

Once back in the United States, White, Ragland, and Lott embarked on a lecture tour to inspire other young women to become missionaries and join them in Africa. The tour succeeded in convincing Dorothy Webster, a teacher from Cleveland, Ohio, and Martha Barber of Chicago, Illinois, to become COGIC missionaries. After completing training, Webster chose to concentrate her missionary efforts in Haiti, while Barber agreed to serve in Africa. In March 1947, Barber and Lott boarded a Pan American clipper at New York's LaGuardia airport and two days later landed at Roberts Field, Monrovia, Liberia. After a few days, a plane transported the two to Cape Palmas and then on to Tubake where they resumed work on COGIC's second mission. Acting on Western concepts of respectability, Lott and Barber believed that a proper place to worship would lend itself to more souls being saved, and in 1948, through the efforts of a coordinated national fundraising campaign, COGIC opened its second church edifice at Tubake and a mission house three years later. The completion of a second church building and mission station elevated COGIC's mission status in Liberia, which did not go unnoticed. The government praised Lott and Barber for improving the lives and living conditions of the people living in the Tubake district. COGIC's second mission also served as the catalyst for the growth of a trading town that took the name Tubake, which became an economic and religious center for the district.[48]

While COGIC missionaries continued working in Cape Palmas, Sarah January formed a third congregation in the capital city of Monrovia. The small congregation grew in number until it became necessary to appoint a pastor and upon the recommendation of January, Mason appointed Valentine Brown, a native of Liberia and recent convert. With the appointment, COGIC now possessed an international presence and jurisdiction over the congregants' power to appoint and remove clergymen, thus giving the denomination an official presence in Africa.[49]

As COGIC missions in Africa became more successful, the national denomination believed it necessary to appoint an overseer and in 1945, Mason appointed Charles Pleas as the bishop of Liberia. In September 1948, Pleas made his first trip to the country, marking the first time that a male member of COGIC visited its congregations and missions in Africa. Pleas found small churches in desperate need of financial assistance and remembered that upon arrival "I found Elder Valentine Brown and a fine group of believers waiting with joy and great expectations and the government of Liberia was very anxious to know about the men leaders of the Church and just what we were like." Pleas further stated he "sought the opportunity to make the acquaintance of governmental officials." He remembered that he had met Liberia's president and was pleased that he treated him "very cordially" as the president understood he was a prominent executive of COGIC.[50]

Since there was no church edifice for the congregation in Monrovia, Pleas, with the help of Brown, procured a site to build a house of worship and with money secured from the Foreign Mission Bands, Pleas bought materials that allowed construction to begin in 1948. Upon completion, he convened the first African convocation of the Church of God in Christ in Liberia, which allowed the three Liberian congregations the opportunity to gather and learn the overall structure of the now international denomination. At the conclusion of the African convocation, Pleas returned to Memphis where he stressed the importance of continued monetary support for the missions and the further expansion of COGIC in Africa. Responding to the call, COGIC's leadership, in 1949, sent Elder O. T. Jones of Atlanta to Monrovia, which ultimately solidified the denomination's foothold in the country.[51]

Influenced by their theology, COGIC missionaries, along with the national denomination, perceived many of the elements of indigenous African culture as backward and non-Christian. Missionaries argued that the gospel alone could not raise Africa from its backward state and the strict adherence to sanctification was needed. Their devotion to sanctification led the denomination to develop an assimilationist policy, which led to the insistence upon conformity to Western behavior and social norms in all their foreign missions.

Although no concrete evidence detailing COGIC's stance on European colonialism exists, one can deduce that the denomination supported Western values in Africa. Elizabeth Robinson taught women of the denomination manners and social grace in the form of sanctification. Therefore, it is not a stretch to believe that she would have subscribed to the theory that Africans could benefit from borrowing the best aspects of Victorian culture, just as many blacks had after the Civil War. Ironically, the denomination's critique and paternalistic view of indigenous African cultures resembled whites' attitude toward black culture in the United States. Unknowingly, COGIC missionaries dispensed their own brand of respectability throughout their foreign missions, which duplicated and imposed middle-class values in their missions just as white northern missionaries had among blacks in the South after the Civil War. Although members continued to practice an emotional brand of worship, their attitude toward social etiquette and social behavior had changed.

Sanctification Brought to the Caribbean

Once COGIC solidified its foothold in Africa, the denomination turned its full attention toward the Caribbean. In 1927, with funds provided by the national denomination, Mattie McCually of Tulsa, Oklahoma, traveled to Trinidad and spent two years on the island. Experiencing limited success, McCually returned to the United States in 1931, an outcome that convinced COGIC's Home and Foreign Mission Department that a male might be more suitable for work on the Islands. Cornelius Hall, a COGIC elder living in Los Angeles and a native of the Turks Islands of the West Indies, volunteered to return to his homeland to render what he referred to as "service to his people." To enable him to travel freely, he built a boat, and for ten years, Hall served as a missionary in the West Indies, evangelizing and spreading COGIC's message from island to island, but in 1947, he tragically disappeared at sea.[52]

After Hall's death, COGIC shifted its foreign mission work to Port-au-Prince, Haiti, sending Dorothy Webster to the island in 1947. As a former French teacher in the Cleveland, Ohio, schools, church officials believed that her language skills would be especially effective in Haiti. Webster's work led to the establishment of the first COGIC congregation, mission, and grade school in Port-au-Prince, but she is most remembered for working to "introduce hundreds of souls to Christianity and waging a war against voodoo."[53] Seeing an opportunity for growth in Haiti, the denomination appointed Joseph Paulseus, a native of Haiti, presiding bishop of the country. With his help, the denomination grew exponentially in Haiti, so much so that by 1955, the church possessed ninety-six congregations with a membership that reached into the thousands. After Bishop Paulseus's death, COGIC continued to grow under the direction of Bishop Joseph St. Juste, also a native Haitian.[54]

As the poorest nation in the Western hemisphere, Haiti's economic conditions resembled those in the Arkansas and Mississippi Delta, and COGIC's message of divine healing, promise of eternal bliss, and divine intervention appealed to Haitians, just as it had to blacks in the Delta. COGIC's Pentecostal theology also remained adept at addressing the social and economic woes of the impoverished nations of the Caribbean, and, therefore, it should be of no surprise that the church directed its missionary efforts toward Jamaica.

The denomination's missionaries first arrived on the island in 1925 where they found a number of Pentecostal groups already working. The Pentecostal Assembly of the World (PAW) had established itself in Jamaica as early as 1917, but COGIC's missionary department also wanted a denominational presence. Missionaries found a thriving agricultural economy that, in many ways, exploited black laborers in a similar manner as America's agricultural economy. Blacks labored long hours in sugarcane fields, but enjoyed none of the economic windfall the crops produced for the nation. The island's black population had experienced little economic progress as the vast majority continued to live in slums, thus producing an ideal environment for the growth of COGIC.[55] In 1925, the national leadership sent Ed Cunningham, a native of the island and COGIC minister, to establish a mission school. Settling in Kingston, he established the first COGIC congregation on the island and as a result of his efforts, the denomination expanded. Although the church did continue to grow, research revealed few specifics about COGIC in Jamaica until immigrants from the island transplanted it to England.[56]

In an attempt to find better wages and living conditions, Jamaican immigrants transplanted the denomination into Europe. England became a prime destination for Jamaican immigrants in the 1950s, and the denomination attracted other immigrants from the West Indies living in the United Kingdom, giving COGIC an instant foothold in Europe. From England, the denomination crossed the English Channel and spread into France where it attracted poor African immigrants. COGIC's brand of Pentecostalism again proved adept at addressing the immediate needs of the poor living in the French suburbs. As always, the denomination offered African immigrants divine healing through uncompromising faith, sobriety, and the hope of employment as employers learned of the honesty and reliability of COGIC congregants.

Just as COGIC would use the Great Migration to expand to the northern section of the United States, it also used the black self-help movement to grow internationally. Similar to Baptists and Methodists, COGIC missionaries dedicated their lives to uplifting blacks whom they believed still lived under a veil of heathenism. Driven by the theory of sanctification and their growing acceptance of middle-class values, COGIC missionaries reproduced paternalistic views toward Africans with whom they worked. As COGIC missionaries uplifted, they also duplicated middle-class values and often displayed blatant racist attitudes toward African culture. While carrying the light of Christianity into the "darkness" of Africa, COGIC missionaries established congregations that would eventually give the Church of God in Christ an international presence. At home, however, the black middle class continued to demonize COGIC, but the denomination's efforts and attitudes in its foreign missions proved that members' class standing and worldview were changing and as congregants moved into urban centers, congregations would quickly adapt and take another step toward mainstream respectability.

5

Memphis, the Hope of a Promised Land

The Achievement of Respectability for the Church of God in Christ

In the first three decades of the twentieth century, African Americans began to move as a million or more left their homes for urban centers of the industrial north. They had grown tired of sharecropping, lynching, and deplorable educational facilities that kept them from properly educating their children. Thomas Jones examined the problem in his study, *Negro Education,* and found that "the average school year for black children in the South lasted only five months and most teachers barely possessed a third grade education." In addition, buildings were in "wretched condition and lacked proper sanitation, lighting, and equipment," making it impossible to deliver an education equal to that of whites.[1] Even after receiving an education, blacks, many times, were exiled to the North because with the acquisition of knowledge, they found it impossible to live under the system of Jim Crow. A woman living in Greenwood, Mississippi, echoed this when she spoke of her son living in the North, stating, "we are afraid to invite him home for a visit because I can not expect him to accept the abuse which we have grown accustomed."[2]

The *Chicago Defender* also helped to pull blacks into the North. Widely circulated in the South, the paper ran editorials designed to cause blacks to question their marginalized status. One editorial argued, "If you freeze to death in the North and be free, why freeze to death in the South and be a slave, where your mother, sister and daughter are raped and burned at the stake; where your father, brother and sons are treated with contempt and hung from poles, riddled with bullets at the least mention that he does not like the way he is treated." The paper called for blacks to "Come North . . . for the hard working man, there is plenty of work."[3] Editorials such as these prompted blacks to sell everything they owned in an attempt to secure passage and with them they brought their religious practices and customs, explaining COGIC's arrival in the great industrial North. Although viewed in the beginning as a storefront denomination, urban centers provided COGIC's congregants with better economic and educational opportunities, which in return allowed the church to alter its image.

As blacks migrated northward, COGIC women often led the effort in establishing the denomination in the region. For instance, Mary Johnson remains the most famous female evangelist credited with "digging out" the first COGIC congregation in the state of Michigan. Born in North Carolina and raised as a devout Baptist, Johnson settled in Memphis after her marriage where, in 1901, she converted to Pentecostalism. She experienced tragedy in 1905 when her husband died, but five years later, she married William G. "Ting-a-Ling" Johnson, a COGIC minister.[4] The two conducted missionary work throughout Arkansas and Tennessee, gaining valuable experience they would later use in establishing churches in the North. Early one morning as the couple prayed, Johnson claimed that God revealed a plan to her and anointed her husband William to write in an unknown language. Unable to decipher the writing, the couple took the paper to Mason, which he interpreted as instructions to move to Michigan to evangelize.[5]

Following what they believed to be divine instructions, the couple moved to Detroit in March 1914; the date not only represented the arrival of the Johnsons but also the founding of COGIC in the state. With no place to live, the two settled in a half-way house on Beaubien Street; wasting no time, they began to preach on the corner of Catherine and Gratiot Streets, which was also the home of a boardinghouse known as the "bear trap" due to its rowdy tenants and unlawful activities. The Johnsons conducted daily meetings, out of which developed the first COGIC congregation in Michigan. As the size of the meetings grew, the congregants found themselves in need of a larger place to worship. With money Mary earned as a laundress, the couple rented a storefront on 630 Beaubien Street. Johnson's laundry salary not only provided a home, but it also secured the first COGIC worship structure in Michigan. William erected a partition to divide the one-room structure; on the residential side of the divided room the couple slept on a rollaway bed and cooked meals on a small stove that also provided heat and they used the other side of the room for worship services. Congregants, made up mostly of women and children, sat on old frame chairs salvaged from trash piles, and William fashioned the first pulpit out of an old produce cart.[6]

Despite poor conditions, the Detroit congregation continued to grow. Hearing of their success, Mason traveled to Detroit in 1915. While there, he appointed William the head pastor of the fledgling congregation. Upon confirmation, William sought to incorporate the denomination in the state, but the congregation failed to meet the required membership numbers, and the state rejected their application. In response, the Johnsons conducted a revival that claimed to have rivaled that of the famous Azusa Street gathering. By the end of the meeting, the congregation possessed the required number for incorporation, and in June 1915, the state of Michigan recognized the Church of God in Christ as an incorporated denomination.[7]

In 1920, as a result of her continued work in the state, Lizzie Robinson appointed Mary Johnson the State Mother of Women's Work in Michigan. Johnson then personally led the expansion of COGIC throughout the state. According to Johnson, "After my husband died he left me with two tents and with them I personally dug out and set up Prayer and Bible Bands in the cities of Ypsilanti, Albion, Jackson, Battle Creek, Lansing, Grand Rapids, Muskegon, Pontiac, Flint, Saginaw, Port Huron, Mt. Clemmons, and Carlton." Johnson not only set up a tent meeting in Ypsilanti, but she raised enough money to purchase a lot and personally managed the construction of the first COGIC church in the town. Later in Mother Johnson's life, Bishop C. L. Morton of Ontario, Canada, requested that she supervise the women there. At the request of Morton, Robinson appointed Johnson the Provincial Mother of Women's Work for Ontario. Johnson worked seven years in Canada and helped establish COGIC congregations in Ontario and elsewhere in Canada. In similar fashion, COGIC spread to other northern states as men and women left everything they owned and followed the Great Migration routes to evangelize. Not only did COGIC grow in the industrial North, but it transformed itself in mid-South cities.[8]

Headed to Memphis

Memphis also became a popular destination for poor blacks leaving the Delta, and the ever-increasing population brought Mason and COGIC a steady flow of converts who transplanted their religious customs and traditions once practiced on Delta plantations into an urban setting. The city "served as the hub of the Mississippi Delta, a crossroad between the South and the mid-West, and an excellent example of a New South city."[9] After the Civil War, Memphis attracted thousands of blacks from the Delta due to mechanization in the cotton fields and an emerging industrial economy. With the influx of blacks entering the city, business leaders enticed industrialists to invest in the economy with the promise of cheap labor and an anti-union climate. Henry Ford opened a plant in 1913 and a second in 1924. Fisher Body Works, a company that produced wooden parts for automobile bodies, began operations in Memphis in the 1920s, while Sears opened a retail outlet and Firestone opened a plant in 1937. Coupled with its vibrant popular culture, Memphis became a regional beacon of progress that appeared to offer more freedom for blacks in contrast to the Delta. Although the black population would grow to constitute a greater percentage of the population than ever before, blacks remained at the bottom of the social hierarchy and incoming migrants encountered an urban environment that reproduced rural forms of paternalism, intimidation, and white supremacy.[10]

Edward Hull "Boss" Crump Jr. dominated the business and political spheres of Memphis. Born in 1874 outside Holly Springs, Mississippi, Crump lost his father at the age of four during the yellow fever epidemic of 1878. Arriving in Memphis in 1894, he pursued a business career and quickly rose in the ranks of the business elites by marrying into a prominent mercantilist family. With his newfound wealth, he bought controlling interest in a carriage and saddlery manufacturing company, but by 1902, he sold his shares and bought two Mississippi plantations and a Coca-Cola franchise and built one of the largest insurance underwriting companies in the South.[11]

Crump's business ambitions naturally led him into city politics. Elected mayor in 1909, his administration began the task of improving the image of Memphis. With the help of the city council, he passed laws that prohibited the carrying of firearms within city limits and cracked down on the entertainment district that remained the source of a great deal of the crimes that plagued the town. In the tradition of the South, he also passed a city ordinance that allowed policemen to arrest any black on the street after midnight.[12] Crump believed that he understood the black man and quickly developed a paternalistic relationship with the local black community. Recognizing the importance of the black vote, he supported blacks' political participation as long as they cast their ballots for the Crump machine, but he ruthlessly put down social protest that hinted at equality between the races.[13] Crump once lamented to the editor of the black Memphis *World*, "You have a bunch of 'Niggers' teaching social equality, stirring up social hatred and I'm not going to stand for it. I've dealt with 'Niggers' all my life and I know how to treat them."[14]

As paternalistic as a Delta plantation owner, Crump also offered blacks favors in the form of welfare, public housing, and political suffrage. The mayor secured employment for those who remained loyal and "knew their place." He pointed to Tom Lee, a local hero who saved thirty-two persons after a stern-wheeler capsized in the Mississippi River, "as an example of how he took care of his blacks." Crump led the efforts in commemorating the heroism of Lee by lobbying city officials to construct a monument in Lee's honor. Over the years, Lee became a town favorite and special source of pride to the white community because, according to Crump, he remained "unassuming and very polite" and remained in his place.[15]

If Crump played the role of the plantation master, the Memphis police department assumed the role of overseer. In an attempt to maintain control over the black population, city officials condoned heavy-handed treatment of blacks. The department became notorious for its harassment and the arresting of blacks for the smallest infractions. As historian Patty Schechter writes, Ida B. Wells remembered that "A colored girl was convicted of assault and sentenced in a local court after getting the best of a white girl during a fight." The altercation resulted from a series of confrontations in which the white girl had refused to allow the black girl to pass on a wooded path. As things escalated, "the brother of the white girl came along to the woods and abused the colored girl." When attacked on the next day, the black girl fought back, but in court, "a judge carried the sentence to the utmost of his power by giving her [the black girl] 11 months 29 days and a half in the workhouse." Episodes like this became all too common as blacks continued to suffer under a Delta culture that had simply been transferred into urban Memphis.[16]

Despite the brutality of the police, the 1920s witnessed the start of an ongoing relationship between Memphis, the Delta, and ultimately the Church of God in Christ. Even with its racial problems, to immigrants "Memphis represented modernity, urbanism, and industrialism, while the roads, highways, and rail lines connecting Memphis to the Delta brought a steady flow of migrants' cultural and religious traditions."[17] Susie Bryant, for example, migrated from the rural Delta to Memphis. Living in Greenwood, Mississippi, Bryant's mother found it impossible to make a living as a sharecropper after the death of her husband. With hopes of finding industrial employment, Bryant's mother took her chances and moved to Memphis. Once there, however, the family found Memphis no better than Mississippi. Bryant remembered the discrimination she felt at Memphis restaurants, especially having to "go to the back door" and not being able to "drink out of the fountains." She also recalled that she and her mother lived in a "shotgun-house" in Memphis, just as they had in Greenwood and Bryant's mother eventually ended up as a domestic after she failed to find industrial work.[18]

Naomi Jones echoed Bryant's sentiments on racism in Memphis. Jones migrated from Canton, Mississippi, at the age of eighteen, "I was just tired and I was going to go to Memphis and get me a job." Life in Mississippi was simply too hard for Jones and she believed that Memphis would be better, but found:

> They had them same signs here as they had in Mississippi . . . You didn't go in a restaurant that said, "Whites Only." To enter the movie, except

on Beale Street, you had to go in the side door . . . And it was just as segregated here as it was in Mississippi. In some instances, I would have to
say more, because this was a bigger city. You would have to use the side
door, back door, and the next door for a rest room.[19]

Jones, like Bryant, found limited employment opportunities and worked as a
domestic servant in the homes of whites. Overall, Jones and thousands of other
black women like her continued to labor as cooks, domestics, and laundresses.
Most never gained industrial employment, locking them into a cycle of poverty,
which they never escaped.[20]

Black men who migrated to Memphis fared economically worse than their
female counterparts. Johnnie Roger Turner, a migrant from eastern Arkansas,
remembered that her family left during the middle of the night and a waiting car
took them to Memphis.[21] Johnnie's father, however, failed to find industrial
employment and, instead, like thousands of other black migrants, the entire
family headed over the Harahan Bridge from downtown Memphis back into
Arkansas to pick cotton. Johnnie recalled, "Every morning you'd get up real early
and the trucks would come by and pick you up and take you to whatever plantation there was where you would pick cotton."[22] Thousands of migrants continued to labor in the fields after they moved into Memphis, but even more
important, they brought with them their religious customs that had once been
practiced on Delta plantations.

Despite the paternalistic efforts of Crump, a large poverty-stricken group of
blacks lived in Memphis. They huddled into areas of the city that were prone to
flooding and lived in poorly built shotgun houses. Over 70 percent of the city's
African American population continued using communal toilets or pit privies
as 90 percent of the white population enjoyed indoor plumbing.[23] The lack of
governmental action to better the living conditions of the poor compounded the
situation. According to historian Keith Wailoo, white Memphians viewed the living conditions of blacks as more of a blight on the looks of the city rather than
a real health hazard. Building codes, inspections, and maintenance presented city
government with costly problems that they preferred to ignore rather than fix.
Many felt that the city should close the black slums instead of improving the
hygienic and health conditions of the people in order to enhance the aesthetics
of the Bluff City.[24]

From Movement to Denomination: The Explosion of Growth

Aware of the mass black migration into the city, Charles H. Mason returned to
Memphis to preach in 1897, conducting his first revivals on street corners and

later in a tent that he referred to as his tabernacle. As word of his tent services spread, his congregation grew to well over a hundred members within two years. Inspired by its swell in numbers, the tent congregation purchased a vacant lot at 392 Wellington Street and built a forty-by-sixty-foot wooden structure that took the name Saints Home Church of God, which represented the first Church of God in Christ structure in Memphis. As the number of migrants from the Delta increased, so did the popularity of COGIC. The promise of divine healing, sobriety, religious dancing, and the continued practice of black folk rituals made the migrants feel at home.[25]

Although the denomination experienced tremendous growth, COGIC never sought out public recognition and in adherence to sanctification, nor did it concern itself with secular matters. During the denomination's early years, Memphis newspapers took little notice or simply ignored its presence. The tenth annual convocation served as a prime example when close to one thousand members bombarded Memphis hotels and restaurants. While whites would have certainly noticed the increase in the black population, local news outlets only briefly mentioned the event. However, as COGIC grew among the poor, black middle-class Memphians began to view the denomination as a threat to racial advancement.[26]

Despite economic and social hardships, a small black middle class had developed in Memphis. In 1920, the city possessed more than fifty black-owned merchant businesses including restaurants, drugstores, laundries, funeral homes, and two newspapers, but saloons and prostitution became the most profitable businesses for blacks. For example, Robert R. Church opened his first saloon in the 1860s, and by 1906 he had become one of the wealthiest black men in the United States. Church settled in Memphis after its capture by Union forces and took advantage of the economic opportunities during the postwar years by investing in real estate and various small businesses, including a hotel and a saloon. He also helped to establish the Solvent Savings and Trust, the first black-owned financial institution based in Memphis. Church's venture into black capitalism prompted the Negro Business League to call for more blacks to enter banking, a call that J. Jay Scott, a funeral director, and H. Wayman Wilkerson answered in 1910 when they formed the Fraternal Savings Bank, giving Memphis two black banking establishments.[27]

In addition to businessmen, a respectable professional class thrived in Memphis. In 1920, black physicians, dentists, and attorneys made up the professional class in the city. Comprised of educated and, often times, light-skinned blacks, the professional class made the political decisions. "The Colored Citizens Association sounded out mayoral candidates and petitioned the city for paved roads, streetlights, neighborhood parks, and one day a week access for blacks to visit the zoo."[28]

Black middle-class Memphians remained aware that the fate of the poor, many of whom were members of Mason's congregation, directly impacted their middle-class status. As a result, progressives like Reverend Sutton E. Griggs, pastor of the Tabernacle Baptist Church, worked to elevate the entire race. Described as an "intellectual among Negro Baptist clergymen," Griggs became alarmed at the increased number of lynchings, black disfranchisement, and the entrenchment of segregation throughout the country. Within the framework of a novel, he decided to highlight the racial problems in the South while presenting a solution. Griggs introduced his readers to a "New Negro" determined to assert his rights, arguing, "if blacks wanted equality, they must create racial organizations to harness the strength of the black race." Griggs also reasoned that "the association must then make a study of the 'retarding forces' within the black community and move to correct and strengthen black institutions such as the home, school, and the church."[29]

Griggs believed the black church also needed to be modernized and focused on improvement of the condition of blacks in this world, rather than in the next. He theorized, "because blacks were introduced to Christianity as hopeless slaves, they turned their thoughts to the death bed, the funeral, the grave, and the hope of a better life in the afterworld." After emancipation, they continued to dwell on the hope of a better life in heaven, but in Griggs's opinion, "religion ought to do more than help a man reach heaven when he dies. It ought to help him to live in this world. It ought to help people meet every problem of life." By redirecting blacks' otherworldly emphasis, he felt the new concept of Christianity could combat white supremacy while uplifting the race.[30]

Similar to most progressives, Griggs called on black Memphians to abandon the style of Christianity practiced by their slave ancestors. A follower of Benjamin Kidd, a British social Darwinist, Griggs taught that religion remained the number-one factor in the development of a race of people. Kidd believed that "what led to racial superiority was not intellectual ability, but the tendency of a race to subordinate themselves for the good of society, a characteristic inculcated by white Christianity."[31] To incorporate Kidd's theory, Griggs adopted the same vocational curriculum as Booker T. Washington's Tuskegee Institute. In order to help blacks cope with their present situation, Griggs's church taught black women domestic science, moral training, and how to become better cooks for white homes. Men learned basic carpentry, masonry, and improved agricultural technologies; thus, by teaching practical skills, Griggs sought to develop a respectable class of blacks who could win the approval of whites.[32]

The strategy of accommodation won Griggs enormous support from the white population of Memphis, but lower-class blacks disagreed with his social assessment. In their opinion, Griggs failed to realize that the vast majority of black Memphians remained unsatisfied with their lives, and according to historian Vittorio Lanterari, "people who had been subjected to a life of misery and persecution tended to demand a passionate religion."[33] Black Memphians during the first three decades of the twentieth century fit Lanterari's classification, as a majority of poverty-stricken blacks continued to use religion in a similar way as their slave ancestors—as an escape from their everyday lives. Men such as Griggs remained unpopular with the masses as "black Memphians typically looked toward the church for emotional fulfillment rather than intellectual stimulation, which led many to make their religious home the Church of God in Christ."[34]

Even though COGIC grew in popularity among the poor, the black middle class remained unimpressed. They argued that Mason's preaching of rewards in the afterlife and lack of a vocal stance on secular issues hindered racial advancement. Men such as Griggs viewed Mason's services as counterproductive to the fight to combat negatively held stereotypes of the race. Progressives believed that as they stressed rational liturgy, proper hygiene, and respectable conduct, Mason's charismatic style of worship impeded their efforts.

As a result, the educated black populace, during the 1920s, continued to view COGIC as a storefront church composed of uncultured preachers and members who continued to be an embarrassment. For instance, when COGIC held large religious meetings, whites' suspicions produced rumors of black magic, wild emotions, and uncontrollable female sexual promiscuity. While untrue and wildly exaggerated, the accusations cast the entire black community in a negative light. To separate themselves, the black elite labeled the congregants of COGIC as fanatical, uneducated, and uncultured "holy rollers." They characterized Pentecostal meetings as "pandemonium where members acted out exhibitions worthy of a mad house."[35] White employers also complained that their servants spent too much time at Mason's services, which often forced them to hire replacements. Historian Tera Hunter pointed this out when she argued that whites viewed religious revivals as a good thing, but when their cooks and washerwomen threw down their work and hurried off to the church, it became a nuisance to whites who depended upon their labor to make their lives comfortable.[36]

COGIC Gave Them Something Tangible

Even with mounting criticism, Mason's following continued to grow. Historian David Tucker explained the growth when he argued, "the elite ridiculed Mason's magic, but the masses remained spellbound." Tucker maintained that "most poor blacks still feared spirits and believed that Mason demonstrated command over the spirit world when he cast out demons and interpreted words spoken in tongues."[37] Outside Memphis, author Zora Neale Hurston concluded that the development of COGIC and other Pentecostal denominations occurred as the result of a deepening class line within the black community. She argued COGIC grew as a "protest against the high-brow nature" of mainstream black churches, which seemed to be overtaking the black population.[38]

Financial success accompanied Mason's increasing membership and in 1924, when the local Royal Circle Hospital failed, COGIC purchased the property and constructed a new worship center to house its national convocation. Further expansion occurred after Griggs's Tabernacle Baptist Church defaulted on their mortgage and COGIC purchased the property. While economic success allowed the denomination to expand in Memphis, on the eve of the Great Depression Mason and COGIC still lacked the respect of whites and middle-class blacks.[39]

The Great Depression allowed the membership of COGIC to continue to grow as it produced an environment in which the fledgling denomination gained a new degree of respectability. When the stock market crashed, Memphis residents took little notice. Local newspapers reported the news but declined to give it headline status and leading businessmen thought that the health of the stock market was simply irrelevant to the local agriculturally based economy of the Bluff City. The *Commercial Appeal* called "talk of a national disaster unbelievably silly," citing local businessmen who predicted "a short duration of hard times that would pass with little notice to the citizens."[40] Early on, they seemed to be correct, as during the first year of the Depression, little changed in Memphis as the city experienced no run on banks and none of the larger financial institutions failed. According to historian Roger Biles, "Memphis was removed from the nation's banking and manufacturing centers in the Northeast and Midwest, so the city experienced a lag time between the stock market crash and the onset of economic difficulty."[41]

By the mid-1930s, however, river trade decreased and unemployment numbers rose. By winter, relief lines formed as thousands lined up in search of a meal but instead of downplaying the economic situation, "the *Commercial Appeal* now reported that so many people jumped off the Harahan Bridge into the Mississippi River that they printed the names and telephone numbers of clergymen and begged people to seek counseling, but soon the paper reported that a preacher had also jumped off the bridge."[42]

While the Great Depression intensified the hardships blacks faced in Memphis, their migration into the city reached an all-time high. Economic hard times encouraged them to uproot from the surrounding rural areas and move into Memphis, but the expanding black community continued to occupy the worst areas of town. To the north, they congregated along the low-lying area of the Wolf River and to the south, they lived in the industrial portion of town. As a result of the filth and squalor, disease became commonplace; for example, health officials attributed frequent outbreaks of typhoid to the use of communal toilets and as unemployment numbers rose, so did the frequency of the outbreaks.[43]

As the Depression deepened, people began to turn toward their religion for solace during the economic hard times. Mason preached a simple message of endurance and self-reliance, which allowed COGIC to become the second-largest black denomination in the city, after the Baptists, with more than twenty separate congregations.[44] The promise of divine healing also allowed the denomination to expand its base among the poor. Proper medical care remained out of reach for many, but Mason promised that with uncompromising faith, God would heal any malady known to man. Mason's revivals during the 1930s became known as the "emergency rooms of the soul" as columns in the *Whole Truth*, the principle periodical of the church, began to be filled with testimonials of people who swore that, with Mason's help, they had been healed by God. One testimonial read:

> I am glad that I can report victory over sin. I wish to tell of the wonderful healing power of God. In September 1933, I was lying on my bed, I had a vision. I saw a man standing near my bedside, who said to me you have a very bad stomach and you will have an operation and after the operation you will have ten days of grievance. Then suddenly the man disappeared. I then turned to the Lord and began to pray. I decided not to have the operation and go through the ten days of grievance. I began to pour out my complaint before the Lord with serious grievance. I sought out Bishop Mason on the tenth day and after prayer I was healed. Before this, after eating I would have terrible gas pains. My stomach would stay swollen and I did not have a waist line. [Now] [m]y stomach feel as it did when I was a girl and I am over 50 years old. The Lord has done a great thing for me whereof I am glad. I desire your prayers.[45]

Other testimonials dealt with more serious health matters. Elder E. B. Stewart, a COGIC minister, testified that he praised God for his goodness as "I have a little son that was born with a rupture," and he "consulted Bishop Mason for prayer; he told me to believe in the Lord and my son would be healed." Stewart followed Mason's instructions and "the Lord completely healed the rupture and now the child is happy, running and playing with other children. I give God all the glory."[46]

In an attempt to educate members on the importance of hygiene and good health, the *Whole Truth* began to run a wellness column. Although peppered with religious undertones, the column offered readers short articles on health-care, food preparation, and body hygiene. Readers could also submit questions to Dr. Nunez, the column's editor, who answered them the following month. How much the column helped in the fight against unsanitary conditions and better health remains unknown, but COGIC's attempt to help the masses slowly began to change the image of the denomination as it moved into the mainstream in Memphis.[47]

Crime and vice generated by the unemployment rate created instability among the poor. On weekends, blacks journeyed to Beale Street to visit the saloons and gambling halls. With the advent of the Great Depression, Beale Street became even more popular, but to white Memphians the street music and lewd behavior only served to confirm their beliefs that blacks were compulsive by nature and prone to violence. The *Press Scimitar* claimed that "Beale Street allowed 'Good-Time Charleys' to strut in the white lights and men to slink in the shadows destroying already impoverished households as men and women squandered household earnings in the gambling halls and saloons."[48] In addition, alcoholism led to domestic strife as men vented their anger toward their socioeconomic conditions on their wives and children. Similar to whites, this also contributed to men abandoning their families, which then led to the economic necessity that forced black women to work outside the home or find a second job, leaving children at home to raise themselves.

COGIC, however, remained adept at addressing the problems of alcoholism and domestic strife. Sanctified adherents could not consume alcoholic beverages, thus making COGIC's membership less susceptible to alcoholism. The denomination also offered hope to husbands who considered abandoning their families. Correspondingly, employers began to take note of COGIC members as a reliable pool of labor that gained a reputation of sobriety, honesty, and punctuality. As COGIC men found employment, they testified to others how membership and faith could lead to a job. Although arguably paternalistic, whites viewed Mason's message of hard work, thrift, and sobriety as being conducive to the social control of blacks. Yet, black religious leaders in Memphis continued to view COGIC as a storefront church and an embarrassment.

In 1936, religious leaders used a fire that occurred during COGIC's convocation as a prime example of the backwardness of the denomination. City newspapers reported that a carnival-like atmosphere surrounded the convocation and on the night of the fire, loud speakers blared, "I'm glad I got religion" as old men sold peanuts and candy near the entrance of the church while worshipers inside danced and shouted. The *Press Scimitar* reported "there were 2,000 Negroes in the large wooden tabernacle and 20 sinners on a bench, with their eyes rolled back into their heads in an effort to be saved when the fire broke out."[49] The paper informed readers that since November 26, five hundred preachers and well over five thousand blacks had been conducting a twenty-four-hour service at Mason's church on Fifth Street. The paper noted that before the fire started, Utah Smith, a COGIC preacher from Hartford, Connecticut, worked the crowd into a frenzy as he stood in the pulpit and chanted, "Ah Jesus, Ah Jesus, Ah Jesus, are you washed in the Blood of the Lamb?"[50]

Fire Chief Klinck told reporters that because of the intense worship service, no one noticed that a fire engulfed the basement until Jerry Johnson, a delegate from New Orleans, smelled smoke. The article joked that what Johnson smelled was not "flapjacks" but rather wood burning and as he yelled "fire," the congregants fought their way out of the building. After extinguishing the fire, authorities found a charred male body amid the debris. COGIC left Memphis in "shock" when church officials refused to cancel the remaining days of the convocation and moved the all-night meetings to Lauderdale and Georgia Street.[51]

The following year, COGIC again angered prominent black leaders when Mason advertised that he wanted to publicly baptize 250 new converts during the annual Cotton Carnival. The city developed the Cotton Carnival as a means to promote consumer interest in cotton during the Depression years, but "unlike the Mardi Gras celebration in New Orleans, the Cotton Carnival claimed no religious significance." From the onset, the carnival remained a business venture looking to stimulate cotton prices, though it failed to produce any real increase in the price.[52]

In 1936, after witnessing the Cotton Carnival parade in which blacks played a limited role in pulling the floats, the black business class sponsored the Cotton Makers' Jubilee. They wanted to highlight the role blacks played in the cotton industry and, on a larger scale, wanted to promote blacks' desire to be regarded as a part of the progressive social and economic interests of Memphis.[53] The problem occurred in 1937 when COGIC announced that during the Cotton Makers' Jubilee, Mason would officiate a mass baptizing at the foot of Beale Street in the Mississippi River before a reviewing stand in a park on the bluff. In protest, Reverend J. J. Walker, pastor of the East End Christian Church, organized the Memphis Ministerial Club for the explicit reason of stopping what they referred to as Mason's "baptizing show."[54]

Dr. Walter White, the elected president of the association, appointed a committee that impressed upon Mason the importance of religious dignity and the "great shame and harm to the entire black community" if he carried out his plan.[55] The Memphis Ministerial Club failed to stop the planned "baptizing show," and left with no other choice, Dr. White turned to the white ministers of

Memphis for their help. Reverend Walker, chairman of the committee, solicited the help of white ministers when he argued in local newspapers:

> The Negro people had the same reaction as the white ministers when they read publicity of the baptizing show. Where established churches have progressed in the type of ministers selected and in the reformation of the church program, storefront churches have become stuffed with cast-offs and religious criminals who will not be denied. While aggressive minorities are pushing forward with intelligent and modern interpretation of a gospel that was once wholly emotionalized, others have glittered with their emotional paroxysms. It is unfortunate that the efforts of the sincere and well-established churches in Memphis, both small and large, have to be hampered by the manipulation of a group—both unorthodox and pagan—of the outer fringes. While the one [mainstream religions] steadily prods at social problems with instruments of a spiritual, physical, and religious nature.[56]

In the end, the ministerial associations, with the aid of city officials, stopped Mason's "baptizing show," but more important, the event illustrated that what was deemed as respectable religious customs and traditions among blacks remained in flux. Middle-class blacks argued that events like Mason's "baptizing show" reinforced social Darwinist arguments that blacks remained socially and culturally inferior to whites, while men such as Dr. White and Reverend Walker argued that sacred religious ceremonies should not be disgraced by administering them in a carnival-like atmosphere. Though the traditional claim was that one needed only a call from God to be ordained a minister, White and Walker argued that the lack of adequate training hampered Mason and kept him from serving in his position in a dignified manner.[57]

COGIC'S March toward Respectability: A Cathedral Worthy of Respect

Although in battle with the local black middle class, COGIC made significant strides among poor blacks and many white city officials who believed Mason to be an honest man. Whites viewed his religious message of hard work, thriftiness, and sobriety as conducive to the social control of blacks during the Depression and because of COGIC's increasing numbers, Mason sought to build a larger headquarters to serve as an annual meeting place for the national convocation. He envisioned a structure that would house the thousands of delegates who traveled to Memphis yearly for the meeting. However, Mason's health continued to deteriorate and on April 12, 1940, he commissioned R. R. Williams to construct the new temple on South Fifth Street.[58] Williams secured the services of W. H. Taylor and U. E. Miller, who drew up the plans for the building and served as the superintendent of construction. Though the Depression hindered the fundraising efforts of the church, Mason used his reputation to secure loans from two banks for costs above the $2,900 raised by the denomination to begin the initial construction.[59]

Problems occurred when the United States entered into World War II and the creation of the War Production Board (WPB) brought the project to a halt. The WPB, created in 1942 to direct America's industrial conversion to war production, switched auto factories to producing tanks, shirt factories to making mosquito netting, and manufacturers of refrigerators, stoves, and cash registers to producing munitions. The war effort required conservation as well as production. "Use it up, wear it out, and make do without" became the prevailing slogan.[60] As a consequence of the government's rationing, by 1944 the new temple remained only partially completed and church officials were unable to obtain the steel and lumber necessary to finish the project. After several failed attempts to secure the materials, the half-completed edifice stood without a roof or floors.[61]

In 1943, COGIC hired William Graber, a local Memphis attorney, and petitioned the WPB to appropriate $48,000 worth of steel and lumber that the Tri-State Iron Company in Memphis agreed to sell, but the WPB turned down COGIC's request, citing that the material would be better used to supply the war effort. Mason then turned to Reverend James L. Delk, a politically connected white COGIC preacher, for help in securing the steel. Born in September 1887 in Pall Mall, Tennessee, Delk converted to Pentecostalism in 1899 and after completion of his law degree, opened a practice in Conway, Arkansas. In 1904, Delk met Mason for the first time when he heard him preaching to a large crowd in Conway. Due to the interracial nature of Pentecostalism, Delk joined the ranks of Holiness in 1914 when Mason ordained him; his preaching led him to Hopkinsville, Kentucky, where he began to pastor one of the largest white Pentecostal congregations in the state. Although no evidence revealed that the white congregation received direction from Memphis, Delk always remained close to Mason, often referring to himself as a COGIC preacher.[62]

At the request of Mason, Delk traveled to Washington, D.C., to work the political wires in an effort to secure the steel needed to complete the temple. Meeting with members of the State Department, officials advised him to meet with Tom Stewart, the ranking senator from Tennessee, who earlier had assisted William Jennings Bryan in the Scopes trial in Dayton, Tennessee. According to Delk, "Senator Stewart got busy and I kept the streets hot going from Sen. Stewart's office to the WPB office down in the Security Building."[63] After a month in Washington, federal officials notified Delk that the problem with the steel appropriation rested in Memphis, not in Washington. In August 1944, Delk traveled to Memphis and with the help of District Attorney General William Gerber, met with Allen Harrison, chairman of the local WPB in Memphis. In September, a telegram from Gerber informed Delk that the federal agency had, for the second time, rejected COGIC's request for the steel. The telegram read:

> I regret to advise you that it has been impossible for me to impress upon the local board to the extent that they will be willing to permit the purchase of the desired steel. They advise it will be impossible to grant the request due to present regulations and increased war demands.[64]

After being rejected, Delk met with Memphis's mayor, Walter Chandler. The mayor acknowledged that he knew of Mason and regarded him as a "fine old gentleman" but explained that the city decided, in conjunction with the WPB, that all nonessential building projects would be placed on hold. Refusing to take no for an answer, Delk traveled back to Washington to meet with Senator Stewart for a second time. According to Delk, "Senator Stewart worked hard day and night and caused the WPB in Washington to override the Memphis office and granted COGIC the privilege of purchasing the $48,000 worth of steel."[65] In return, Delk and Mason agreed to work on behalf of the Democratic Party in Tennessee. An excerpt from a letter to Delk read that "COGIC's and your agreed willingness to work on behalf of the Democratic Party is certainly appreciated."[66]

Newspapers throughout the South carried the news of the steel appropriation. A Memphis *Press Scimitar* article headline read "Temple Given WPB Priority." The piece stated that COGIC secured the priority from the War Production Board for the completion of the Church of God in Christ tabernacle, known as Mason Temple. The article further stated that COGIC contracted Tri-State Iron Works to furnish the material that would complete the structure, which would hold over 20,000 people at its completion.[67] The *Chattanooga Times* also ran an article that greatly improved the image of COGIC in Memphis. The article bragged that through its influence with the War Production Board and Senator Tom Stewart, the Church of God in Christ secured a priority for $48,000 worth of steel when no white church or contractor could do so.[68]

Overnight the WPB gave COGIC local respectability. The ability to purchase the steel in a time of war gave white Memphians the impression that COGIC was politically connected in the nation's capital. Mason's message, reputation of honesty, and now perceived political strength made COGIC a well-respected black denomination in Memphis. Evidence of this could be seen when Mayor Walter Chandler wrote Mason a personal letter congratulating him on the completion of what Chandler called "a handsome edifice that will serve to bring the people of Memphis together."[69]

In 1945, COGIC completed construction of Mason Temple, dedicating the building at their thirty-eighth annual convocation in December of that same year. The *Commercial Appeal* referred to the building as:

> The largest convention hall owned by any Negro church group in America with a total estimated cost of $275,679. The main building covers some 29,672 square feet and boasts a seating capacity of 7500 with seats that are in theater style, upholstered in red and deeply cushioned. The main floor of the auditorium measures 134 by 135 feet with a horseshoe balcony that measures 35 by 133, an elevated rostrum 25 by 48; a circle chancel, 7 by 64; two choir lofts, each 24 by 60.[70]

A public address system connected all parts of the building, which enabled persons in any of the many sub-assembly rooms or in the 500-seating capacity dining room in the basement to hear proceedings at all times. Reporters who were granted access to the building found numerous offices and suites of offices, including those of Bishop Mason and Bishop McEwen that were all grouped around the auditorium on the top level. Church leaders also incorporated a barbershop, shoeshine parlor, and hair salon to ensure that delegates adhered to a respectable grooming standard. To accommodate a large number of older members, Mason Temple also housed a fully staffed and equipped emergency ward consisting of two hundred beds designed to assist parishioners in case of medical emergencies. To complete the building, the Department of Women raised an additional $1,600 to place a neon sign out front that read Church of God in Christ.[71]

The denomination had come a great distance since the first delegates held their initial convocation in a tent at the corner of Fifth Street, but the completion of Mason Temple meant much more than the fulfillment of the dreams of sharecroppers. On a local level, the temple gave COGIC credibility as white Memphians now overwhelmingly viewed COGIC as a mainstream religious organization that had grown in number with the increasing flow of Delta immigrants. Even the local black middle class began to accept COGIC as an established denomination; yet, nationally, most blacks continued to view COGIC as a storefront church that existed on the periphery of black religious life. In the 1930s and 1940s, however, the demographics of COGIC's membership began to change as the Great Migration routes opened the industrial North for the growth of the denomination in the region. As members who lived there came into contact with new progressive beliefs and ideas, their increased expectations pulled the denomination into the national civil rights movement, which would eventually lead to national creditability.

6

"Dar He"

COGIC and the National Civil Rights Movement

As blacks progressed in America, the fulfillment of their hopes and dreams would lie in the struggles of the civil rights movement, and organizations such as the National Association for the Advancement of Colored People, the National Urban League, and Congress for Racial Equality would lead the way. Black religious organizations also joined in the fight as the Baptist Southern Christian Leadership Conference and its charismatic leader Dr. Martin Luther King Jr. became synonymous with the struggle for black equality.[1] The African Methodist Episcopal denomination also voiced their opinions about the inhumane treatment of African Americans, while the Church of God in Christ instructed its membership to maintain the position of "of the world but not in the world" related to issues of political and social equality. However, as COGIC's membership became increasingly more urban and educated, this position would not always be followed and after closer examination, it becomes clear that COGIC often found itself at the center of several national civil rights events as the movement intensified into a national crusade, allowing the denomination to rise to national respectability.

On Saturday, September 3, 1955, the sub-headlines of the *Chicago Defender* read "Howard Raps Apathy of Urban Negro." The article detailed the words of Dr. Theodore Roosevelt Howard, the recently elected president of the National Medical Association. Described as a dynamic and militant leader in the fight for black rights in his home state of Mississippi, Howard addressed a crowd that assembled in celebration of the oldest black residence in Chicago. The house, 119 years old, now served as the parsonage for Bishop Louis Henry Ford, pastor of St. Paul Church of God in Christ. During his keynote address, Howard impeached those who, "after coming from the South, forgot about conditions back home and about the equally bad conditions in Chicago," and "won't walk half a block to register to vote and forget about the NAACP." Howard ended the speech by making an emphatic pledge that "we are going to stay [fighting] until segregation and discrimination are wiped out in America, including Mississippi."[2] The speech, on most days, would have made the headline of Chicago's premiere black newspaper, instead the *Defender* bumped Howard to the sub-headlines as the paper's main caption read "Lynched Kidnapped Chicago Boy: Mother Waits in Vain For Her Bo." The two stories shared the front page and would become intimately intertwined in the days to come since the Chicago teen, missing in Mississippi and feared dead, belonged to Bishop Louis Ford's denomination, the Church of God in Christ.[3]

In August 1955, Emmett Louis Till boarded a train in Chicago, Illinois, headed for summer vacation in his mother's home state of Mississippi. Till had chosen to spend a portion of his summer holiday with his great-uncle Mose Wright and cousins in the small town of Money. Similar to thousands of other blacks, Till's family fled the South during the Great Migration and settled in Chicago with the hope of finding better employment and social equality. However, they continued to maintain strong family ties to the South as family members often visited one another during holidays, but not long after arriving in Mississippi, Till broke one of the most entrenched social taboos in southern culture, he made a sexual advance at a white woman.[4]

On August 24, 1955, while standing in front of Bryant's Grocery Store and at the urging of several older boys, Till walked into the corner market to "look at the pretty lady and buy bubble gum." Upon leaving, he supposedly muttered "goodbye baby" to Carolyn Bryant, who was working behind the counter. Aware of the transgression, Bryant followed Till outside where in a show of bravery, the Chicago youth allegedly whistled at her.[5] Three days later, in an act of revenge, Roy Bryant, the husband of Carolyn, and his half-brother J. W. Milam arrived at Mose Wright's home around 2:00 A.M. Milam carried a pistol in his right hand and a flashlight in the left as he yelled, "Preacher, preacher, we want the boy who did the talking."[6] Wheeler Parker, Till's cousin asleep in the next room, was awakened when he heard a voice threaten to blow the teen's head off if the young man failed to refer to him as sir. As Bryant and Milam carried Till from the home, the Wrights begged that they be allowed to pay money for the boy's wrongdoing or that the men simply whip Till. The family's pleading would be in vain; three days later some fifteen miles north of Money, a young fisherman discovered Till's body floating in the Tallahatchie River. He had been severely beaten, shot in the head, and bound to a 150-pound cotton-gin pulley that kept his body partially submerged underwater. Authorities arrested Bryant and

Milam and charged the two with the murder of Emmett Till—the lynching would set off a national firestorm that forced both civil rights and religious organizations to take a stand.[7]

In the late nineteenth century, southern whites began to express their profound anxieties about the increase of blacks' rights through the use of violence in the form of lynching. They often justified these violent acts as a needed tool to control the beastly sexual desires of black men for white women. For example, South Carolina senator Benjamin Ryan Tillman echoed the sentiment when he declared that he would rather his three daughters be "killed by a tiger or bear than to have any of them robbed of their womanhood by a black fiend." NAACP investigations revealed that between the years of 1889 and 1900 southern whites killed, maimed, or castrated over 1,189 black men.[8]

By 1955, however, blacks had progressed to the extent that violent acts such as the one committed by Milam and Bryant would not be tolerated. In an open letter to President Eisenhower, William Henry Huff, attorney for the Chicago branch of the NAACP, wrote, "The dastardly act on the part of these criminal-minded persons is so outrageous that it opens the door for condemnation even from the president of the U.S." He urged Eisenhower to speak out and to see that a thorough investigation be conducted of this unwarranted and horrific event.[9] Roy Wilkins, national director of the NAACP, argued that it appeared that Mississippi had decided to maintain white supremacy by murdering children and that the killers of the boy "felt free to lynch him" because "there is in the entire state no restraining influence of decency, not even in the state capital, among the daily newspapers, the clergy, nor any segment of the so-called better citizens." The National Urban League, the sister organization of the NAACP, at its national convention, passed a resolution branding the slaying an atrocity that "hits all of America between the eyes" and called on officials in southern states to move promptly to redeem the good name of America.[10]

Prominent Illinois officials such as Mayor Richard Daley and Governor William Stratton also joined in the condemnation of Mississippi. Mayor Daley, in a wire to the president, declared that the people of the city had been gravely shocked at the brutal murder of Emmett Till and "we join together with all decent citizens in urging swift prosecution of those who are guilty of the act." Governor Stratton weighed in on the controversy by instructing the state's attorney general to write Mississippi officials and urge a full investigation to ensure that justice be done. Even the ranking senator from Illinois addressed the lynching, stating:

> I am shocked and horrified by the murder of Emmett Till. Everything possible must be done to bring those responsible for this heinous crime to justice. Even before the final word was received of his murder, I was

in touch with the F.B.I. and asked for a report on the events surrounding his abduction and urged them to intervene in the case.[11]

Religious denominations also became outspoken critics of the murder and the state of Mississippi. The slaying of Emmett Till was "worse than a lynching and as cruel as the crime was, it showed the people of Mississippi what their campaign of hate has done,"[12] Dr. Joseph H. Jackson, president of the National Baptist Convention of the U.S.A., Inc., told delegates at the organization's seventy-fifth annual session. Jackson also condemned officials for their poor handling of the case and called upon delegates to pass a resolution to urge the people, both black and white to discontinue the methods of hate. The African Methodist Episcopal Church became one of the most outspoken religious denominations in the condemnation of the lynching. Bishop W. J. Wall of the AME Zion Church in Chicago said, "In destroying him [Till] the attempt was made to destroy desegregation in Mississippi by holding him up as the bloody flag of awe to strike terror to the hearts of the advocates of school freedom." Wall pointed out that two men already had been murdered as part of a "program of terrorization of people of color seeking their citizen rights." He concluded by noting, "the boy [Till] has become the symbol of the fight in the South and in America at large."[13]

Bishop H. Thomas Primm of New Orleans, presiding bishop of Louisiana and Mississippi, called for his congregants to wear a black ribbon in a two-day protest of the lynching.[14] The Reverend T. J. Griffen, a Baptist minister from the north side of Chicago, held a rally in which fifteen hundred citizens protested the inhumane treatment of Till. While speaking to the crowd, Griffen called for immediate enactment of a federal antilynching law and the intervention of the federal government to guarantee free election and to bring the reign of terror against the black citizens of Mississippi to an end.[15]

The Chicago teen's murder unified blacks behind one cause and because of their anger, class differences and religious affiliations gave way to their demands for justice. The Church of God in Christ, at first glance, seemed visibly absent in the protest, but upon closer examination, the denomination and its leadership were actually at the center of the event. As Clenora Hudson-Weems argued, "Chicago received more than its share of southern blacks, as it became a Mecca for those relocating from Mississippi, which gave the city and the Mississippi Delta a strong connection."[16] Southern blacks did not only physically relocate to northern urban centers, but they also brought with them their southern culture and religion, which explains the arrival of COGIC in Chicago. Members met in what became known as "storefront" churches, which progressive blacks disdained, but as COGIC's memberships grew, the denomination became a mainstay of black Christian life in the North. Even though the Till family fled Mississippi, they maintained a strong tie with their southern denomination. Emmett's granduncle served as the pastor of the East Money Church of God in Christ and his mother worshiped at Roberts Temple Church of God in Christ in Chicago.

Bo Comes Home with the Aid of COGIC

At the Illinois Central Station in Chicago, five men lifted a soiled paper-wrapped bundle from a huge brown wooden Victorian box. The bundle contained the remains of Emmett Till and at first sight of the make-shift coffin, Till's mother Mamie Bradley wailed, "Oh God, oh God, my only boy." Limp from grief, Bradley was seated in a wheelchair while a huge crowd of spectators watched as she cried, "Lord, you gave your only son to remedy a condition, but who knows but what the death of my only son might bring an end to lynching." Filled with sorrow, Bradley was not alone on that horrible day; two local COGIC ministers, Bishop Louis Ford and the Reverend Isaiah Roberts, accompanied her and pushed the wheel chair as she screamed, "Let me pray." Both clergymen helped her out of the chair and to her knees where she prayed, "Lord take my soul, show me what you want me to do, and make me able to do it," as reporters and media captured the moment for history. Bradley, a devout COGIC member, would make it through the most difficult time of her life with the help of her denomination. Although COGIC never used the event to underscore the social inequalities of blacks in America, its support of a member would indirectly bring the denomination into the spotlight of the national civil rights movement.[17]

Bradley insisted that her son's remains be buried in Chicago and not Mississippi, but due to the condition of the body, funeral director A. A. Rayner advised not to have an open casket. She, however, remained adamant about allowing the nation "to see what racism in America had done to her child." Bradley's decision allowed thousands to see the teen's body and was crucial in building national outrage. Juan Williams noted that the display of Emmett's body "without question moved black America in a way the Supreme Court ruling on desegregation could not match."[18] People were simply shocked and horrified as they viewed Till's remains at Roberts Temple Church of God in Christ, an event that arguably sparked the national civil rights movement.[19]

It Happened at Roberts Temple Church of God in Christ

William Roberts founded Roberts Temple in 1925; born in Okalona, Mississippi, in May 1876, Roberts, at the age of twenty-three, moved to Memphis in search of work. While there, he joined the Holiness movement and, in 1904, became a member of Mason's Wellington Street congregation. He served as a deacon and later assistant pastor to Mason until 1916 when a group of women invited him to Chicago to establish a COGIC ministry. Roberts accepted the invitation and relocated to Chicago with his oldest son Isaiah with the remainder of his family arriving the following year. Initially, Roberts's ministry experienced hard times; established blacks frowned upon the arrival of recently relocated blacks from the South. Disdain often centered around what they referred to as the lack of right and proper religious practices associated with Pentecostalism. Also, transplants set up temporary churches in storefronts, something progressives believed to be improper, but, in spite of difficulties, Roberts's following continued to grow, and in 1925, he and his congregants purchased two lots on Fortieth and State Street to build a worship structure. Completed later in the year, Roberts Temple Church of God in Christ could seat 1,000 persons and over the years, the church became a mainstay in the religious life of blacks living in Chicago. The church would again show its importance when, in 1955, it opened its doors to one of the most important funerals in African American history.[20]

Till's coffin lay in state at Roberts Temple Church of God in Christ for four days as an estimated 250,000 people filed by. The viewing line stretched down the block as shocked, mortified, and appalled people cried, fainted, and wept upon first sight of the body. G. H. Milara remembered that "I had tears in my eyes and when I looked at that little boy, I fainted."[21] As time progressed, the crowd grew angry and Chicago police had to be called to maintain order, but the crowd's shock and outrage never subsided. Even during the last day of viewing, Reverend Luke Ward, a junior COGIC minister, had to be given first aid when he fainted as he viewed the body.[22]

During the two-hour funeral, thousands packed the church and an even larger overflow crowd gathered outside as a public address system carried the service to those unable to be seated. Reverend Isaiah Roberts, the son of the founder of Roberts Temple Church of God in Christ and current pastor, officiated the services. In his remarks, Roberts commented on the problem of lynching, declaring that "the lynching of Till is a black mark against the United States," and he called for justice and a swift trial of the boy's slayers.[23] Next, Bishop Louis Ford delivered the eulogy in which he lambasted Mississippi and the United States for the continued mistreatment of blacks. Citing an example of a recent mistake made in Texas when owners of a restaurant seated an Indian diplomat in the black section of the restaurant, Ford asked, "Who is going to apologize to the Negro?" "How do we expect to be the leaders of the world when we are mistreating Negroes in the South?" "We don't need to send any more missionaries to Africa; we need to send them to the back woods of Mississippi."[24]

The vocal stance of both Roberts and Ford departed from the usual position of COGIC clergymen on secular topics; they usually remained quiet on civil and social rights issues. At its inception, sharecroppers and day laborers made up the majority of the denomination's membership and clergymen remained aware that using their pulpits and churches for civil rights activities could lead to their eviction off land they sharecropped or even worse, being killed. Whites constantly used blacks' economic concerns as a means of discouraging civil rights activities, and COGIC members, in the early years, remained tied to whites economically more so than any other black denomination's membership, which coupled with theological restrictions, muted all protest from COGIC. So when Roberts Temple became the convergence point of the civil rights movement during Till's funeral, this action marked a clear departure of the denomination's usual stance. Similar to the Sixteenth Street Baptist Church in Birmingham, Alabama, which served as the epicenter for civil rights activities in the 1960s, Roberts Temple served the same purpose in 1955. More important, however, COGIC's actions demonstrated the denomination's dissatisfaction with black oppression and its move toward social activism.[25]

A COGIC Preacher Stands Up to Be Counted

In 1955 Mose Wright personified the socioeconomic condition of COGIC members in the South. The *Chicago Defender* described the sixty-four-year-old Wright as "a lover of outdoors and good for picking 200 pounds of cotton any day."[26] In recent years, Wright had shunned the pleas of his wife to leave Mississippi, but after the murder of his nephew, he planned to move, though not before he finished gathering his cotton crop for the year. A sharecropper on a twenty-five-acre plot, Wright argued that he had "too much to run away and leave" as he expected to turn an unprecedented profit of $1,000 on his crop. The article also pictured Wright standing waist high in a field with his hired help as both smiled at the camera while holding cotton balls in their hands. The picture harkens old black stereotypes and the use of words and phrases such as "little Church of God in Christ preacher," plantation, and cotton picker revealed the way in which many educated blacks continued to view COGIC.[27]

The paper continued the condescending tone in its description of Wright's wife, Elizabeth. She had achieved her dream a few weeks earlier when the family purchased a washing machine, but fearing retaliation, she would not return to use it. The paper's unusual emphasis on the recent purchase of a washing machine, something most northern blacks owned or could access, further marginalized the family and the denomination in the eyes of the general public, which hurt the NAACP's call for mass protests against Mississippi. In the end, the Wrights' perceived lack of sophistication hurt the civil rights organization's efforts to sustain a national campaign.[28] However, when J. W. Milam and Roy Bryant stood trial for the murder, Mose Wright, the "little COGIC preacher," served as the prosecution's star witness. A man with a thin and wiry frame, gray hair, and jutting chin, Wright took the stand and made history—standing in the witness box, Wright pointed a lean, accusatory finger toward both Milam and Bryant and in a loud voice declared, "There they are!" Although the jury would find both Milam and Bryant not guilty, the actions of Wright were profound. Serving as a witness and testifying against two white men in Mississippi placed his entire family in danger. More important, the testimony showed the active participation of a COGIC minister who, in the face of danger and economic ruin, delivered testimony in a case that caught the attention of the world.[29]

The NAACP and Mamie Bradley tried to turn Till's lynching into a nationally sustained civil rights campaign, and Roberts Temple even raised money for the effort. In a picture in the September 17 issue of the *Chicago Defender*, Reverend Roberts is shown presenting Bradley with a three-hundred-dollar check.[30] Additionally, the denomination participated in spiritual mobilization drives designed to educate the public on the dangers of segregation and its impact on the black community. Although secularly based, COGIC viewed the campaign as religious in nature and, therefore, members felt comfortable participating. The drives were short lived and rendered no measurable results, which prompted Bradley, along with the help of the NAACP, to petition the federal authorities for help, requesting a hearing before the United States Senate subcommittee on civil rights, but the Senate never granted their wish. The *Chicago Defender* captured Bradley's lobbying efforts in an October issue when the paper printed a photo that showed her standing on the steps of the United States Capitol pointing toward the Dome with a caption that read "Maybe I can get help here." Even more remarkable, Reverend Isaiah Roberts stood next to her, illustrating the denomination's continued support in the months after the funeral.[31]

In the end, Bradley, the NAACP, and COGIC failed to establish a broad coalition and the relationship between the three ended badly. Bradley traveled at the request of the NAACP making guest appearances around the country and the civil rights organization raised money to hire lawyers to continue to investigate Till's murder. Records, however, indicate a complicated relationship. Bradley remembered that Roy Wilkins, the NAACP's national director, became concerned that she intended to be paid for her speaking engagements and appearances and as it turned out, a financial dispute between Bradley and Roy Wilkins did arise.[32]

Scheduled to make a series of speeches on the West Coast, Bradley agreed to an honorarium with a booking agent, but when Wilkins learned of the news, "he became very distraught and put his foot down and said he did not agree" and, according to Bradley, "he accused me of capitalizing on my son's death."[33] Wilkins canceled the remainder of Bradley's NAACP-sponsored appearances, which further discredited her with the national organization and the general public. Once the object of universal sympathy, Bradley became the target of accusations from those who previously supported her as reports now complained that she had turned from a grief-stricken mother to an arrogant celebrity full of her own importance.[34] In an open letter published in the newspaper, Bradley's lawyer also seemed to indict her as he stated that a recommendation had been made that she should free herself of those who wished to turn a profit off her son's case. The lawyer also revealed that once news of the formal break between Bradley and the NAACP leaked, his office decided to no longer handle her case, stating, "I, therefore, request to be relieved as your attorney and hope you will receive other counsel to represent you in any matter which should follow."[35] Bradley's subsequent disgrace also hurt the denomination's image as old stereotypes of uneducated storefront preachers who looked to make an easy dollar began to resurface. The NAACP also most likely believed that Bradley was being influenced by her denomination and consequently, in the end, the issues of class and respectability kept Bradley and the NAACP from uniting.

Although Bradley and the NAACP never succeeded in establishing a broad base coalition, Till's lynching did move and galvanize black America. As Harvard Sitkoff writes, it is undeniable that the Till murder had something to do with the emergence of the civil rights movement.[36] The event overwhelmingly caused blacks to stand up for their rights as many felt that their perceived silence somehow condoned the act. Till's murder also stirred an activist spirit in the black youth, which would cause them to join the civil rights movement. A teenager at the time of Till's death, activist Anne Moody remembered, "I started to hate all white people who were responsible for the murders of blacks," but even more, "I hated Negroes, I hated them for not standing up and not doing something about the murders. In fact, I think I had a stronger resentment toward Negroes for letting the whites kill them than toward the whites."[37] Student Nonviolent Coordinating Committee (SNCC) activist Cleveland Sellers recalled that the Till case had a profound effect upon his development and led him to the movement. Sellers remembered, "Till was only three years older than me and I identified with him and I tried to put myself in his place to imagine what he was thinking when those white men took him from that house."[38]

The Till incident angered blacks enough to make them stand up for their rights. Even those who had a history of silence—namely, COGIC—found it hard to maintain their stance. The denomination's activism can be seen in the testimony of Till's granduncle and COGIC preacher Mose Wright, as well as in the words of Reverend Roberts and Bishop Ford when they turned Roberts Temple Church of God in Christ's pulpit into their personal soapbox as they condemned the actions of Mississippi during Till's funeral. The denomination even supported Mamie Bradley in her failed request for a congressional investigation. Similar to Moody and Sellers, the Till case awakened an activist spirit within the denomination's membership and no person personified this more than Medgar Evers.

Born COGIC and Unsatisfied: Medgar Evers

Born in Decatur, Mississippi, in 1925, Medgar Evers represented a critical turning point in the lives of second-generation COGIC members. Named after his great-grandfather, a Mississippi slave, Evers lived in a state that had not changed racially since the times of his grandparents,[39] a state known for its repressive Jim Crow laws. Mississippi culture dared blacks to step out of their prescribed place. However, James Evers, Medgar's father, proved the exception. James refused to believe that his skin color made him less of a man than any white person in Decatur. Referred to as a "gruff man," whites feared him, and rather than cross him, they often maintained their distance. Through hard work as a laborer, the elder Evers acquired a small plot of land and, although not middle class by any means, landownership allowed him to provide the basic necessities for his family. James was not devoutly religious, yet he maintained membership in a local Baptist church and served as a deacon.[40]

Jessie Evers, Medgar's mother, also had a profound influence on her son's life. Similar to thousands of other black women in the South, she worked as a domestic for several local white families, and unlike Medgar's father, Jessie was devoutly religious. A member of the Church of God in Christ, she forced her children to accompany her to worship services as many as three to four times a week. In these services, Medgar learned the Pentecostal doctrine of sanctification, which emphasized a strict sense of right and wrong and the golden rule to do unto others what you would have them do unto you. Charles Evers, Medgar's brother, remembered that, even though their mother forced them to attend church on a regular basis, "a lot [of] young people resented the Church because it promised heaven in the sweet by and by and lulled people into accepting a subhuman life on earth."[41] Charles remembered his mother as different from many religious blacks who believed in suffering on earth for a place in heaven, "Mama was a different kind of religious person; she was not the type who believed in praying and sitting down. She taught us: 'You pray, and then you get up and go after it'" and her activist spirit would be inherited by her sons.[42]

Medgar's parents could read and write, and they stressed the profound importance of education. James allowed his sons to attend high school, and with the acquisition of an education, Medgar's worldview proved incompatible with the religious doctrine of "of the world but not in the world" propagated by COGIC. Historian and Evers biographer Michael Williams theorized that the lynching of Willie Tingle, a family friend, also had a profound affect on Evers that would change the way he viewed life as well as religion. Local whites lynched Tingle for a suspected sexual gaze at a white woman, and without protest from blacks, whites tied Tingle to a pole and shot him to death. They allowed Tingle's body to remain tied to the pole for days to serve as a constant reminder of the punishment if blacks dared to transgress against southern culture. According to Williams, "Evers and his brother Charles walked past that very spot on a daily basis and even once locals removed the body, the victim's bloody clothing continued to hang as a reminder." What bothered Evers even more "was the fact that people acted as if the man never existed; they refused to talk about the event; there was no news, no protest, and most of all, no condemnation from the black pulpits" and from that day forth, the lynching changed Evers's outlook and he began to view religion and preachers with disdain and a certain suspicion.[43]

As World War II intensified, Evers, like thousands of other blacks, joined the military. Participating in combat in both Germany and France, Medgar, for the first time, received a broader view of the world outside of Mississippi and the experience gave Evers increased expectations of his country. Wanting to exercise his rights as a citizen, once back home in Mississippi, he and his brother Charles registered to vote. However, as time for voting drew near, whites bombarded the family with threats against their lives. Evers remembered, "All we wanted to be was ordinary citizens," he declared. "We fought during the war for America and Mississippi was included. Now after the Germans and the Japanese hadn't killed us, it looked as though the white Mississippians would."[44] Evers fought back the only way he could; he enrolled in Alcorn A&M College and as he acquired a college education, he grew increasingly dissatisfied with his mother's religion and its lack of active participation in black equality. Although discontent, Medgar achieved what his parents had not—a college education that allowed him to claw his way into the middle class as a business owner.[45]

Evers's life represents the stringent pressure placed on many second-generation COGIC members. As they became educated, they recognized the profound inconsistencies of their religious doctrine with their desire to fight for equal rights; Evers's sense of pride and the need to fight against Jim Crow arguably pushed him out of his mother's denomination. While still wary of preachers, he must have viewed the Baptist denomination as more compatible with his need to engage in the growing civil rights movement. In addition, the denomination's Southern Christian Leadership Conference (SCLC) had taken a bold public stance against segregation, vowing to work to end Jim Crow. COGIC's leadership, however, never made such public statements nor possessed a protest organization, which might explain Evers's departure from the denomination in his adulthood.

On the night of June 12, 1963, while serving as the field secretary for the NAACP in Mississippi, Evers's life came to an end. After returning home from the New Jerusalem Baptist Church, Evers stepped out of his car, and as he stood in his driveway, Byron de la Beckwith, a known white supremacist, shot him in the back. Evers died later that night, but his work would not be in vain, as marchers across the state of Mississippi protested his murder, bringing unwanted national media attention to the state. In death, Evers became one of the most celebrated heroes of the NAACP and the civil rights movement. During his ten-year career with the organization, he worked to bring thousands of new members into its ranks in Mississippi and registered scores of blacks throughout the state to vote.[46]

Remembered as a "martyr of the movement,"[47] Evers's life came to represent the bravery blacks displayed during their fight for freedom; visibly absent and never analyzed are the religious contradictions he harbored. As an attendant of a COGIC congregation in his youth, the denomination's strict adherence to distancing itself from secular events and movements "pushed" Evers out of its ranks as an adult and into the Baptist denomination. Yet, this never stopped COGIC members from claiming Evers as one of their own as the denomination continues to view him as a civil rights icon with COGIC roots and values that were shaped by his education, war experience, and sanctification.

COGIC Opened Its Doors for Malcolm

A civil rights icon in his own right, Malcolm X also shares an unusual association with COGIC. Although the Nation of Islam and the denomination share no direct religious connections, the two organizations would intersect in 1965 at Faith Temple Church of God in Christ in Harlem, New York. Known for his fiery rhetoric and uncompromising views, Malcolm X indicted whites for their maltreatment of blacks in America. After serving a prison term and his subsequent conversion to Islam, he assumed the role of official spokesman for the Nation of Islam. Well known for the strict discipline imposed on its members, the Nation became the fastest-growing black religious movement in urban America in the mid-twentieth century. An opponent of the passive nonviolent movement, the Nation stressed racial pride and insisted that integration would not remedy the economic ills that plagued black America. As a devout Muslim, in 1964, Malcolm completed the Hajj, his mandatory pilgrimage to Mecca, and while in the holy city, he witnessed Muslims of all races and nationalities worshiping together as brothers. Convinced that this interracial cooperation could be duplicated in the United States, Malcolm, upon his arrival home, announced his plans to leave the Nation of Islam.[48]

Scheduled to deliver a speech at the Audubon Hotel in Harlem on February 21, 1965, gunmen fatally shot Malcolm X, and hospital officials publicly announced his death at 3:30 that same afternoon.[49] Locked in a bitter dispute with members of the Nation of Islam, Malcolm's funeral services seemed in doubt as both the Baptist and Methodist congregations in Harlem shied away from allowing their facilities to be used for the funeral. Actively engaged in the civil rights movement, both denominations realized that opening their doors for the funeral might associate their faiths with Black Nationalism, thus hurting their credibility among white moderates.[50] However, Bishop A. A. Childs allowed Malcolm's body to be rolled into Faith Temple Church of God in Christ, as "none of Harlem's gaping cathedrals would open the doors."[51]

Alvin Childs, a popular COGIC evangelist from Chicago, in 1948 conducted a successful revival in Harlem, and attendees insisted that he establish a permanent ministry. In the beginning, Childs had thirty members, but soon his numbers began to swell. The fledgling congregation possessed no real worship structure, and similar to many other COGIC ministers, Childs purchased a large circus tent and erected it on 124th and St. Nicholas Avenue where people gathered until members secured a permanent worship structure. Congregants raised enough money ($175,000) to purchase an old theater at 1763 Amsterdam Street, and in 1952 they moved into their new edifice, quickly making the transition from perceived storefront church to a cornerstone of the Sugar Hill community in which the church is located.[52]

Faith Temple became one of the fastest-growing black churches in the city and, by the early 1960s, the congregation boasted a membership of well over three thousand. Similar to all black churches, Faith Temple became more than a place where locals received spiritual guidance, the church also served as a self-help institution. Additionally, Faith Temple began to broadcast a weekly radio address on local and national stations such as WJRN, WHOM, WADO, and WTHE, where thousands listened on a regular basis for the next twenty years. Childs brought the message of COGIC into the homes of blacks on the East Coast, and by 1965, Faith Temple had become entrenched into the black religious life of New York. More significantly, in February when the congregation decided to open its doors for the funeral of Malcolm X, COGIC would once again indirectly connect itself to the national civil rights movement.[53]

An estimated fifteen hundred people packed Faith Temple to pay their final respects to the slain controversial black leader and as actor and close friend Ossie Davis delivered the eulogy, a COGIC facility again allowed blacks from different denominations and classes to unify. Unlike the local Baptists and Methodists, the general public viewed COGIC as apolitical on the issues of civil rights and their perceptions allowed Faith Temple, to not only host the funeral, but also permitted Malcolm's family to adhere to the Islamic burial traditions. Faith Temple existed to serve the Sugar Hill community and the COGIC congregation provided one of the greatest services by allowing the funeral of Malcolm X to be held within their building. As a result of COGIC distancing itself from civil rights issues, the church experienced no repercussions and with the regeneration of Malcolm's popularity in the following years, Faith Temple's leadership and members were lauded for their decision, which again placed COGIC squarely within the history of the movement.

COGIC, King, and the Memphis Sanitation Strike

In 1967, Memphis sanitation workers placed COGIC on a direct collision course with the national civil rights movement. Representing the largest black denomination in Memphis, COGIC's membership made up a large percentage of the dissatisfied workers. In 1964, a Tennessee advisory committee found that blacks in Memphis held only 2.2 percent of the white-collar jobs in the city. Black women continued to labor as domestics, earning five dollars a day at best working as school janitors for fifty-eight cents an hour and as full-time hospital workers for as little as eighty-two dollars a month.[54]

Men also worked in labor-intensive occupations cleaning ditches and clearing vacant lots and as sanitation workers. James Robinson's life personified the problem of blacks locked in a desperate cycle of poverty. In an attempt to escape the nearby cotton fields of Arkansas and Mississippi, Robinson explained in an interview, "I was born in Earle, Arkansas, and we lived in the country and my father was a sharecropper; the five of us boys could pick a bale of cotton a day." He revealed that he had only a tenth-grade education and had little hope of ever working as anything but a laborer.[55] Robinson found employment as a sanitation worker and remembered that conditions in the occupation proved not much better than the plantation. The city provided no place for black workers to use the bathroom, no suitable facilities for lunch, and even worse, the pay remained awful. Workers' jobs required them to perform some of the most degrading acts, yet they made a mere 94 cents to $1.14 an hour, making a full week's pay of $45.60 before taxes. Their low wages placed them below the established poverty line, thus rendering sanitation workers eligible for welfare in spite of completing a full week's work.[56]

The 1960s was a volatile time in the United States, giving rise to social unrest throughout the country. Often the result of political and social inequality, the decade added another element to the fragile mix: poverty. Across the country, blacks continued to lag behind whites economically, and in Memphis, blacks fared no better. As the home of the Church of God in Christ, the sheer size of the denomination forced whites to listen to the voices of COGIC's leadership, as they remained well aware that COGIC possessed the numbers to influence the outcome of local elections. For example, J. O. Patterson Jr., son of Senior Bishop J. O. Patterson Sr., had been elected to the Tennessee state legislature largely due to the voting bloc his father's denomination represented.[57]

Under Mason's direction, COGIC and city officials maintained a civil relationship. Mayors of the city often made guest appearances at COGIC's international convocation and city officials from time to time presented Mason with awards, which white politicians always made sure the local media covered. Referred to as a simple, honest man, Mason understood the nature of his relationship with local white leaders. In his younger years he had often preached against lynching, but as the denomination solidified itself in Memphis Mason made no such public statements nor did he vocalize his opinions about the civil rights movement. COGIC, for the most part, kept a safe distance from the movement and maintained a good relationship with white Memphians.

National Respectability and Creditability

With the death of Mason in 1961, COGIC, for the first time in its history, experienced a change in leadership. Though the denomination would not formally elect J. O. Patterson Sr. to serve as the new senior bishop until November 1968, Patterson had already grown to be a powerful force within COGIC's ranks. Although he had been close to Mason, Patterson Sr. would steer the denomination in a different direction when it came to the issue of civil rights. In years past, COGIC had always distanced itself from social and political issues; however, as the civil rights movement moved into a different phase and with Martin Luther King's promise to concentrate efforts on economic improvements, COGIC decided that the denomination must join the movement.

On February 12, 1968, when black sanitation workers left their jobs and began their strike, few suspected the walkout would escalate into a national event. Tired and disgusted workers demanded to unionize, but city officials resisted. As the strike intensified, COGIC became intimately involved, because the denomination owned one of the largest black religious facilities in the city: Mason Temple. COGIC allowed workers to use the church as a meeting place, and on February 17, as some two thousand people listened to speeches by black ministers, J. O. Patterson Sr., the son-in-law of Charles Mason, stood before the crowd and proclaimed, "What's mine is yours if you need it." The denomination followed up on its promise throughout the strike by donating money, food, and clothing to the strikers. Patterson's words marked a beginning of a new era in COGIC's history as the international denomination now openly involved itself in a civil rights campaign.[58]

Waging the "People's War Against Poverty," Dr. Martin Luther King Jr. viewed Memphis and the strike as an opportunity to highlight his new campaign and, against the better judgment of his colleagues, King flew to Memphis on March 18, 1968. An estimated nine thousand people had gathered inside COGIC's headquarters by 7:00 P.M. and an even larger crowd stood outside of Mason Temple waiting for King to make his address from the pulpit at 9:00.[59] Historian Michael Honey writes, "As the civil rights leader made his way through the side door of the church, a standing room only crowd greeted him." In a speech lasting a little over an hour, King stated, "We have Baptists, Methodists, Episcopalians, Presbyterians, and members of the Church of God in Christ, we are all together." As he ended his speech, he argued that blacks must unite beyond class lines and explained, "The Negro 'haves' must join hands with the Negro 'have-nots' in this fight."[60] King's address garnered the strikers national attention, but more important, it also brought COGIC into the rank and file with other mainstream black religious denominations as an active participant in the strike. Protesters used Mason Temple for strategy sessions, and as a symbol of their support, congregants collected money in metal trashcans that were passed around during mass rallies held at the church.

Trouble arose on March 28, as King readied to lead a mass march in Memphis. The city erupted in violence when marchers and protestors clashed with local police, leaving one person dead. To restore order, officials called out the National Guard and the courts issued an injunction that kept King from leading the march. The civil rights icon left the city but returned on April 3, 1968, determined to lead a mass nonviolent march. Once again, Mason Temple would serve as the backdrop for one of the most important events in the history of the civil rights movement.[61]

Tired and under the weather, King arrived in Memphis and planned to spend a restful evening at the Lorraine Hotel. However, when Ralph David Abernathy arrived at Mason Temple alone, he could see the disappointment on the faces of the more than two thousand people who had assembled to hear King. A violent thunderstorm rolled through Memphis, and "the windows of

Mason Temple shook," as news spread that King would make an unscheduled appearance. The civil rights leader appeared before the crowd around 9:30 P.M. King stood in the pulpit that Charles Harrison Mason built, beneath a large portrait of the bishop hanging from the ceiling, and delivered his last public address, "I've Been to the Mountain Top."[62] On that April night, King, the embodiment of the cult of respectability, looked into the waiting eyes of a crowd composed of large numbers of COGIC members. Finally, the black middle class had found a common cause with the Church of God in Christ that transcended class and religious differences—the basic dignity of man. King's speech solidified what the death of Emmett Till could not—the establishment of a coalition that linked the black middle class to the black poor, which included COGIC.

The following day, James Earl Ray assassinated Dr. Martin King Jr., which many argued brought an end to the national civil rights movement, but with the death of King, COGIC did something it had never done: it refused to retreat to the shadows of American history. The denomination continued its involvement in the strike, and on April 12, COGIC again opened the doors to Mason Temple, allowing Reverend Gardner Taylor, president of the Progressive Baptist Convention, to address a crowd of six hundred. In the speech, he argued that change must be brought to America and the help of all was needed. Adhering to the remarks, COGIC would remain intimately involved in the strike until its end four days later.[63]

The national membership would express their approval of the involvement of the denomination in the strike when in November they elected J. O. Patterson Sr. to serve as senior bishop. The selection of Patterson, who openly departed from COGIC's inward-looking stance on secular issues, signaled a dramatic shift for the denomination, revealing that the Church of God in Christ had, in fact, completed a slow progression that began with sharecroppers in rural Arkansas, Mississippi, and Tennessee into a mainstream religious denomination that ended with the establishment of a coalition with the black middle class. In the end, the Memphis Sanitation Strike provided COGIC with a common ground that united outward-looking religious progressives such as King with the inward-looking restorationist membership of the Church of God in Christ.

Afterword

Wandering in the Wilderness

On November 17, 1961, Charles Harrison Mason died at the age of ninety-five, leaving the denomination with no clear directive for the future. As thousands packed Mason Temple on November 25 and Bishop Ozro Thurston Jones Sr., Mason's friend and fellow Holiness minister, eulogized the senior bishop, everyone must have wondered what would be next. At the end of the memorial, congregants laid the founder's body to rest in a marble vault in the lobby of the temple that he, with the help of laborers, domestics, and sharecroppers, built.[1]

Mason's death marked the beginning of what scholars have referred to as a phase known as "Wandering in the Wilderness"[2] in which COGIC looked for leadership and a direction for the future. Due to old age and declining health, Mason, in 1951, appointed a five-man supervisory committee to which he delegated executive powers.[3] The group, known as the Executive Commission, carried out the business of the denomination, which included the ability to appoint and remove state bishops. After Mason's death, the board elected a twelve-man General Assembly, which COGIC's 1926 constitution mandated to oversee and execute the business of the denomination. Bishops elected A. B. McEwen chairman of the assembly, but due to his longtime relationship with Mason and his seniority on the Executive Commission, members of the General Assembly appointed Bishop O. T. Jones Sr. to serve as head of the church.[4]

Born in Fort Smith, Arkansas, in 1891, the seventh child of Merion and Mary Jones, Jones Sr. enjoyed a lifelong relationship with Mason during which he helped to codify the doctrine of the denomination. His parents stressed the importance of education and not only did Jones Sr. graduate high school as class valedictorian, but he also attended Temple University in Philadelphia. Jones Sr., as senior bishop, pushed an agenda of education and the strengthening of the denomination's youth auxiliaries. His administration, however, would be short lived as a dispute arose at the 1964 National Convocation over the legitimacy of the position of "senior bishop" and the proper role of the Executive Board.[5]

Ending a three-year battle in the courts in Tennessee, the denomination agreed that the General Assembly, not the chancery court of Shelby County, would decide the future and direction of COGIC. In January 1968, the denomination convened a constitutional convention in Memphis. Lasting six days and in ten general sessions, delegates debated on "whether Bishop Jones, Sr. or the Executive Board would have ultimate authority over the Church."[6] In similar fashion as the founding fathers of the United States who drew up the Virginia and New Jersey Plans, delegates at the Memphis convention also composed two plans known as the Majority and Minority Reports.[7]

The Majority Report called for the abolishment of both the Executive Board and the position of senior bishop. They would be replaced with a General Assembly of twelve elected bishops to govern the church as well as the election of a presiding bishop who would serve four-year terms in office. In contrast, the Minority Report wanted to continue the structure of supervisory oversight that had begun under Mason. The report called for only a senior or a presiding bishop to be elected by a majority vote of the General Assembly and the bishop could not be removed from office except by death or disability, as his tenure in office would be for life. In the end, delegates adopted the Majority Report by a vote of 1,046 to 232,[8] setting into motion the system used to elect presiding bishops, their term length, and COGIC's overall governance structure that is still used today.[9]

The New Frontier of Educational Growth

COGIC entered into the new frontier of its history in November 1968 when the denomination elected its first General Board and Presiding Bishop James Oglethorpe (J. O.) Patterson. Born the son of William and Mollie Patterson on July 21, 1912, in Derma Calhoun County, Mississippi, Patterson married Deborah Mason, the daughter of C. H. Mason, and as a result, he experienced a meteoric rise in the denomination. In 1952, his father-in-law appointed him to the Executive Board and in 1968 congregants elected him their senior bishop. During Patterson's tenure, the denomination continued to grow into a religious mainstay and nothing symbolized the shift more than COGIC's participation in the Memphis sanitation strike. Patterson allowed workers to use Mason Temple as a meeting place and although nine months away from his election as presiding bishop, on February 17, 1968, Patterson moved the denomination into the mainstream when he stood before a crowd of striking workers in Mason Temple and proclaimed, "What's mine is yours if you need it."[10]

Martin Luther King Jr.'s "Mountain Top" speech delivered at Mason Temple on April 3, 1968, also pulled COGIC into the mainstream. According to theologian Alonzo Johnson, "Dr. King's last public rally at COGIC's headquarters represented a broader shift taking place in the Church during this period."[11] As the denomination continued to progress into the "1970s and 1980s, it changed from a more insular, morally rigorous holiness identity to an internationally recognized Pentecostal identity."[12] Patterson also embarked on a modernization campaign, making much-needed improvements to Mason Temple by paving parking lots and providing lighting and security, but most of all, he made tremendous strides in the area of education.[13]

In an effort, for the first time, to determine an accurate count of the number of members, Patterson established a Department of Research. With a function similar to the U.S. Census Bureau, Patterson produced the most accurate count in the denomination's history, and the survey also enabled him to project future revenues through tithes. In 1970, he improved the denomination's image when he established the C. H. Mason Theological Seminary in Atlanta, Georgia, marking a turning point for the denomination in the realm of education. With the opening of the seminary, COGIC completed its transformation from a denomination composed of sharecroppers, laundry women, and domestics to one that now offered its members a Master of Divinity as well as a Master of Christian Education. In addition to the seminary, Patterson created a system of local Bible colleges in several states to further educate COGIC's members. Recognizing the financial difficulties most members faced, Patterson established the C. H. Mason Memorial Scholarship Fund to help students defray the cost of school tuition. With these improvements in education, COGIC shattered the stereotype that the denomination did not support the advances of black education. Patterson would serve the church from 1968 to 1989 and without question, he modernized the denomination, making it a religious mainstay.[14]

COGIC Moves into the Political Arena

In 1990, upon the death of J. O. Patterson, the General Assembly elected Bishop Louis Henry Ford of Chicago to serve as the new presiding bishop. Born in Clarksdale, Mississippi, on May 23, 1914, Ford joined COGIC at an early age and spent his entire life serving the denomination. He attended Saints Industrial College and over the years, became the institution's most distinguished alumnus as he rose in rank within the church. In the early 1930s, Ford moved to Chicago, Illinois, where he helped to grow the denomination in the city. He founded

St. Paul Church of God in Christ in 1936 and, with a thriving radio ministry, he delivered the message of Holiness to thousands throughout the Midwest. Ford also made a national name for himself when he played an integral role in the funeral of Emmett Till and, as a result, the NAACP, in 1966, selected him to serve as a member of their national executive committee. While serving on the national civil rights organization's steering committee, Ford learned the value of staying politically connected and the importance of forming alliances with secular organizations. For instance, in the early 1970s, while maintaining his COGIC roots, he accepted a position to serve as a special advisor to Chicago's mayor Richard Daley and in turn became a trusted member of the Daley political machine.[15]

In 1989, at the age of seventy-five, Ford became the presiding bishop of the Church of God in Christ. As bishop, he employed the lessons he had learned over the years and connected COGIC to secular politics more than any other leader in the past. Although politically savvy, Ford, according to Ithiel C. Clemmons, "longed for the Church he discovered as a child while growing up in Mississippi and his tenure as presiding bishop would be centered around an unapologetically restorationist vision."[16] He believed that COGIC should remain engaged in secular events in the public sphere, but also felt that the denomination should not compromise its core Holiness beliefs in the process. His "restorationist" vision also extended to the symbolic institutions of the denomination, particularly national properties such as Mason Temple and Saints Junior College. A proud graduate of the institution, Ford's administration directed much-needed resources to the school and also commissioned and funded construction projects on the campus, which included "a one million dollar Deborah Mason Patterson All Purpose Facility Center."[17]

Although a restorationist, Ford still continued the self-help work of COGIC while also raising the national political profile of the denomination. In the 1990s, he returned to the secular organization that gave him his start when he formed an alliance with the NAACP and the National Urban League in an effort to feed, clothe, and provide better jobs for blacks in inner cities. COGIC, along with the NAACP, engaged in clothing drives and donated money to inner-city missions. Using skills he had honed as a member of the Chicago political machine, Ford led yearly delegations composed of the denomination's senior bishops to visit then governor William Jefferson Clinton in Little Rock, Arkansas. The bishop and the governor became friends and "in November 1993, when then presidential candidate Clinton visited the 84th Annual Holy Convocation, Clinton asked Ford and the denomination for their blessing and for help in his bid for the presidency."[18]

Politically shrewd, Clinton recognized the potential voting bloc the denomination represented and Ford understood the vast amount of political patronage he could deliver to COGIC by supporting Clinton's candidacy. "Through his friendship with President Clinton, Bishop Ford harnessed resources for a spillway in Holmes County, Mississippi, the birthplace of COGIC, to correct a serious flooding problem that the residents had endured for over a century." While remaining true to his Holiness-Pentecostal roots, "Ford broadened the view of the black Pentecostal tradition from direct acts of charity to infusing the denomination in the arena of public policy."[19] Recognizing the importance of involving the denomination in the political realm, COGIC continues to grant local, state, and federal politicians the opportunity to use its pulpits, but only with the notion that campaign promises must be kept.

Leadership for 2000 and Beyond

Three years into his term, Ford unexpectedly died on March 31, 1995, and his death marked a generational shift in the leadership of COGIC. In November 1995, the General Assembly elected Chandler David Owens as the fifth presiding bishop of the denomination. The first of the presiding bishops not born in Mississippi, Owens became the most popular and charismatic leader of COGIC since the death of its founder. Owens's father had been a COGIC minister; therefore, Chandler, himself, began to preach at an early age and those who knew him during his childhood referred to him as a "boy preacher."[20] Owens argued that he brought to the office a more collegial leadership and based his administration on the slogan "Vision 2000 and Beyond," but many members accused him of abusing his power.[21] In a bitter dispute over the right to remove a COGIC pastor of an 800-member congregation in Florida, Owens told a circuit court judge, "I have the authority to make all of the decisions within the Church without any disruption or confirmation." He further stated, "a board must approve my decisions, [The General Assembly] but they remain mine to make." Owens concluded, "The [P]ope has the right to send a priest to a Catholic church, and the right to remove him. I have the same authority." However, Owens would not get to lead COGIC beyond 2000.[22]

The controversy surrounding Owens grew and, in November 2000, during the annual National Convocation, Gilbert Earl Patterson, the nephew of late presiding bishop J. O. Patterson, defeated Chandler Owens with 59 percent of the vote in a hotly contested race. The election marked the first time in the history of COGIC that the denomination voted out a presiding bishop. The action left many wondering about the direction of the church. Born September 22, 1939, in Humboldt, Tennessee, Gilbert Earl Patterson's family relocated to Memphis two months after his birth. Due to his uncle's marriage to the founder's daughter, G. E. Patterson, during his childhood, came into regular contact with Mason and other early leaders of the church. However in 1952, life changed when Patterson's father received leadership of a Detroit, Michigan, congregation and the family relocated. It would be in Michigan, at the age of sixteen, that Patterson joined the ranks of the clergy.[23]

In 1961, Patterson returned to Memphis to attend Lemoyne Owen College, a historically black institution in the city, and while enrolled, he also began to co-pastor Holy Temple Church of God in Christ where he matured into a seasoned clergyman. By 1975, Patterson was ready to begin his own congregation so he purchased and remodeled an old Baptist edifice at 547 Mississippi Boulevard. He named the new church Temple of Deliverance the Cathedral of Bountiful Blessing and his congregation exponentially grew. Within three years the membership had outgrown the church and, in need of added space, Patterson commissioned the building of a new sanctuary. COGIC economically empowered the black community when it granted the contract valued at $1.2 million to a black-owned construction company.[24]

Over the years, G. E. Patterson became one of the most well liked ministers in Memphis. He conducted a vibrant television ministry, which brought him to the attention of local whites and into the homes of thousands of blacks across the mid-South. While not as politically savvy as Ford, Patterson possessed a charismatic personality and when Owens proved vulnerable in the 2000 convocational election, G. E. Patterson was the logical choice to lead the denomination into the twenty-first century. Historians and theologians are still assessing his seven-year tenure, but we do know that he proved to be a "philanthropic bishop," donating generously to his alma mater Lemoyne Owen College and a host of other charities throughout Memphis. He also represented the modernity of the twenty-first century as he drove himself around town in a late model Lincoln Navigator with personalized plates that read COGIC-1. The leadership had, in fact, come a long way since the times of Mason when he used to make the walk from Lexington to Durant to catch the train in order to spread his Holiness message.

In March 2007 as news of the death of Bishop G. E. Patterson spread throughout the city, Memphians paused as television stations interrupted local programming to deliver the details. The city seemed to be in shock until the day of the funeral when all local television stations carried the "home going" services of the late presiding bishop. As dignitaries filed into the service, cameras caught glimpses of President Bill Clinton, Governor Phil Bredesen of Tennessee, future first lady Michelle Obama, and Reverend Jesse Jackson. The memorial service displayed the pomp of a state funeral as all the above dignitaries spoke to the crowd about their fondness and interactions with Patterson. Overall, the funeral represents the completion of the evolution of COGIC as a denomination built upon the backs of laborers and sharecroppers to one that gained national respect as former and future heads of state traveled to Memphis to pay their final respects to the late presiding bishop of the Church of God in Christ.

With the death of Patterson, and the election of Charles E. Blake as senior bishop, COGIC has moved into one of its most public phases in the denomination's history. A native of Arkansas, Blake's life, in many ways, represents the experience and expectations of COGIC's present membership. Blake's father left Arkansas for California during the 1940s and was instrumental in establishing the church in the city of Los Angeles. Today, however, the son not only leads the largest COGIC congregation in the nation, the West Angeles Church of God in Christ, but he also serves as the presiding bishop. In many ways, the West Angeles church runs counter to the restorationist nature of Holiness and sanctification as the mega-congregation boasts a wealthy influential membership with members such as A-list actors Denzel Washington and Angela Bassett. However, with the infusion of money and an educated membership, the church now stands at a crossroad and only the future will decide if the principles of sanctification can actually be achieved in a modern-day global transnational denomination.

Notes

Preface

1. For more information, see Jerma Jackson, *Singing in My Soul: Black Gospel Music in a Secular Age* (Chapel Hill: University of North Carolina Press, 2004); Teresa L. Reed, *The Holy Profane: Religion in Black Popular Music* (Lexington: University Press of Kentucky, 2003).

Acknowledgments

1. For example, one of the court cases used had been misfiled for years, and it was through the efforts of historian Elton Weavers that the case was found.

Introduction: The Roots of the Study

1. David Daniels, "The Cultural Renewal of Slave Religion: Charles Price Jones and the Emergence of the Holiness Movement in Mississippi" (Ph.D. diss., Union Theological Seminary, 1992), 7; Evelyn Brooks Higginbotham, *Righteous Discontent: The Women's Movement in the Black Baptist Church, 1882–1920* (Cambridge, Mass.: Harvard University Press, 1993), 7–12; Glenda Elizabeth Gilmore, *Gender and Jim Crow: Women and the Politics of White Supremacy in North Carolina, 1896–1920* (Chapel Hill: University of North Carolina Press, 1996); Paul Harvey, *Redeeming the South: Religious Culture and Racial Identities among Southern Baptists, 1865–1925* (Chapel Hill: University of North Carolina Press, 1997), 111.

2. Arthur E. Paris, *Black Pentecostalism: Southern Religion in an Urban World* (Amherst: University of Massachusetts Press, 1982), 19.

3. "The Church in the Southern Black Community," last modified March 9, 2012, http://docsouth.unc.edu/church/intro.html.

4. Higginbotham, *Righteous Discontent,* 205.

5. Daniels, "The Cultural Renewal of Slave Religion," 13; Carter G. Woodson, *The History of the Negro Church*, 3rd ed. (Washington, D.C.: Associated Publishers, 1972), 228.

6. Jesse E. Lipford, "Sanctifying the Unholy: Black Pentecostalism, the Church of God in Christ and African American Culture," *West Tennessee Journal of History Society* 56 (Spring 2000): 40; Vinson Synan, *The Holiness Pentecostal Movement in the United States* (Grand Rapids, Mich.: William B. Berdmans Publishing, 1971), 167–168. For more detailed numbers, see Eileen W. Lindner, *Yearbook of American and Canadian Churches, 2001* (Nashville: Abingdon Press, 2001).

7. Grant Wacker, *Heaven Below: Early Pentecostals and American Culture* (Cambridge, Mass.: Harvard University Press, 2001), 6, 59, 104, 145, 146–147, 227–229, 231, 236); also James Goff and Grant Wacker, *Portraits of a Generation: Early Pentecostal Leaders* (Fayetteville: University of Arkansas Press, 2002).

8. Daniels, "The Cultural Renewal of Slave Religion."

9. John Giggie, *After Redemption: Jim Crow and the Transformation of African American Religion in the Delta, 1875–1915* (New York: Oxford University Press); Randall Stephens, *The Fire Spreads: Holiness and Pentecostalism in the American South* (Cambridge, Mass.: Harvard University Press, 2008); Anthea D. Butler, *Women in the Church of God in Christ: Making a Sanctified World* (Chapel Hill: University of North Carolina Press, 2007).

10. Giggie, *After Redemption.*

11. Elton Weavers, "The Metamorphosis of Charles Harrison Mason: The Origins of Black Pentecostal Churches in Tennessee," *West Tennessee Journal of History Society* 56 (Spring 2000).

12. See John Giggie, "God's Long Journey: African Americans, Religion, and History in the Mississippi Delta" (Ph.D. diss., Princeton University, 1997) for more information about the larger context of how this fight between so called progressives and conservative affected blacks' consumer culture in the Arkansas and Mississippi Delta.

13. Theodore Kornweibel, "Bishop C. H. Mason and the Church of God in Christ during World War I: The Perils of Conscientious Objection," *Journal of Southern Studies* (Winter 1987): 261–281.

14. Walter L. Williams, *Black Americans and the Evangelization of Africa 1877– 1900* (Madison: University of Wisconsin Press, 1982).

15. Sylvia M. Jacobs, *Black Americans and the Missionary Movement in Africa*, (Westport, Conn.: Greenwood Press, 1982).

16. Butler, *Women in the Church of God in Christ*, 3.

17. Clenora Hudson-Weems, *Emmett Till: The Sacrificial Lamb of the Civil Rights Movement* (Troy, Mich.: Bedford Publisher Press, 1994).

18. Synan, *The Holiness-Pentecostal Movement*, 35; George A. Smith, *The History of Georgia Methodism from 1786 to 1866* (Atlanta, 1913), 396–398. Story also told in Weavers, "The Metamorphosis of Charles Harrison Mason," 38.

19. Synan, *The Holiness-Pentecostal Movement*, 36–37. Also see Delbert R. Rose, *A Theology of Christian Experience* (Minneapolis: Bethany Fellowship, 1965), 52.

20. Synan, *The Holiness-Pentecostal Movement*, 37, 41; Arthur E. Paris, *Black Pentecostalism: Southern Religion in an Urban World* (Amherst: University of Massachusetts Press, 1982), 17.

21. Synan, *The Holiness-Pentecostal Movement*, 46–47.

22. Synan, *The Holiness-Pentecostal Movement*, 50–51; *Journal of General Conference, Methodist Episcopal Church, South, 1894*, 25–26.

23. Synan, *The Holiness-Pentecostal Movement*, 53.

1. In the Beginning, There Stood Two

1. Mason's early biographical narrative has been reprinted in countless anniversary, homecoming, and unpublished church booklets. In the early 1970s, academics also began to recount the story and since that time, it has appeared in dissertations, articles, and most recently, book chapters. Citing every source where the material appears is nearly impossible and, for that reason, I will refer only to the materials I personally used to narrate the story.

2. Manuscript census returns, Tenth Census of the United States, Populations Schedules, Conway County, Arkansas, 1880. The exact birth date of Mason may never be known. The oral history of the church claims that Mason's biological father's name was Jerry Mason, who served and died in the Civil War. Mason's surviving relatives placed his birth date on his obituary as 1862. Other historians, such as Elton Weavers, in the "The Metamorphosis of Charles Harrison Mason," place Mason's birth after the Civil War in 1866. No concrete primary source materials exist that proved or disproved the 1862 or 1866 date of birth. In an effort to remain as accurate as possible, the 1866 birth date along with the name Jeremiah given as the father in the 1880 Arkansas Census Report will be used in this monograph.

3. Peter Randolph, *Slave Cabin to the Pulpit, The Autobiography of Reverend Peter Randolph* (Boston: James H. Earle, 1893), 196–204; also quoted in Milton C. Sernett, *African American Religious History Documentary History* (Durham, N.C.: Duke University Press, 1999), 66.

4. Albert J. Raboteau, *Slave Religion: "The Invisible Institution" in the Antebellum South* (New York: Oxford University Press, 2004), 213; also see John Blassingame, *The Slave Community: Plantation Life in the Antebellum South* (New York: Oxford University Press, 1979), 131.

5. Additional information on Reconstruction can be found in Eric Foner, *Reconstruction, 1863–1877* (New York: Harper & Row, 1988).

6. For more information on the system of sharecropping, see Gerald D. Jaynes, *Branches Without Roots: Genesis of the Black Working Class* (New York: Oxford University Press, 1985); Ronald Davis, *Good and Faithful Labor: From Slavery to Sharecropping in the Natchez District* (Westport, Conn.: Greenwood Press, 1982); R. Douglass Hurt, *African American Life in the Rural South, 1900–1950* (Columbia: University of Missouri Press, 2003).

7. *Times-Picayune* (New Orleans), July 1878. The fever spread throughout Memphis into mid-October, infecting over 17,000 and killing 5,150. Over 90 percent of whites who remained contracted yellow fever, and roughly 70 percent of these died. Blacks also contracted the fever in large numbers and the total number of deaths among them living in the city remains unknown.

8. *Arkansas Gazette*, December 12, 1879, 8. Thanks to Ken Barnes, who during conversation alerted me to the existence of this source. The newspaper article is in reference to Benjamin "Pap" Singleton, a black man who led a group of blacks called the Exodusters out of the Deep South into Kansas in search of what they called their "promise land" after the Civil War. For more details, see Nell Irvin Painter, *Exoduster: Black Migration to Kansas after the Civil War* (Lawrence: University Press of Kansas, 1986).

9. Kenneth Barnes, *Who Killed John Clayton: Political Violence and the Emergence of the New South, 1861–1893* (Durham, N.C.: Duke University Press, 1996), 42.

10. Vertie L. Carter, *Dr. E. C. Morris: May 7, 1855–September 5, 1922* (Little Rock, Ark.: VLC Research and Biographical Technical Enterprise, 1999), 11–12.

11. Although the official history states that the Masons settled in the town of Plumerville, research in Conway County revealed that most blacks settled in Howard, a black pocket community of Plumerville. Most black women worked in

the homes of whites who lived in Plumerville. Also, if the Masons continued to work as sharecroppers in the county, the probability that they lived in Howard and gave their address as Plumerville would be consistent with other blacks who were known to do so.

12. Walter L. Fleming, *Documentary History of Reconstruction: Political Military, Social, Religious, Educational, and Industrial, 1865–1906* (New York: McGraw Hill Book Company, 1966), 167.

13. Elsie W. Mason, *The Man Charles H. Mason: Sermons of His Early Ministry* (n.p., 1979), 7; Clemmons, *Bishop C. H. Mason,* 3–6.

14. U.S. National Library of Medicine. I was unable to confirm the information but Clemmons in *Bishop C. H. Mason and the Roots of the Church of God in Christ,* 4, stated that Charles's father Jeremiah died as a result of the yellow fever epidemic in Memphis in 1878.

15. James Counts, *The History and Life Work of Elder C. H. Mason, Chief Apostle and His Co-Laborers* (n.p., c. 1920), 13; Story also recounted in Daniels, "The Cultural Renewal of Slave Religion," 90–92, and Weavers, "The Metamorphosis of Charles Harrison Mason," 39. Also see Sharla M. Fett, *Working Cures: Healing, Health and Power on Southern Slave Plantations* (Chapel Hill: University of North Carolina Press, 2002).

16. Elnora Lee, *A Man Greatly Used by God* (n.p., c. 1955), 3.

17. Elder William Dean of Lexington, Mississippi, interviewed by author, October 5, 2005. For more details on the black religious transformation, see Giggie, *After Redemption.*

18. Leon F. Litwack, *Trouble in the Mind: Black Southerners in the Age of Jim Crow* (New York: Alfred A. Knopf Publishing, 1998), 380.

19. Mason, *The Man Charles H. Mason,* 8; Lee, *A Man Greatly Used by God,* 3.

20. Mason, *The Man Charles H. Mason,* 9. According to Ithiel C. Clemmons in *Bishop C. H. Mason,* Mason turned to Dr. Morris in 1893 after the traumatic breakup of his first marriage. Clemmons further argues that Morris was the father Mason had missed in young adulthood and benefited from Morris's mediation and administration skill. From around the nation, both black and white leaders sought his principled and common-sense guidance. By observing Morris, Mason developed leadership skills and a pragmatic approach to group interaction. While I agree that Morris and Mason probably knew each other, I found no proof of such a close relationship that Clemmons alleges the two had.

21. Carter, *Dr. E. C. Morris,* 51.

22. Carter, *Dr. E. C. Morris,* 7; Todd E. Lewis, "Elias Camp Morris (1855–1922)," *Encyclopedia of Arkansas History and Culture,* http://encyclopediaofarkansas.net.

23. Carter, *Dr. E. C. Morris,* 51. According to Paul Harvey's *Redeeming the South,* 236, Morris avoided any exclusive emphasis on artisan training, suggesting that the forces of the present age would not tolerate old methods of thinking.

24. Mason, *The Man Charles H. Mason,* 9. Story also recounted in David Daniels, "The Cultural Renewal of Slave Religion," 93; Weavers, "The Metamorphosis of Charles Harrison Mason," 40; Giggie, "God's Long Journey," 213.

25. Daniels, "The Cultural Renewal of Slave Religion," 93.

26. Mason, *The Man Charles H. Mason,* 10.

27. Harvey, *Redeeming the South,* 111.

28. Giggie, "God's Long Journey," 196; Giggie, *After Redemption,* 165–166.

29. Tom Dillard, "Scipio A. Jones," *Arkansas Historical Quarterly* (Winter 1972): 218.

30. Willard B. Gatewood, *Aristocrats of Color* (Bloomington: University of Indiana Press, 1990), 72.

31. *Arkansas Baptist Vanguard* (May 1894).

32. Giggie, *After Redemption,* 165–166.

33. Giggie, "God's Long Journey," 198.

34. Giggie, "God's Long Journey," 198.

35. Weavers, "The Metamorphosis of Charles H. Mason," 39–40. Weavers argues that Mason's introduction to the Holiness movement was in fact due to reading Amanda Smith's autobiography, but my extensive research found no primary source material to prove that claim. For more information about African American religious identify after the Civil War, see Lawrence W. Levine, *Black Culture and Black Consciousness: Afro-American Folk Thought from Slavery to Freedom* (New York: Oxford University Press, 1977); Harvey, *Redeeming the South;* ; Paul Harvey, *Freedom's Coming: Religious Culture and the Shaping of the South from the Civil War through the Civil Rights Era* (Chapel Hill: University of North Carolina Press, 2005).

36. Elsie W. Mason, *The Man Charles H. Mason: Sermons of his Early Ministry* (n. p., 1979), 10. Mason stated that some of the worst sinners in the town converted during his first revival and this let him know that God wanted him to continue.

37. Litwack, *Trouble in the Mind,* 385.

38. Mason, *The Man Charles H. Mason,* 10; Dean Interview.

39. For a more detailed view of how blacks viewed southern cities and economic opportunities, please see Tera Hunter, *To 'Joy My Freedom: Southern Black Women's Lives and Labors after the Civil War* (Cambridge, Mass.: Harvard University Press, 1997).

40. Gatewood, *Aristocrats of Color,* 92.

41. Gatewood, *Aristocrats of Color,* 93.

42. Giggie, *After Redemption,* 176.

43. Giggie, *After Redemption,* 176.

44. Harvey, *Redeeming the South,* 107–108.

45. Daniels, "The Cultural Renewal of Slave Religion," 28–29; "Autobiographical Sketch of Charles Price Jones, Founder of the Church of Christ (Holiness), U.S.A.," in *History of Church of Christ (Holiness) U.S.A., 1895–1965,* ed. Otho B. Cobbins (New York: Vintage Press, 1966), 22; Clemmons, *Bishop C. H. Mason,* 6–7.

46. Elder William Dean of Lexington, interviewed by author, October 5, 2005. The first church established by Mason in Lexington, Mississippi, also took the name St. Paul. Elder Dean, the current senior pastor, remains convinced that this is where the name originated.

47. Daniels, "The Cultural Renewal of Slave Religion," 29–30.

48. "Autobiographical Sketch of Charles Price Jones," 22.

49. "Autobiographical Sketch of Charles Price Jones," 25–26.

50. "Autobiographical Sketch of Charles Price Jones," 24.

51. Daniels, "The Cultural Renewal of Slave Religion," 31.

52. "Autobiographical Sketch of Charles Price Jones," 24.
53. "Autobiographical Sketch of Charles Price Jones," 23.
54. Daniels, "The Cultural Renewal of Slave Religion," 20–23; Clemmons, *Bishop C. H. Mason*, 11–12.
55. Daniels, "The Cultural Renewal of Slave Religion," 19. By this time I believe that Mason and Jones are traveling and preaching together on a regular basis.
56. Vernon L. Wharton, *The Negro in Mississippi, 1865–1890* (New York: Harper & Row Publishing, 1965), 259; Patrick Thompson, *History of the Negro Baptist in Mississippi* (Jackson, Miss.: R. W. Bailey, 1899), 26.
57. *Report of the Freedmen's Aid Society, M. E. Church, 1874.* Extracts from letters.
58. Wharton, *The Negro in Mississippi*, 259.
59. Giggie, "God's Long Journey," 212.
60. Patricia A. Schechter, *Ida B. Wells Barnett and American Reform, 1880–1930* (Chapel Hill: University of North Carolina Press, 2001), 64–65; also see Giggie, "God's Long Journey," for a closer look at African American religion in the Arkansas and Mississippi Delta during post-Reconstruction.
61. John Hope Franklin, *From Slavery to Freedom: A History of African American Freedom* (New York: McGraw Hill, 2000), 286–87.
62. Daniels, "The Cultural Renewal of Slave Religion," 76–78.
63. Jones published criticisms of the Baptist Church and its new traditions in the *Truth* in the same manner as William Christian did while using the *Arkansas Baptist Vanguard* as his medium.
64. Mason, *The Man Charles H. Mason*, 12.
65. McCoy, *Yes Lord*, 27.
66. McCoy, *Yes Lord*, 28; St. Paul Church of God in Christ, *The 2004 Year Book.* Story also told by Jessie Fields of Lexington, Mississippi, interviewed by author, September 13, 2005.
67. McCoy, *Yes Lord*, 28.
68. Mason, *The Man Charles H. Mason*, 13.
69. Fleming, *Documentary History of Reconstruction*, 259.
70. Historical Census Browser. http://fisher.lib.virginia.edu/collections/stats/histcensus/index.html (accessed June 5, 2011); also see Wharton, *The Negro in Mississippi*, 169. Today Holmes County comprises seven municipalities: Cruger, Durant, Goodman, Lexington, Pickens, Tchula, and West and smaller rural settlements named after local churches.
71. For more information on James Z. George, see Lucy Peck, "The Life and Times of James Z. George" (Master's thesis, Mississippi State University, 1964); May Spencer, "Senator James Zachariah George of Mississippi: Bourbon or Liberal?" *Journal of Mississippi History* 16 (July 1954): 164–83. George served as a member of the Mississippi secession convention and signed the ordinance of secession. During the war, he served in the Confederate army attaining the rank of brigadier general of state troops. Afterward he resided in Jackson, Mississippi, before being appointed chief justice of the state supreme court in 1879; elected as a Democrat to the United States Senate in 1880; reelected in 1886, and again in 1892, serving from March 4, 1881, until his death on August 14, 1897.
72. The Mississippi Department of Archives and History, "Works Progress Administration Records," Record Group 60, Jackson, Mississippi, J. W. Lowen and

Charles Sallis, eds., 161. Whites in the county referred to this act as the Holmes County Plan after the statewide Mississippi Plan of 1875 designed to intimidate and frighten blacks away from voting.

73. "Holmes County Today and Yesterday," *Lexington Advertiser*, sesquicentennial edition, August 28, 1986.

74. Fleming, *Documentary History of Reconstruction*, 333.

75. Historical Census Browser. http://fisher.lib.virginia.edu/collections/stats/histcensus/index.html (accessed June 5, 2011). The second public school district opened in Holmes County in 1902 in the city of Lexington and the third in Durant in 1903. COGIC opened Saints School in Lexington in 1918. The opening afforded blacks the opportunity to educate their own children in a setting other than the one-room black school operated by the county's school district.

76. Blassingame, *The Slave Community*, 131.

77. St. Paul Church of God in Christ, *The 1987 Year Book*, 1. The official membership roster shows that Paul R. Favors, John Lee, Anthony Lee, Edward F. Copper, and Charles Pleas served as the first deacons in the Lexington congregation. Members included Anthony Lee, Wilks Lee, Francis Lee, Cornelius Thurmond, William Thurmond, Leticia Thurman, Lee Corbin, Wash Owen, Minor Washington, Addie Golden, Mary Mimms, Francis Miller, Lula McCullough, Francis Broy, Horace Broy, Joseph Redmon, John L. Conic, Emma Conic, Cornelius Porter, Lizzie Porter, Kitty Clark, Richard Clark, Kin Green, Mollie McCollugh, Charles Nash, and Henry Mimms.

78. McCoy, *Yes Lord*, 27.

79. Booker T. Washington, *Up From Slavery: An Autobiography By Booker T. Washington* (New York: Bantam Book, 1901), 73.

80. "Rules of Government of the Churches of God in Christ" (Jackson: Published privately, 1906), 4.

81. "Rules of Government of the Churches of God in Christ," 4.

82. "Rules of Government of the Churches of God in Christ," 8.

2. We Will Let the Courts Speak for Us

1. *Los Angeles Daily Times*, April 1906; also quoted in Marne L. Campbell, "'The Newest Religious Sect Has Started in Los Angeles': Race, Class, Ethnicity, and the Origins of the Pentecostal Movement, 1906–1913," *Journal of African America History* 95 (Winter 2010): 1–25; Stephens, *The Fire Spreads*, 193–195; Estrelda Alexander, *The Black Fire: One Hundred Years of African American Pentecostalism* (Downers Grove, Ill.: InterVarsity Press, 2011).

2. *The Azusa Mission: The Greatest Pentecostal Outpouring Ever Known in the United States* (n.p., c. 1952), 1. Story also recounted in Leonard Lovett, "Black Holiness-Pentecostalism: Implication for Ethics and Social Transformation" (Unpublished Ph.D. diss., Emory University, 1979), 54–61; Weavers, "The Metamorphosis of Charles Harrison Mason," 43; Arthur E. Paris, *Black Pentecostalism: Southern Religion in an Urban World* (Amherst: University of Massachusetts Press, 1982), 23–24; Clemmons, *Bishop C. H. Mason*, 43–45.

3. *The Azusa Mission*, 1.

4. Marne L. Campbell, "The Newest Religious Sect Has Started in Los Angeles:

Race, Class, Ethnicity, and the Origins of the Pentecostal Movement, 1906–1913,"
Journal of African America History 95 (Winter 2010): 9.

5. Stephens, *The Fire Spreads,* 188. For a detailed biographical sketch of
Charles F. Parham, see Mrs. Charles F. Parham, *The Life of Charles F. Parham:
Founder of the Apostolic Faith Movement* (Birmingham, Ala.: Commercial Printing
Company, 1930).

6. Parham, *The Life of Charles F. Parham,* 137. Leonard Lovett, in the "Black
Holiness-Pentecostalism" account, remembered the series of events in a different
manner. In late 1905 Charles Parham and William J. Seymour met each other
through their mutual friend, a black woman named Mrs. Lucy Farrow. As a result,
when Parham came to the Houston area and set up a short-term Bible school,
Farrow was instrumental in getting Seymour enrolled.

7. *The Azusa Mission,* 1–2; also see Allan Anderson, *Spreading Fires: The
Missionary Nature of Early Pentecostalism* (New York: Orbis Publishing, 2007).
Anderson argues that the Azusa revival served as the true beginning of the modern
Pentecostal movement as black and white believers came to receive the Holy Spirit
at the hands of Seymour. Once they left, they carried the message of speaking in
tongues back to their communities and countries, which spread Pentecostalism to
the masses.

8. Anderson, *Spreading Fires,* 2; also see the *Los Angeles Times,* April 18, 1917.

9. Mason, *The Man Charles H. Mason,* 14. Also see Weavers, "The
Metamorphosis of Charles Harrison Mason," 43.

10. Dovie Marie Johnson of Lexington, Mississippi, interview by author,
October 5, 2005.

11. McCoy, *Yes Lord,* 28–29; Lee, *C. H. Mason,* 9.

12. Mason, *The Man Charles H. Mason,* 14; also see McCoy, *Yes Lord,* 29.

13. McCoy, *Yes Lord,* 29; Mason, *The Man Charles H. Mason,* 18–19. Also see
Lovett in "Black Holiness-Pentecostalism," 58–59.

14. Elsie W. Mason, *The Man Charles H. Mason: Sermons of his Early Ministry*
(n.p., 1979), 19. For more information on how Seymour's movement spread
throughout the country and abroad, see Anderson, *Spreading Fires.*

15. Cheryl J. Sanders, *The Holiness-Pentecostal Experience in African American
Religion and Tradition* (New York: Oxford University Press, 1996), 11–12.

16. McCoy, *Yes Lord,* 32.

17. McCoy, *Yes Lord,* 34.

18. Historical Census Browser. http://fisher.lib.virginia.edu/collections/stats/
histcensus/index.html (accessed June 5, 2011).

19. Weavers, "The Metamorphosis of Charles Harrison Mason," 46.

20. "Fanatical worship of Negroes," *Commercial Appeal,* May 22, 1907; also
quoted in David M. Tucker, *Black Pastors and Leaders* (Memphis: Memphis State
Press, 1975), 91; Weavers, "The Metamorphosis of Charles Harrison Mason," 45.

21. For more information on class and religion within the African American
community, see Glenda E. Gilmore, *Gender and Jim Crow: Women and the Politics
of White Supremacy in North Carolina, 1896–1920* (Chapel Hill: University of North
Carolina Press, 1996), and Higginbotham, *Righteous Discontent.*

22. *Apostolic Faith,* May 1907.

23. Butler, *Women in the Church of God in Christ.*

24. "Negro House Boy Makes Funny Talk At Police Station," *Commercial Appeal* (Memphis), 1907.

25. "Negro House Boy Makes Funny Talk At Police Station," *Commercial Appeal* (Memphis), 1907.

26. "Negro House Boy Makes Funny Talk At Police Station," *Commercial Appeal* (Memphis), 1907.

27. "Negro House Boy Makes Funny Talk At Police Station," *Commercial Appeal* (Memphis), 1907.

28. *Apostolic Faith*, May 1907.

29. Weavers, "The Metamorphosis of Charles Harrison Mason," 45.

30. *Avant et al. v. Mason et al.*, Shelby County Chancery Court 1907, Number 14777.

31. "The Report of the Council," *Truth* (Jackson), September 1907.

32. *Avant et al. v. Mason et al.*

33. McCoy, *Yes Lord,* 33–34; For a more detailed history of the Holy Convocation, see Clemmons, *Bishop C. H. Mason,* 73–75.

34. Weavers, in "The Metamorphosis of Charles Harrison Mason," 45.

35. McCoy, *Yes Lord,* 7.

36. http://fisher.lib.virginia.edu/collections/stats/histcensus/index.html.

37. *Avant et al. v. Mason et al.*

38. *Avant et al. v. Mason et al.*, Scott's Deposition. At the time of the lawsuit Henry Scott worked for Steward Brothers of Memphis, Tennessee, lived at 464 Wicks Avenue, Memphis. He had been a member of the Wellington Street congregation and also helped build the first church structure.

39. *Avant et al. v. Mason et al.*, Scott's Deposition.

40. *Avant et al v. Mason et al.* The fifty-two-year-old Avant moved to Memphis in 1867. In 1907 when the lawsuit was filed he worked as an Express-man and claimed that he was among the first to join the Wellington Street congregation in 1890. In 1907 Avant listed 672 LeRose Street in Memphis as his home address.

41. *Avant et al. v. Mason et al.*, Avant's Deposition. Also see Harvey, *Redeeming the South,* 133.

42. *Avant et al. v. Mason et al.*, Searcy's Deposition. Searcy listed his address in Memphis as 214 Turley Street and his age as fifty-four.

43. *Avant et al. v. Mason et al.*, Searcy's Deposition.

44. Wharton, *The Negro in Mississippi,* 264.

45. *Avant et al. v. Mason et al.*, Avant's Deposition.

46. *Avant et al. v. Mason et al.*, Avant's Deposition.

47. *Avant et al. v. Mason et al.*, Avant's Deposition.

48. *Avant et al v. Mason et al.*, Jones's Deposition. In 1907 Jones stated that he had lived in Jackson thirteen years. He led three congregations; one was five miles east of Jackson in Peoria, and another was a small congregation seventeen miles south of Jackson by rail.

49. *Avant et al v. Mason et al.*, Jordan's Deposition. I. L. Jordan lived in Hollywood, Mississippi. Jordan stated that prior to Mason's visit to California, the worship ordinances were baptizing and foot washing and administering the Lord's Supper.

50. The congregation most likely received the help of the supervisory tribunal

in Jackson to file this suit. The plaintiffs' case hinged on the concept of "original use." In chapter 2, the Mississippi State Supreme Court ruled against Jones and his followers at Mt. Helm based on the concept that Mr. and Mrs. Helms donated the property for the use of a Baptist church and not a sanctified church. Jones, Scott, Avant, and Reaves knew that this remained their best chance of retaining the property.

51. *Avant et al. v. Mason et al.* Information obtained from a copy of the actual injunction found in the court docket.

52. *Avant et al. v. Mason et al.* Information obtained from the actual Plea of Abatement found in the court docket.

53. *Avant et al. v. Mason et al.*, Mason's Deposition.

54. *Avant et al. v. Mason et al.*, Mason's Deposition.

55. *Avant et al. v. Mason et al.*, Mason's Deposition.

56. *Truth* (Jackson), June 1906.

57. *Avant et al. v. Mason et al.*, Edward Driver's Deposition.

58. *Avant et al. v. Mason et al.*, Mason's Deposition. This testimony comes from Mason's second deposition in the court case. The actual page numbers for the second deposition are 88–108.

59. *Avant et al. v. Mason et al.*, Mason's Deposition.

60. *Avant et al. v. Mason et al.*, Mason's Deposition.

61. *Avant et al. v. Mason et al.*, Mason's Deposition.

62. *Avant et al. v. Mason et al.*, Mason's Deposition.

63. The Plaintiffs' names as they appeared on the original bill of complaint in 1907: Henry Avant, Sydney Reaves, Henry Scott, Lulu Washington, Annie Neal, Mattie Lark, Maud Washington, Edmund Mosby, Robert Turner, Jerry Phipps, Samuel Davis Jr., Richard Miller, Lulu Haskins, Clara Rady, Mary Randolph, Ethel Neal, Annie Neil, Martha Johnson, Annie Woods, and Peter Jones.

64. William Frazier, Derrick Johnson, Jim Murphy, Rebecca Carroll, Susie Ford, Julia Thomas, Fannie Buntyn, Fannie Rogers, Lucy Cohen, Minnie Yates, Millie Roberts, Bob Roberts, Benjamin Roberts, William Phillips, Susie Philips, Hugh Philips Jr., Jerry Philips, Milton Sanders, Calvin Rucker, Eliza Heint, Lavinia Cartwright, Sebastian BebBolt, Milton Sanders Jr., Sara Peters, Jesse Smith, Minnie Minuet, Eliza Jew, George Spark, Lavinia Turley, Lucy Rose, Theodore Powers, Mamie Taylor, Amanda Taylor, Amanda Allen, Amanda Montgomery, William Montgomery, Delia Maxwell, Lottie Parks, Gertrude Clayton, Mary Clayton, Annie Sullivan, Elizabeth Taylor, John Maxwell, Emma Reed, Mollie Frazier, Clara Clements, Katie Frazier, Hattie Frazier, William Bryant, Daisy Latimore, Virginia Wilson, Lula Brooks, Fletcher Flake, Lucinda Jackson, Clara Hanson, Jim Lowry, Julia Roberts, Mamie Roberts, John Washington, Levy Mason, Holt Roberts, George Thompson, Mary Warren, Eliza Harris, Ruben Warren, Eliza Warren, Alva Jones, Mabel Jones, Sam Jones, Indiana Washington, Emma Page, Hollie Page, Mollie Page, Ruthie Page, Sara Newell, Minnie D. McLellan, Tom Newell, Louisa Newell, Clarence Hones, Mollie Houston, Elvira Duggery, Arthur Washington, Nicey Davis, I. E. Hightower, Hannah Lindsey, Beatrice Keeper, Richard Cobb, Ruth Craig, William Hughes, Mary Miller, Linda Prince, Johnnie Mitchell, Charlie Mitchell, Martha Jenkins, Lillie McCall, Elisa BenBolt, Edgar Rodgers, Maria Hall, Mandy Allen, Allie Menter, J. C. Copeland, Dicy Wale, A. M. Fraizer, George Buchanan, Henry

Westfield, Eleanor Rucker, David Ayer, Mary Jacobs, Zie Jacobs, Viola Jacobs, Caroline Johnson, C. L. Wheeler, R. A. Wheeler, Lizzie Wheeler, Saint Samuel, Sara Thomas, Easter Webb, Queen Minuet, and Hattie Lee.

65. *Avant et al. v. Mason et al.,* Adams's Deposition.

66. *Avant et al. v. Mason et al.,* Adams's Deposition.

67. *Avant et al. v. Mason et al.,* Adams's Deposition.

68. *Avant et al. v. Mason et al.,* Adams's Deposition.

69. *Avant et al. v. Mason et al.,* Adams's Deposition.

70. *Avant et al. v. Mason et al.,* Adams's Deposition.

71. *Avant et al. v. Mason et al.,* Adams's Deposition.

72. *Avant et al. v. Mason et al.,* Judge's Ruling found in the court jacket.

73. *Avant et al. v. Mason et al.,* Opinion of the Western District of the Tennessee Supreme Court.

74. *Avant et al. v. Mason et al.,* 3.

75. *Avant et al. v. Mason et al.,* 6.

76. *Avant et al. v. Mason et al.,* 7.

77. *Mason et al. v. Avant et al.,* Counter Suit Deposition.

78. *Mason et al. v. Avant et al.,* Counter Suit Deposition. Court records show that Mason sued for sixteen months rent at $30.00 a month totaling $480.00. He also sued to recoup $128.00 spent on the large gospel tent, $120.00 to replace the roof, $150.00 for the roof and ceiling, and sixteen months offering for $109.00 per month totaling $1,744.00 plus the sum of $101.00 in interest.

79. *Mason et al. v. Avant et al.,* Counter Suit Deposition. Turner stated that he was forty years old and his residence was 2111 Monroe Street. He had lived in Memphis for about twenty years and for the last five he worked in real estate. He stated that if the building were cut up into rooms for rent each room would bring about $30.00–35.00 a month because of its proximity to downtown and if put into the shape of a hall it would rent from $15.00 to $25.00 a month.

80. *Mason et al. v. Avant et al.,* Counter Suit. Henry Shelton stated that he was fifty-three and lived at 2096 Vinton Avenue. When asked if the building were cut up into rooms and rented, Shelton stated that each room ought to rent for $40.00–$50.00 each.

81. *Mason et al. v. Avant et al.,* Jordan's Counter Suit Deposition.

82. *John A. Lee v. Charles Mason,* Holmes County Chancery Court Number 1505. The names of the dissenting members and Mason's followers' names are unknown. The jacket to the court case was found in the chancery court in Lexington, but all the filed materials were missing. A timeline of the court case can be discerned by the recorded dates of motions and petitions filed by both the defendants and plaintiffs, but the actual details of the case remain obscure without the case depositions and rulings.

3. Mason Told Us Not to Fight

1. William A. Sweeny, *History of the African American Negro in the Great World War* (New York: Johnson Reprinting Company, 1970), 78–79.

2. *Crisis* 16 (July 1918): 111; also quoted in Mark Whalan, *The Great War and the Culture of the New Negro* (Gainesville: University of Florida Press, 2008), 18.

3. Tom Dillard, "Scipio A. Jones," *Arkansas Historical Quarterly* (Winter 1973): 212.

4. *Common Wealth* (Greenwood), April 1917.

5. Kornweibel, "Bishop C. H. Mason," 265; The sermon in its entirety can be found in Mason, *The Man Charles H. Mason,* 36. Also see Theodore Kornweibel, *"Investigate Everything": Federal Effort to Ensure Black Loyalty during World War I* (Bloomington: University of Indiana Press, 2002).

6. Mason, *The Man Charles H. Mason,* 39. Also quoted in Tucker, *Black Pastors and Leaders,* 98.

7. Mason, *The Man Charles H. Mason,* 39.

8. Kornweibel, "Bishop C. H. Mason," 265; Mason, *The Man, Charles Harrison Mason,* 36–39.

9. Stewart Halsey Ross, *Propaganda for War: How the United States Was Conditioned to Fight the Great War of 1914–1918* (Jefferson, N.C.: McFarland & Company, 1996), 3 and 218. Also see Kendrick Clements, *The Presidency of Woodrow Wilson* (Lawrence: University Press of Kansas, 1992), and *Freedom Daily,* April 2002.

10. Chandler Owen personified the attitude of many middle-class blacks who opposed the war. Owen was born in Warrenton, North Carolina, in 1889 and graduated from Virginia Union University in 1913. While attending Columbia University in 1916, he became friends with A. Philip Randolph, the future labor leader, and joined the Socialist Party of America. The two became known as the Harlem Lenin and Trotsky. They also started a Marxist journal in 1917 called the *Messenger* and were jailed and mocked by many in the black community for their opposition to the war.

11. For more on the Espionage and Sedition Acts, please see David M. Kennedy, *Over Here: The First World War and American Society* (New York: Oxford University Press, 1980); also see Ross, *Propaganda for War.*

12. Jeanette Keith, *Rich Man's War, Poor Man's Fight* (Chapel Hill: University of North Carolina Press, 2004), 119; Agent McElveen, Memphis, Tenn., April 20, 1917, "In Re: Anonymous Communication Endeavoring Prevent Negro Enlistment," OG 3057, Reel 8.

13. Editorial, *Washington Bee* (Washington, D.C.), April 7, 1917.

14. Arlyn J. Parish, "Kansas Mennonites During World War I," *Fort Hays Studies* no. 4 (May 1968): 17.

15. Parish, "Kansas Mennonites," 19.

16. Kornweibel, "Bishop C. H. Mason," 262.

17. Stephens, *The Fire Spreads,* 262.

18. Kornweibel, "Bishop C. H. Mason," 261.

19. Stephens, *The Fire Spreads,* 261.

20. Keith, *Rich Man's War,* 133. Also see Paul Murray, "Blacks and the Draft: A History of Institutional Racism," *Journal of Black Studies* 2, no. 1 (September 1971): 18; Kornweibel, "Bishop C. H. Mason," 266.

21. McCoy, *Yes Lord,* 37.

22. Special Agent M. M. Schaumbuger to Bureau, September 25, 1917. Casefile OG227347.

23. Stephens, *The Fire Spreads,* 261.

24. Grant Wacker, *Heaven Below: Early Pentecostals and American Culture* (Cambridge, Mass.: Harvard University Press, 2001), 245.

25. Special Agent M. M. Schaumbuger to Bureau, September 25, 1917.

26. Special Agent M. M. Schaumbuger to Bureau, September 25, 1917. Also see Kornweibel, "Bishop C. H. Mason," 267.

27. Special Agent M. M. Schaumbuger to Bureau, September 25, 1917.

28. Murray, "Blacks and the Draft," 61. For more information about whites' worry about possible black uprisings, see Keith, *Rich Man's War,* 142–147.

29. *Commonwealth* (Greenwood), 1918.

30. Parish, "Kansas Mennonites," 37.

31. Parish, "Kansas Mennonites," 38.

32. Harry D. Gully to Bureau, April 2, 1918.

33. Bureau of Investigations File. Casefile 64788, p. 2.

34. Harry D. Gully to Bureau, April 2, 1918.

35. Keith, *Rich Man's War,* 166. Keith also showed that Pat Harrison won the election handily with 56,715 votes to Vardaman's 44,154. Vardaman attributed the loss in part to voter intimidation. Harrison carried the Delta, Gulf Coast, Black Belt, and piney woods counties, but Vardaman won twenty-four counties, mostly in the northeastern hills. In his farewell letter to the people of Mississippi, Vardaman claimed that President Wilson had more power than any other man in the United States. For a more detailed account of the life of James K. Vardaman, see George C. Osborn, *James Kimble Vardaman, a Southern Commoner* (Jackson, Miss.: Hederman Brother Publishing, 1984), and William Holmes, *The White Chief: James K. Vardaman in Mississippi Politics* (Baton Rouge: Louisiana State University Press, 1970).

36. Harry D. Gully to Bureau, April 2, 1918.

37. Harry D. Gully to Bureau, April 2, 1918. Bacon also informed Gully that another white preacher named Cohen preached at the church in August 1917, but was unable to give any information other than his last name.

38. Harry D. Gully to Bureau, April 2, 1918. Mason is apparently referring to the large number of German speaking officers who served in the Union army and commanded black troops during the Civil War. For a more detailed account, see Martin W. Ofele, *German-Speaking Officers and the U.S. Colored Troops, 1863–1867* (Gainesville: University of Florida Press, 2004).

39. Harry D. Gully to Bureau, April 2, 1918.

40. Harry D. Gully to Bureau, April 2, 1918. Special Agent Gully also interviewed James Lee, a resident of Lexington, and an ordained preacher in Mason's church. From this interview Gully found out the names of Harry Mims, Wash Brooks, Robert Booker, and John Collin, who preached at ten other COGIC churches scattered throughout the county. After interviewing all the men they stated that they did not preach against the war, although they knew it was part of the creed of COGIC.

41. Kornweibel, "Bishop C. H. Mason," 270; also see the *Commercial Appeal* (Memphis), April 18, 1918, and Weavers, "The Metamorphosis of Charles Harrison Mason," 47.

42. Special Agent McKivean at Memphis Office to Bureau, April 18, 1918. Casefile 64788. According to oral accounts, not all COGIC preachers survived the

harassment. In northwest Michigan Elder Manugrum, a COGIC preacher, was fatally shot for his perceived opposition to World War I.

43. Special Agent McKivean at Memphis Office to Bureau, April 18, 1918. Mason told McElveen that Reverend Johnson was arrested in Dallas, Texas, and was later released upon showing proper paperwork.

44. Special Agent McKivean at Memphis Office to Bureau, April 18, 1918.

45. Special Agent Eugene Palmer at Jackson Office of Bureau, June 1918.

46. Kornweibel, "Bishop C. H. Mason," 272.

47. For more information concerning the transformation of black religious traditions in the Mississippi Delta, see Giggie, "God's Long Journey," 196. Also see Yvonne Chireau, *Black Magic: Religion and the African American Conjuring Tradition* (Berkeley and Los Angeles: University of California Press, 2003), and Jeffery Anderson, *Conjuring in African American Society* (Baton Rouge: Louisiana State University Press, 2005).

48. Palmer at Jackson Office to Bureau, June 1918; Kornweibel, "Bishop C. H. Mason," 72.

49. Palmer at Jackson Office to Bureau, June 1918.

50. Jessie Fields, Lexington, interviewed by author, October 18, 2005.

51. Elder William Dean, interviewed by the author, September 2005.

52. McCoy, *Yes Lord*, 37.

53. Jessie Fields, Lexington, interviewed by author, October 18, 2005. On the day of this interview I personally saw the so-called dungeon where Mason was held. Today murals are painted on the walls of the room depicting several events in Mason's life, including this episode. Another account exists in McCoy, *Yes Lord*, 38, McCoy stated that when Mason was released to be taken to the train station clouds immediately began to gather causing the "outdoors" to become dark. As authorities proceeded to the train station, a car ran over the sheriff's son and lightning knocked down his wife and blew down the jailhouse fence.

54. Palmer at Jackson Office to Bureau, June 1918.

55. Palmer at Jackson Office to Bureau, June 1918.

56. Agents of the Los Angeles Bureau to Bureau Headquarters, July 29, 1918; Kornweibel, "Bishop C. H. Mason," 267, 271–275; For more biographical information and the Church of God in Christ in California, see Clemmons, *Bishop C. H. Mason*, 82–87.

57. Agents of the Los Angeles Bureau to Bureau Headquarters, July 29, 1918.

58. Agents of the Los Angeles Bureau to Bureau Headquarters, July 29, 1918. Agents of the Los Angeles to Bureau, July 29, 1918. This postcard bore the postmark Washington, D.C., but has a return address written in the upper-left-hand corner 180 E. High Street, Norfolk, Va. Agents also noted in their files that they saw another postcard that put Holt in Lexington around July 2, 1918.

59. Agents of the Los Angeles Bureau to Bureau Headquarters, July 29, 1918.

60. Agents of the Los Angeles Bureau to Bureau Headquarters, July 29, 1918.

61. Agents of the Los Angeles Bureau to Bureau Headquarters, July 29, 1918.

62. Agents of the Los Angeles Bureau to Bureau Headquarters, July 29, 1918.

63. Agents of the Los Angeles Bureau to Bureau Headquarters, July 29, 1918.

64. Agents of the Los Angeles Bureau to Bureau Headquarters, July 29, 1918. This file was sent to agents in Jackson, Mississippi, for the prosecution of Mason.

65. Texas agents to Bureau, October 10, 1918; Mason's troubles in Texas are also recounted in Kornweibel, "Bishop C. H. Mason," 273–276.

66. Texas agents to Bureau, October 10, 1918. Hattie McElmore, Henry Baker Bookie Griffin, George Morris, Robert Wilkerson, Roscoe LittleJohn, Bethal LittleJohn, Lewis Harold, Joe Graves, Aron Black, Mr. and Mrs. Davis, Tom French, Hattie Black, Sarah McElmore, Alex Taylor, Minnie Taylor, and Henry Baker, all who paid 25 cents.

67. Texas agents to Bureau, October 10, 1918. Kornweibel, "Bishop C. H. Mason," 276.

68. Texas agents to Bureau, October 10, 1918.

69. Texas agents to Bureau, October 10, 1918.

70. Texas agents to Bureau, October 10, 1918.

71. Texas agents to Bureau, October 10, 1918.

72. Parish, "Kansas Mennonites," 31.

73. Texas agents to Bureau, October 10, 1918.

74. Texas agents to Bureau, October 10, 1918.

75. Parish, "Kansas Mennonites," 48–49.

76. Parish, "Kansas Mennonites," 48–49.

77. Texas agents to Bureau, October 10, 1918.

78. Texas agents to Bureau, October 10, 1918. Pierson stated that he bought one of the little books and paid fifteen cents for it, and paid the twenty-five cents to get his name on the church register.

79. Texas agents to Bureau, October 10, 1918.

80. Texas agents to Bureau, October 10, 1918.

81. Texas agents to Bureau, October 10, 1918.

82. Texas agents to Bureau, October 10, 1918.

83. Texas agents to Bureau, October 10, 1918.

84. Texas agents to Bureau, October 10, 1918. Agents secured from Black, the congregation's secretary, the church register in which appears the names of the members of the church, their ages and the twenty-five cents as indicated in the above statements. Among these names there are 40 whose ages range form 18 years old to 45, and, for the purpose of ascertaining whether any of those had failed to register, an unknown informant searched, but found only three who had not registered at the proper time.

85. Grant Wacker, *Heaven Below: Early Pentecostals and American Culture* (Cambridge, Mass.: Harvard University Press, 2001), 247.

86. Kornweibel, "Bishop C. H. Mason," 274.

87. Kornweibel, "Bishop C. H. Mason," 274.

88. Kornweibel, "Bishop C. H. Mason," 275–276.

89. Kornweibel, "Bishop C. H. Mason," 276.

90. Kornweibel, "Bishop C. H. Mason," 277. Also see Div. Supt, C. E. Breniman to Div. Supt. H. G. Clabaugh, August 31, 1918. As to Special Agent Dewitt Winn, the Spanish flu epidemic is believed to have killed over 500,000 people in the United States alone and American soldiers returning home from war likely introduced this new strain of flu into the American population. More American soldiers died as a result of the flu once they returned home than in actual combat. For a detailed account of America during the flu epidemic of 1918, see Carol R. Byerly, *Fever of*

War: The Influenza Epidemic in the U.S. Army during World War I (New York: New York University Press, 2005).

4. Come Over to Macedonia and Help

1. Words used by COGIC missionary Elizabeth White in 1937 as she traveled throughout the United States in search of other women who would join her in Africa.
2. Louis R. Harlan, "Booker T. Washington and the White Man's Burden," *American Historical Review* 71 (January 1967): 441–467.
3. Walter Williams, *Black Americans and the Evangelization of Africa, 1877–1900* (Madison: University of Wisconsin Press, 1982), 98; Samuel Miller to Samuel Armstrong, January 11, 1880. A.B.C.F.M. Papers, collection 6, vol. 30, no. 344.
4. Williams, *Black Americans*, 43; also see Henry M. Turner speech in *A.M.E. Budget, 1883*, 130.
5. Williams, *Black Americans*, 45; also see Africa *A.M.E. Church Review* (April 1892): 467–468.
6. Williams, *Black Americans*, 98; also quoted in Josephus R. Coan, "The Expansion of Missions of the African Methodist Episcopal Church in South Africa" (Ph.D. diss. Hartford Seminary, 1961), 49–51.
7. Williams, *Black Americans*, 102; also see *Voice Mission*, September 1, 1899, 4.
8. Williams, *Black Americans*, 64 and 67.
9. Williams, *Black Americans*, 69; also see James Melvin Washington, *Frustrated Fellowship: The Black Baptist Quest for Social Power* (Macon, Ga.: Mercer Press, 1986).
10. Williams, *Black Americans*, 69.
11. Williams, *Black Americans*, 108; James J. Cole, *Africa in Brief* (New York: Freeman Steam Printing Establishment, 1896), 23.
12. Williams, *Black Americans*, 108–109.
13. According to Sylvia M. Jacobs in *Black Americans and the Missionary Movement in Africa* (Westport, Conn.: Greenwood Press, 1982), the leading black institutes of higher education whose students actively sought to work in Africa were Fisk University, Howard University, Atlanta University, Lincoln University, New Orleans University, Philander Smith College, and Hampton Institute.
14. Williams, *Black Americans*, 87.
15. Williams, *Black Americans*, 87–88.
16. Williams, *Black Americans*, 93; also see Amanda Smith, *An Autobiography: The Story Of The Lords Dealing With Amanda Smith, The Colored Evangelist* (Chicago: Meyer & Brother, 1893).
17. Williams, *Black Americans*, 75 and 93–94. Also see Photograph Collection, Sheppard Papers.
18. Kenneth Barnes, *Journey of Hope: The Back to Africa Movement in Arkansas in the Late 1800s* (Chapel Hill: University of North Carolina Press, 2004), 109.
19. Barnes, *Journey of Hope*, 109–110. Also see Minutes of 25th Annual Conference, November 16, 1892, Newport, pp. 388–389, Arkansas AME Records.
20. Barnes, *Journey of Hope*, 119–121. Also see Liberia Bulletin, 16, February 1900, Sherrill to Leonard, October 6, 1906, Missionary Correspondence, roll 5.

21. Biographical information about Elizabeth Robinson can be found in Clemmons, *Bishop C. H. Mason*, 110; Elijah L. Hill, *Women Come Alive* (Arlington, Tex.: Perfecting the Kingdom Press, 2005), 11–20; Butler, *Women in the Church of God in Christ*, 12–15; *The Official Quarterly Guide Senior YPWW* (Memphis: Church of God in Christ Publishing, 2001), 21–22.

22. Butler, *Women in the Church of God in Christ*, 15–18.

23. Charles H. Pleas, *Fifty Years Achievement from 1906–1956* (Memphis: Church of God in Christ Press, 1906), 24; *Church of God in Christ: The Official Quarterly Guide Senior YPWW*, 36–37.

24. "History of Saints Industrial College," *The St. Paul Eighteenth Annual Homecoming Year Book*, 29. Also see Butler, *Women in the Church of God in Christ*, 99.

25. *The Official Quarterly Guide Senior YPWW*, 26–27.

26. Similar information also covered in Butler, *Women in the Church of God in Christ*, 42–43.

27. McCoy, *Yes Lord*, 41; Clemmons, *Bishop C. H. Mason*, 113; Butler, *Women in the Church of God in Christ*, 42–43.

28. Pleas, *Fifty Years Achievement*, 12–13; Dorcas also mentioned in Butler, *Women in the Church of God in Christ*, 46.

29. Butler, *Women in the Church of God in Christ*, 46–47.

30. Mary C. Terrell, *A Colored Woman in a White World* (Washington, D.C.: Ransdall, 1940), 298.

31. Cheryl Townsend Gilkes, "Together and in Harness: Women's Traditions in the Sanctified Churches," *Signs, Journal of Women in Culture and Society* 10, no. 41 (Summer 1985): 685.

32. Benjamin T. Moore, *A Handbook for Saints* (N.p., c. 1944), 31.

33. Darlene Clark Hine, "Rape and the Inner Lives of Black Women in the Middle West: Preliminary Thoughts on the Culture of Dissemblance," in *Unequal Sisters: A Multicultural Reader in U.S. Women's History*, ed. Ellen Carol Dubois and Vicki L. Ruiz (New York: Routledge, 1990), 292–297.

34. Butler, *Women in the Church of God in Christ*, 46–47.

35. Butler, *Women in the Church of God in Christ*, 47.

36. CPleas, *Fifty Years Achievement*, 25.

37. Jerry R. Ramsey III, *Year Book of the Church of God in Christ For the Year 1926* (Memphis: Church of God in Christ Publishing, 1926), 148.

38. Pleas, *Fifty Years Achievement*, 25–28.

39. Williams, *Black Americans*, 107; *Voice of Missions* (September 1, 1899): 4.

40. Pleas, *Fifty Years Achievement*, 27–28; Higginbotham, *Righteous Discontent*, 34.

41. Pleas, *Fifty Years Achievement*, 26.

42. Hunter, *To 'Joy My Freedom*, 168.

43. Hunter, *To 'Joy My Freedom*, 175.

44. Leonard Lovett, "Black Holiness-Pentecostalism, Implications for Ethics and Social Transformation" (Unpublished Ph.D. diss., Emory University, 1979), 25.

45. German Ross, *History and Formative Years of the Church of God in Christ* (Memphis: Church of God in Christ Publishing House, 1969), 69. Also see Lovett, "Black Holiness-Pentecostalism," 25–26; Tucker, *Black Pastors and Leaders*, 93.

46. Pleas, *Fifty Years Achievement*, 26.

47. Pleas, *Fifty Years Achievement*, 26–27.
48. Pleas, *Fifty Years Achievement*, 27–28.
49. Pleas, *Fifty Years Achievement*, 29.
50. Pleas, *Fifty Years Achievement* 29.
51. Pleas, *Fifty Years Achievement*, 29–30.
52. Pleas, *Fifty Years Achievement*, 25.
53. Pleas, *Fifty Years Achievement*, 30.
54. Pleas, *Fifty Years Achievement*, 30.
55. For more information on the island nation of Jamaica, see J. Mursell Phillippo, *Jamaica: Its Past and Present State* (London: Dawson Publishing, 1969).
56. Pleas, *Fifty Years Achievement*, 31.

5. Memphis, the Hope of a Promised Land

1. Emmett J. Scott, *Negro Migration during the War* (New York: Oxford University Press, 1920), 18–19.
2. Scott, *Negro Migration during the War,* 24.
3. Scott, *Negro Migration during the War,* 31.
4. Mary Mangum Johnson, *The Life and Works of Mother Mary Mangum Johnson: Founders of the Church of God in Christ in the state of Michigan* (Detroit, Mich.: published privately by Johnson/Barber, 1936), 9; *Historic Moments in Northeast Michigan,* The Diamond Jubilee Year Book, 1914–1989; Clemmons, *Bishop C. H. Mason,* 85–86; Butler, *Women in the Church of God in Christ,* 60–67.
5. Johnson, *The Life and Works of Mother Mary Mangum Johnson,* 10.
6. Johnson, *The Life and Works of Mother Mary Mangum Johnson,* 12–13.
7. Johnson, *The Life and Works of Mother Mary Mangum Johnson,* 12–13
8. Johnson, *The Life and Works of Mother Mary Mangum Johnson,* 19–22.
9. Laurie B. Green, "Battling the 'Plantation Mentality': Race, Gender and Freedom in Memphis during the Civil Rights Era" (Ph.D. Diss., University of Chicago, 1999), 12; Hunter, in *To 'Joy My Freedom,* makes a similar observation about Atlanta after the Civil War. Hunter argues that blacks in Atlanta had great hope about their future even though they had to overcome racism and cultural obstacles before they would enjoy full citizenship.
10. Biles, *Memphis in the Great Depression* (Knoxville: University of Tennessee Press, 1986), 19; William D. Miller, *Mr. Crump of Memphis* (Baton Rouge: Louisiana State University Press, 1964), 202.
11. Biles, *Memphis in the Great Depression,* 32–33; David M. Tucker, *Memphis since Crump: Bossism, Blacks and Civic Reformers, 1948–1968* (Knoxville: University of Tennessee Press, 1980), 23–25.
12. Miller, *Mr. Crump of Memphis,* 79.
13. Miller, *Mr. Crump of Memphis,* 77.
14. Tucker, *Memphis since Crump,* 19.
15. Biles, *Memphis in the Great Depression,* 26; *Commercial Appeal,* July 22, 1925.
16. Patricia A. Schechter, *Ida B. Wells Barnett and American Reform, 1880–1930* (Chapel Hill: University of North Carolina, 2001), 7.
17. Laurie B. Green, "Battling the 'Plantation Mentality': Race, Gender and

Freedom in Memphis during the Civil Rights Era" (Ph.D. Diss., University of Chicago, 1999), 23.

18. Green, "Battling the 'Plantation Mentality,'" 22–24. Susie Bryant's account can also be found in Behind the Veil: Documenting African American Life in the Jim Crow South Collection, Center for Documentary Studies, Special Collections, Duke University, Durham.

19. Green, "Battling the 'Plantation Mentality,'" 65–66.

20. Green, "Battling the 'Plantation Mentality,'" 65–66.

21. Green, "Battling the 'Plantation Mentality,'" 68–69.

22. Green, "Battling the 'Plantation Mentality," 68–69.

23. Biles, *Memphis in the Great Depression*, 90.

24. Wailoo, *Dying in the City of the Blues*, 54–70.

25. Author unknown, *Church of God In Christ: The Hour Glass Report Reflections of Past and Present*, 6. St. Paul Church of God in Christ, *The 1987 Year Book*, 23. Reports reveal that the structure was painted gray with two bathrooms and a very small space for worship.

26. Tucker, *Black Pastor and Leaders*, 97; *Commercial Appeal*, December 5, 1917.

27. Tucker, *Memphis since Crump*, 16.

28. Tucker, *Memphis since Crump*, 16. G. P. Hamilton, *The Brighter Side of Memphis* (Memphis: G. P. Hamilton, 1908), 17. Hamilton shows that the two main black societal organizations in the 1920s were the Primrose Club and the Toxoway Tennis Club. Once a year the organizations hired the riverboat steamer *Charles Organ* for riverboat parties where W. C. Handy provided the music for scripted dances.

29. Tucker, *Black Pastors and Leaders*, 73–75. For more information on Griggs, please see Finnie D. Coleman, *Sutton E. Griggs and the Struggle against White Supremacy* (Knoxville: University of Tennessee Press, 2007); Sutton E. Griggs, *The Story of My Struggles* (Memphis: National Public Welfare League, 1914), 8–10; Sutton E. Griggs, *Guide to Racial Greatness or the Science of Collective Efficiency* (Memphis: National Public Welfare League, 1923), 209.

30. Tucker, *Black Pastors and Leaders*, 75 and 79.

31. Tucker, *Black Pastors and Leaders*, 82.

32. Tucker, *Black Pastors and Leaders*, 79.

33. Quote taken from Tucker, *Black Pastors and Leaders*; Vittorio Lanterari, *The Religion of the Oppressed: A Study of Modern Messianic Cults* (New York: Knopf, 1963), 4.

34. Tucker, *Black Pastors and Leaders*, 87.

35. Synan, *The Holiness Pentecostal Movement*, 144.

36. Hunter, *To Joy My Freedom*, 69.

37. Quoted in Weavers, "The Metamorphosis of Charles Harrison Mason," 46; Tucker, *Black Pastors and Leaders*, 91–92.

38. Lipford, "Sanctifying the Unholy," 43; Synan, *The Holiness Pentecostal Movement*, 144; Zora Neale Hurston, *The Sanctified Church: The Folklore Writings of Zora Neale Hurston* (Berkeley: Turtle Island Press, 1923), 103.

39. Tucker, *Black Pastors and Leaders*, 99.

40. Biles, *Memphis in the Great Depression*, 52; *Commercial Appeal*, October 30, 1930.

41. Biles, *Memphis in the Great Depression*, 52. During the first year of the depression few businesses failed and unemployment remained low in Memphis—2.8 percent for whites and 3.5 for blacks.

42. Biles, *Memphis in the Great Depression*, 52–53; Thomas H. Baker, *The Memphis Commercial Appeal* (Baton Rouge: Louisiana State University Press, 1971), 282.

43. Biles, *Memphis in the Great Depression*, 90–92; Leigh D. Fraser, "A Demographic Analysis of Memphis and Shelby County, Tennessee, 1820–1972" (M.A. thesis, Memphis State University, 1974), 10–18.

44. T. O. Fuller, *Pictorial History of the American Negro* (Memphis: Pictorial History, 1933), 72; Tucker, *Black Pastors and Leaders*, 99.

45. L. A. Berry, "Mario, Ark, Testimony," *Whole Truth* 7, no. 10 (October 1931): 4.

46. Elder E. B. Stewart, "Testimony," *Whole Truth* 8, no. 7 (August 1932): 6.

47. *Whole Truth* 10, no. 1 (February 1934): 8.

48. *Press Scimitar*, March 2, 1935; also quoted in Biles, *Memphis in the Great Depression*, 88.

49. *Press Scimitar*, December 8, 1936.

50. *Press Scimitar,* December 8, 1936. The same article quoted Bishop Mason as saying, "The tabernacle on Fifth Street was built in 1924 at a cost of $20,000."

51. *Press Scimitar*, December 8, 1936.

52. Biles, *Memphis in the Great Depression*, 66–67.

53. Biles, *Memphis in the Great Depression*, 67.

54. *Press Scimitar*, May 5, 1937.

55. *Press Scimitar,* May 5, 1937.

56. *Commercial Appeal*, May 10, 1937.

57. *Press Scimitar*, May 5, 1937.

58. St Paul Church of God in Christ, *The 1987 Annual Year Book.*

59. Author unknown, *The Church of God in Christ: The Hour Glass Report: Reflections of Past and Present*, 16.

60. Clements, *The Presidency of Woodrow Wilson*, 37.

61. Rev. James L. Delk, *He Made Millions of People Happy* (N.p., 1944), 28.

62. Delk, *He Made Millions of People Happy*, 3 and 6–7. Delk personally knew Senator Alben W. Barkley and Senator Harry S. Truman, both from Missouri; and Senator Tom Stewart and Senator K. D. McKeller, both of Tennessee; and Senator Happy Chandler of Kentucky. Delk also mentioned in Ithiel C. Clemmons, *Bishop C. H. Mason*, 23.

63. Delk, *He Made Millions of People Happy*, 16.

64. Delk, *He Made Millions of People Happy*, 16

65. Delk, *He Made Millions of People Happy*, 18.

66. Delk, *He Made Millions of People Happy*, 20.

67. *Press Scimitar*, October 20, 1944. Actual financial reports stated that, in 1941, COGIC raised $23,751.51; in 1942, $20,110.02; in 1943, $42,069.00; and in 1944, $21,555.80. According to COGIC financial records, the total cost of Mason Temple was $207,323.06.

68. *Chattanooga Times*, October 11, 1944.

69. *Church of God in Christ The Hour Glass Report: Reflections of Past and Present,* 13; Walter Chandler to Bishop Charles H. Mason, October 12, 1945.

70. *Commercial Appeal,* December 11, 1945; *Church of God in Christ The Hour Glass Report: Reflections of Past and Present,* 6.

71. *Commercial Appeal,* December 11, 1945; *Church of God in Christ The Hour Glass Report: Reflections of Past and Present,* 8–9.

6. "Dar He"

1. The chapter title here reflects those words remembered in history as the broken English Mose "Preacher" Wright used in court to identify one of the men who took Emmett L. Till from his home.

2. *Chicago Defender,* September 3, 1955.

3. *Chicago Defender,* September 3, 1955.

4. *Chicago Defender,* September 3, 1955.

5. *Chicago Defender,* September 3, 1955. Accounts in the *Chicago Defender* show that Thelton Parke, 19; Maurice Wright, 16; Simeon Wright, and Ruth Mae Crawford, 18 all residents of Money were present that day.

6. *Chicago Defender,* September 3, 1955.

7. *Chicago Defender,* September 3, 1955; for more detailed accounts of the events of that night, see Hudson-Weems, *Emmett Till,* and Simeon Wright, *Simeon's Story: An Eyewitness Account to the Kidnapping of Emmett Till* (Chicago: Lawrence Hill Books, 2010).

8. Charles F. Robinson, *Dangerous Liaisons: Sex and Love in the Segregated South* (Fayetteville: University of Arkansas Press, 2003), 75–76.

9. *Chicago Defender,* September 10, 1955.

10. *Chicago Defender,* September 10, 1955.

11. *Chicago Defender,* September 10, 1955.

12. *Chicago Defender,* September 17, 1955.

13. *Chicago Defender,* September 15, 1955.

14. *Chicago Defender,* September 17, 1955.

15. *Chicago Defender,* September 24, 1955.

16. Hudson-Weems, *Emmett Till,* 31. Also see Mary E. Abrums, *Moving the Rock: Poverty and Faith in a Black Storefront Church* (Lanham, Md.: AltaMira Press, 2010).

17. *Chicago Defender,* September 10, 1955.

18. Preliminary Landmark Report for Roberts Temple Church of God in Christ, November 3, 2005, 13.

19. Hudson-Weems, *Emmett Till,* 8–11.

20. Author unknown, *COGIC Heroes of Faith: William Roberts 1876–1954* (Published privately), 3.

21. *Chicago Defender,* September 10, 1955.

22. *Chicago Defender,* September 10, 1955.

23. *Chicago Defender,* September 10, 1955.

24. *Chicago Defender,* September 10, 1955.

25. For more information on the civil rights and religious and economic

motivations, see Charles Marsh, *God Long Summer: Stories of Faith and Civil Rights* (Princeton, N.J.: Princeton University Press, 1997). In Marsh's book he discusses the economic pressure that the landowner placed upon Fannie Lou Hamer, who wanted to register to vote. She would later be evicted because of her civil rights activities. Also, he explains why Douglass Hudgins remained quiet out of economic fear that his congregation would replace him if he supported any aspect of the movement.

26. *Chicago Defender*, September 17, 1955.

27. *Chicago Defender*, September 17, 1955.

28. *Chicago Defender*, September 17, 1955.

29. *Chicago Defender,* September 24, 1955.

30. *Chicago Defender*, September 17, 1955.

31. *Chicago Defender*, October 15, 1955.

32. Hudson-Weems, *Emmett Till,* 102–105.

33. Hudson-Weems, *Emmett Till,* 105.

34. *Chicago Defender*, November 26, 1955.

35. *Chicago Defender*, November 26, 1955.

36. Quote take from Stephen J. Whitfield, *A Death in the Delta: The Story of Emmett Till* (Baltimore: Johns Hopkins University Press, 1991), 89; Harvard Sitkoff, *The Struggle for Black Equality* (New York: Hill and Wang Publishing, 1993), 44.

37. Whitfield, *A Death in the Delta,* 92.

38. Whitfield, *A Death in the Delta,* 95.

39. Jennie Brown, *Medgar Evers* (Los Angles: Melrose Square Publishing Company, 1994), 25. For more information on Medgar Evers, see Myrlie Evers-Williams and Manning Marable, *The Autobiography of Medgar Evers: A Hero's Life and Legacy Revealed Through His Writings Letters and Speeches* (New York: Civitas Books, 2005), and Salter, *Jackson, Mississippi.*

40. Brown, *Medgar Evers,* 25–28.

41. Brown, *Medgar Evers,* 30–31.

42. Brown, *Medgar Evers,* 31.

43. Interview with Michael Williams, August 1, 2010.

44. Jack Mendelsohn, *The Martyrs: Sixteen Who Gave Their Lives for Racial Justice* (New York: Harper Publishing, 1966), 65.

45. Mendelsohn, *The Martyrs,* 65.

46. Brown, *Medgar Evers,* 22; Michael Williams, *Medgar Evers: Mississippi Martyr* (Fayetteville: University of Arkansas Press, 2011), 3–4. Also see Maryanne Vollers, *Ghost of Mississippi: The Murder of Medgar Evers, the Trial of Bryon De La Beckwith, and the Hunting of the New South* (Canada: Little, Brown, and Company, 1995).

47. Phrase used by Michael Williams and also title of his recent biography on Evers.

48. For more information about the life of Malcolm X, see Alex Haley, *The Autobiography of Malcolm X* (New York: Random House, 1967) and Robert E. Terill, *The Cambridge Companion to Malcolm X* (New York: Cambridge University Press, 2010).

49. Allison S. Draper, *The Assassination of Malcolm X* (New York: Rosen Publishing Group, 2002), 9–13.

50. For more information about religion and its role in the civil rights movement, see Carson, *God's Long Summer.*

51. http://www.childesmemorialtemple.com/history.html.

52. http://www.childesmemorialtemple.com/history.html.

53. http://www.childesmemorialtemple.com/history.html.

54. Michael Honey, *Going Down Jericho Road: The Memphis Strike, Martin Luther King's Last Campaign* (New York: W. W. Norton and Company, 2007), 50–52. For information on the Memphis Sanitation Strike, see David Garrow, *Bearing the Cross* (Norwalk, Conn.: Easton Press, 1986); Selma Lewis, "Southern Religion and the Memphis Sanitation Strike" (Ph.D. diss., University of Memphis, 1976).

55. Honey, *Going Down Jericho Road,* 56.

56. Honey, *Going Down Jericho Road,* 57, 305.

57. Honey, *Going Down Jericho Road,* 141, 142.

58. Honey, *Going Down Jericho Road,* 149.

59. Honey, *Going Down Jericho Road,* 292.

60. Honey, *Going Down Jericho Road,* 297.

61. Honey, *Going Down Jericho Road,* 345–62.

62. Honey, *Going Down Jericho Road,* 415–416, also see Gerald Posner, *Killing the Dream: James Earl Ray and the Assassination of Martin Luther King, Jr.* (New York: Random House, 1998), and "Mountaintop Speech," Mason Temple, Memphis, Tennessee, April 3, 1968.

63. Honey, *Going Down Jericho Road,* 485.

Afterword

1. Clemmons, *Bishop C. H. Mason,* 125; Weavers, "The Metamorphosis of Charles Harrison Mason," 50; *Press Scimitar,* November 25, 1961.

2. Clemmons, *Bishop C. H. Mason,* 126. Clemmons disagrees that this was a period of wondering, but I assert in this afterword that it in fact was because the denomination struggled to find direction with each change in leadership.

3. The five-man commission was composed of Bishops A. B. McEwen, J. O. Patterson Sr., U. E. Miller, S. M. Crouch, and O. T. Jones.

4. *The Official Quarterly Guide Senior YPWW* 38–39; *The Hour Glass Report: Reflection of the Past and Present* 26.

5. *The Official Quarterly Guide Senior YPWW,* 39–40; *The Hour Glass Report,* 26–27; Clemmons, *Bishop C. H. Mason,* 125–126.

6. *The Hour Glass Report,* 27.

7. *The Hour Glass Report,* 27.

8. *The Hour Glass Report,* 27.

9. *The Hour Glass Report,* 27.

10. Honey, *Going Down Jericho Road,* 49.

11. Clemmons, *Bishop C. H. Mason,* 127. For more on the life and works of Dr. Martin Luther King Jr., see Garrow, *Bearing the Cross.*

12. Clemmons, *Bishop C. H. Mason,* 127.

13. *The Hour Glass Report,* 30.

14. *The Official Quarterly Guide Senior YPWW,* 45.

15. *The Official Quarterly Guide Senior YPWW,* 47–48.

16. Clemmons, *Bishop C. H. Mason,* 130.

17. Clemmons, *Bishop C. H. Mason,* 131.

18. Clemmons, *Bishop C. H. Mason,* 133.
19. Clemmons, *Bishop C. H. Mason,* 133.
20. *The Official Quarterly Guide Senior YPWW,* 50.
21. Clemmons, *Bishop C. H. Mason,* 133.
22. *Charisma Magazine,* November 2000.
23. *The Official Quarterly Guide Senior YPWW,* 52.
24. *The Official Quarterly Guide Senior YPWW,* 53–54.

Bibliography

Archival Sources

Alexander and Shirlene Stewart Pentecostal Personal Collection, 1925–1993.
The Arkansas Historical Commission (Little Rock, Arkansas)
> Arkansas Baptist College Papers.
The Flowers Heritage Pentecostal Center (Springfield, Missouri)
> The Black Southern Holiness Collection.
Memphis-Shelby County Public Library, Memphis Room (Memphis, Tennessee)
> Clippings File—Black Churches.
Mississippi Department of Archives and History (Jackson, Mississippi)
> The Mississippi Department of Archives and History. "Works Progress Administration Records," Record Group 60, Jackson, Mississippi, J. W. Lowen and Charles Sallis, eds.
The Schomburg Center for Research in Black Culture (New York, New York)
> The Sherry Dupree African American Pentecostal and Holiness Collection, 1876–1989.
The University of Memphis Special Collection Room (Memphis, Tennessee)
> The Charles H. Mason and the Church of God in Christ Collection.

Government Documents

BOI Reports on the investigation of Charles H. Mason: The Church of God in Christ and other religious dissenters of World War I, 1917–1918.
The City of Chicago. Preliminary Landmark Report for Roberts Temple Church of God in Christ, November 3, 2005.
Historical Census Browser. http://fisher.lib.virginia.edu/collections/stats/histcensus/index.html.

Church of God in Christ Primary Sources

Annual Report from the National Convocation. *The 1926 Yearbook.*
Author unknown. *COGIC Heroes of Faith: William Roberts 1876–1954.* Published privately.
Author unknown. *The Hour Glass Report: Reflections of Past and Present.* Memphis: Church of God in Christ Publishing, n.d.
Author unknown. *The Azusa Street Mission: The Greatest Pentecostal Outpouring Ever Known in the United States.* Memphis: Church of God in Christ Publishing, n.d.
The Church of God in Christ. *The Official Quarterly Guide Senior YPWW.* Memphis: Church of God in Christ Publishing, 2001.
Counts, James. *The History and Life Work of Elder C. H. Mason, Chief Apostle and His Co-Labors.* Memphis: N.p., 1919.

Delk, James. *He Made Millions of People Happy.* N.p., 1944.
"History of Saints Industrial College." *The St. Paul Eighteenth Annual Homecoming Year Book.*
Johnson, Dovie Marie. *Down Behind the Sun: The Story of Arenia C. Mallory.* Memphis: Riverside Press, 1973.
Johnson, Mary M. *The Life and Work of Mother Mary Mangum Johnson: Founder of the Church of God in Christ in the state of Michigan.* Detroit: N.p., c. 1936.
Lee, Elnora. *A Man Greatly Used by God.* N.p., 1955.
Mason, Elsie W. *The Man Charles H. Mason: Sermons of His Early Ministry.* N.p., 1979.
Mason, Mary. *The Late Apostle Speaks.* N.p., 1966.
McCoy, Eugene B. *Yes Lord.* N.p., 1922.
Moore, Benjamin T. *A Handbook for Saints.* N.p., 1944.
Pleas, Charles. *Fifty Years Achievement from 1906–1956.* Memphis: Church of God in Christ Publishing, 1956.
Ramsey, Jerry R. *Year Book of the Church of God in Christ For the Year 1926.* Memphis: Church of God in Christ Publishing, 1926.
Ross, German K. *History and Formative Years of the Church of God in Christ.* Memphis: Church of God in Christ Publishing, 1956.
Rules of Government of the Churches of God in Christ. Jackson: Published privately, 1906.
St. Paul Church of God in Christ. *The 1987 Yearbook.*

Interviews

Bryant, Susie. Interview in Behind the Veil: Documenting African American Life in the Jim Crow South Collection, Center for Documentary Studies, Special Collections, Duke University, Durham, N.C.
Dean, William Elder. Interview by author, tape recording, Lexington, Miss., October 6, 2005.
Fields, Jessie. Interview by author, tape recording, Lexington, Miss., September 13, 2005.
Johnson, Dovie Marie. Interview by author, tape recording, Lexington, Miss., October 5, 2005.
Jones, Naomi. Interview in Behind the Veil: Documenting African American Life in the Jim Crow South Collection, Center for Documentary Studies, Special Collections, Duke University, Durham, N.C.
Turner, R. Johnson. Interview in Behind the Veil: Documenting African American Life in the Jim Crow South Collection, Center for Documentary Studies, Special Collections, Duke University, Durham, N.C.
Williams, Michael. Interview by author, via telephone, Fayetteville, Ark., August 1, 2010.

Court Cases

Avant et al. v. Mason et al. Shelby County Chancery Court, 1907, Number 14777.
Mason et al. v. Avant et al. Counter Suit. Number 14777.
John A. Lee v. Charles Mason. Holmes County Chancery Court, 1908, Number 1505.

Mt. Helm Baptist Church et al. v. Charles Price Jones et al. Supreme Court of
Mississippi, 1901, Number 10041.

Newspapers and Periodicals

Apostolic Faith (Los Angeles)
Arkansas Baptist Vanguard
Arkansas Gazette
Charisma
Chattanooga Times
Chicago Defender
Christian Index
Commercial Appeal
Commonwealth
Crisis
Lexington Advertiser
Liberia Bulletin
Los Angeles Times
Post (Vicksburg)
Press Scimitar
Times-Picayune
Voices of Missions
Washington Bee
Whole Truth

Internet Sources

Documenting the American South. "The Church in the Southern Black
Community." Last modified March 9, 2012.
http://docsouth.unc.edu/church/intro.html.
The History of Faith Temple Church of God in Christ.
http://www.childesmemorialtemple.com/history.html.

Primary Book Sources

Banks, Lowell, Sr. *Historical Church of the Living God 1889–1964.* Published
privately, 1964.
Bartleman, Frank. *What Really Happened at Azusa Street?* Edited by John Walker.
Northridge, Calif.: Voice Publishers, 1962.
Boothe, Charles Octavius. *The Cyclopedia of the Colored Baptists of Alabama.*
Birmingham: Alabama Publishing Co., 1895.
Carter, Verti L. *Dr. E. C. Morris: May 1855–September 5, 1922.* Little Rock: Privately
printed, 1940.

Christian, William. *Poor Pilgrim's Work.* Texarkana, Ark.: N.p., 1916; rpt., Del City, Okla.: Model Printing Co., 1976.

Cobbins, Otha B., ed. *History of Church of Christ (Holiness) U.S.A. 1895–1965.* New York: Vantage Press, 1966.

Cole, James J. *Africa in Brief.* New York: Freeman Steam Printing Establishment, 1896.

Griggs, Sutton E. *Guide to Racial Greatness or the Science of Collective Efficiency.* Memphis: National Public Welfare League, 1923.

Griggs, Sutton E. *Light on Racial Issues.* Memphis: National Public Welfare League, 1921.

Griggs, Sutton E. *The Story of My Struggles.* Memphis: National Public Welfare League, 1914.

Hamilton, G. P. *The Brighter Side of Memphis.* Memphis: G. P. Hamilton, 1908.

Moore, Joanna P. *In Christ's Stead: Autobiographical Sketches.* Chicago: Women's Baptist Home Mission Society, n.d.

Morris, E. C. *Sanctification, Sermons, Addresses and Reminiscences.* Reprint edition. New York: Arno Press, 1980.

Parham, Charles F. *The Life of Charles F. Parham: Founder of the Apostolic Faith Movement.* Birmingham: Commercial Printing Company, 1930.

Randolph, Peter. *Slave Cabin To The Pulpit: The Autobiography of Reverend Peter Randolph.* Boston: James H. Earle, 1893.

Ridgel, Alfred L. *Africa and African Methodism.* Atlanta: Franklin Publishing Company, 1896.

Smith, Amanda (Berry). *An Autobiography: The Story of the Lord's Dealings With Mrs. Amanda Smith, The Colored Evangelist.* Chicago: Meyer & Brother, 1893.

Thompson, Patrick H. *The History of Negro Baptists in Mississippi.* Jackson, Miss.: R. W. Bailey Printing Co., 1898.

Theses and Dissertations

Brown, Gloria M. "Blacks in Memphis, Tennessee, 1920–1955: A Historical Study." Ph.D. diss., Washington State University, 1982.

Butler, Anthea. "A Peculiar Synergy: Matriarchy and the Church of God in Christ." Ph.D. diss., Vanderbilt University, 2001.

Daniel, David. "The Cultural Renewal of Slave Religion: Charles Price Jones and the Emergence of the Holiness Movement in Mississippi." Ph.D. diss., Union Theological Seminary, 1992.

Fraser, Leigh D. "A Demographic Analysis of Memphis and Shelby County, Tennessee, 1820–1972." M.A. thesis, Memphis State University, 1974.

Giggie, John. "God's Long Journey: African Americans, Religion, and History in the Mississippi Delta." Ph.D. diss., Princeton University, 1997.

Green, Laura B. "Battling the Plantation Mentality: Race, Gender and Freedom in Memphis During the Civil Rights Era." Ph.D. diss., University of Chicago, 1999.

Lewis, Selma. "Southern Religion and the Memphis Sanitation Strike." Ph.D. diss., University of Memphis, 1976.

Lovett, Leonard. "Black Holiness-Pentecostalism: Implication for Ethics and Social Transformation." Ph.D. diss., Emory University, 1979.

McDuff, Rose Marie. "The Ethnohistory of Saint's Home Church of God in Christ, Los Angeles, California." M.A. thesis, State University, Sacramento, 1973.

Peck, Lucy. "The Life and Times of James Z. George." M.A. thesis, Mississippi State University, 1964.

Shopshire, James M. "A Socio-Historical Characterization of the Black Pentecostal Movement in America." Ph.D. Diss., Northwestern University, 1975.

Tinney, James S. "Competing Theories of Historical Origins for Black Pentecostalism." Annual Meeting of the American Academy of Religion, New York City, 1979. Unpublished.

Articles

Campbell, Marne L. "'The Newest Religious Sect Has Started in Los Angeles': Race, Class, Ethnicity, and the Origins of the Pentecostal Movement, 1906–1913." *Journal of African America History* 95 (Winter 2010).

Clark, William A. "Sanctification in Negro Religion." *Social Forces* 15 (October 1936).

Dillard, Tom. "Scipio A. Jones." *Arkansas Historical Quarterly* (Winter 1972).

Fleming, Walter. "Pap Singleton, The Moses of the Colored Exodus." *American Journal of Sociology* 15, no. 1 (July 1909).

Gilks, Cheryl Townsend. "Together and in Harness: Women's Tradition in the Sanctified Church." *Signs* 10, no. 2 (Summer 1985).

Harlan, Louis R. "Booker T. Washington and the White Man's Burden." *American Historical Review* 71 (January 1967).

Kornweibel, Theodore. "Bishop C. H. Mason and the Church of God in Christ during World War I: The Perils of Conscientious Objection." *Journal of Southern Studies* (Winter 1987).

Lewis, Todd E. "Elias Camp Morris (1855–1922)." *Encyclopedia of Arkansas History and Culture*. http://encyclopediaofarkansas.net.

Lipford, Jesse E. "Sanctifying the Unholy: Black Pentecostalism, the Church of God in Christ and African American Culture." *West Tennessee Journal of History Society* 56 (Spring 2000).

Murray, Paul. "Blacks and the Draft: A History of Institutional Racism." *Journal of Black Studies* 2, no. 1 (September 1971).

Spencer, May. "Senator James Zachariah George of Mississippi: Bourbon or Liberal?" *Journal of Mississippi History* 16 (July 1954).

Weavers, Elton. "The Metamorphosis of Charles Harrison Mason: The Origins of Black Pentecostal Churches in Tennessee." *West Tennessee Journal of History Society* 56 (Spring 2000).

Secondary Works

Abrums, Mary E. *Moving the Rock: Poverty and Faith in a Black Storefront Church.* Lanham, Md.: AltaMira Press, 2010.

Alexander, Estrelda. *The Black Fire: One Hundred Years of African American Pentecostalism.* Downers Grove, Ill.: InterVarsity Press, 2011.

Anderson, Allan. *Spreading Fires: The Missionary Nature of Early Pentecostalism.* New York: Orbis Publishing, 2007.

Anderson, Jeffery. *Conjuring in African American Society.* Baton Rouge: Louisiana State University Press, 2005.

Baker, Thomas H. *The Memphis Commercial Appeal.* Baton Rouge: Louisiana State University Press, 1971.

Barnes, Kenneth. *Who Killed John Clayton? Political Violence and the Emergence of the New South, 1861–1893.* Durham, N.C.: Duke University Press, 1998.

Barnes, Kenneth. *Journey of Hope: The Back to Africa Movement in Arkansas in the Late 1800s.* Chapel Hill: University of North Carolina Press, 2004.

Biles, Roger. *Memphis in the Great Depression.* Knoxville: University of Tennessee Press, 1986.

Blassingame, John W. *The Slave Community: Plantation Life in the Antebellum South.* Revised and enlarged edition. New York: Oxford University Press, 1979.

Brown, Jennie. *Medgar Evers.* Los Angeles: Melrose Square Publishing Company, 1994.

Butler, Anthea D. *Women and the Church of God in Christ: Making a Sanctified World.* Chapel Hill: University of North Carolina Press, 2007.

Byerly, Carol R. *Fever of War: The Influenza Epidemic in the U.S. Army during World War I.* New York: New York University Press, 2005.

Chireau, Yvonne. *Black Magic: Religion and the African American Conjuring Tradition.* Berkeley and Los Angeles: University of California Press, 2003.

Clements, Kendrick. *The Presidency of Woodrow Wilson.* Lawrence: University Press of Kansas, 1992.

Clemmons, Ithiel. *Bishop C. H. Mason and the Roots of the Church of God in Christ: Centennial Edition.* Memphis: Church of God in Christ Publishing, 2001.

Cohen, William. *At Freedom's Edge: Black Mobility and the Southern White Quest for Racial Control.* Baton Rouge: Louisiana State University Press, 1991.

Coleman, Finnie D. *Sutton E. Griggs and the Struggle against White Supremacy.* Knoxville: University of Tennessee Press, 2007.

Crawford, Charles W. *Yesterday's Memphis.* Miami, Fla.: E. A. Seemann Publishing, 1976.

Davies, Ronald. *Good and Faithful Labor: From Slavery to Sharecropping in the Natchez District.* Westport, Conn.: Greenwood Press, 1982.

Draper, Allison S. *The Assassination of Malcolm X.* New York: Rosen Publishing Group, 2002.

Dubois, Ellen Carol, and Vicki L. Ruiz. *Unequal Sister: A Multicultural Reader in U.S. Women's History.* New York: Routledge, 1990.

Du Bois, William Edward Burghardt. *The Negro Church.* Atlanta: Atlanta University Press, 1903.

Dupree, Sherry Sherrod. *African-American Holiness Pentecostal Movement: An Annotated Bibliography.* New York: Garland Publishers, 1996.

Evers-Williams, Myrlie, and Manning Marable. *The Autobiography of Medgar Evers: A Hero's Life and Legacy Revealed Through His Writings Letters and Speeches.* New York: Civitas Books, 2005.

Fett, Sharla M. *Working Cures, Healing, Health, and Power on Southern Slave Plantations.* Chapel Hill: University of North Carolina Press, 2002.

Fisher, H. L. *The History of the United Holy Church of America Inc.* N.p.: c. 1944.

Fleming, Walter L. *Documentary History of Reconstruction: Political Military, Social,*

Religious, Educational, and Industrial, 1865–1906. New York: McGraw Hill Book Company, 1966.

Foner, Eric. *Reconstruction, 1863–1877*. New York: Harper & Row, 1988.

Franklin, John H. *From Slavery to Freedom: A History of African American Freedom*. New York: McGraw Hill, 2000.

Frazier, E. Franklin. *The Negro Church*. New York: Schoken Books, 1964.

Frey, Sylvia R. *Come Shouting to Zion*. Chapel Hill: University of North Carolina Press, 1998.

Fuller, T. O. *Pictorial History of the American Negro*. Memphis: Pictorial History, 1933.

Garrow, David J. *Bearing the Cross: Martin Luther King, Jr., and the Southern Christian Leadership Conference*. Norwalk, Conn.: Easton Press, 1986.

Gatewood, Willard B. *Aristocrats of Color*. Bloomington: University of Indiana Press, 1990.

Genovese, Eugene D. *Roll, Jordan, Roll: The World the Slaves Made*. New York: Pantheon Books, 1974.

Giddings, Paula. *When and Where I Enter: The Impact of Black Women on Race and Sex in America*. New York: Bantam Books, 1984.

Giggie, John M. *After Redemption: Jim Crow and the Transformation of African American Religion in the Delta, 1875–1915*. New York: Oxford University Press, 2008.

Gilmore, Glenda. *Gender and Jim Crow*. Chapel Hill: University of North Carolina Press, 1996.

Goff, James, and Grant Wacker. *Portraits of a Generation: Early Pentecostal Leaders*. Fayetteville: University of Arkansas Press, 2002.

Gottlieb, Peter. *Making Their Own Way: Southern Blacks' Migration to Pittsburgh, 1916 to 1930*. Urbana: University of Illinois Press, 1987.

Gregory, James N. *The Southern Diaspora: How the Great Migration of Black and White Southerners Transformed America*. Chapel Hill: University of North Carolina Press, 2005.

Haley, Alex. *The Autobiography of Malcolm X*. New York: Random House, 1967.

Harvey, Paul. *Redeeming the South: Religious Cultures and Racial Identities among Southern Baptists, 1865–1925*. Chapel Hill: University of North Carolina Press, 1997.

Harvey, Paul. *Freedom's Coming: Religious Culture and the Shaping of the South from the Civil War through the Civil Rights Era*. Chapel Hill: University of North Carolina Press, 2005.

Henri, Florette. *Black Migration: Movement North, 1900–1920*. Garden City, N.Y.: Anchor Press, 1975.

Herskovits, Melville J. *Cultural Relativism*. New York: Vintage Books, 1972.

Higginbotham, Evelyn Brooks. *Righteous Discontent: Women's Movement in the Black Church, 1880–1920*. Cambridge, Mass.: Harvard University Press, 1986.

Hill, Elijah L. *Women Come Alive*. Arlington, Tex.: Perfecting the Kingdom Press, 2005.

Holmes, William. *The White Chief: James K. Vardaman in Mississippi Politics*. Baton Rouge: Louisiana State University Press, 1970.

Honey, Michael A. *Going Down Jericho Road: The Memphis Strike, Martin Luther King's Last Campaign*. New York: W. W. Norton & Company Press, 2007.

Hudson-Weems, Clenora. *Emmett Till: The Sacrificial Lamb of the Civil Rights Movement.* Bloomington: Parity Press, 2000.

Hunter, Tera. *To 'Joy My Freedom: Southern Black Women's Lives and Labor after the Civil War.* Cambridge, Mass.: Harvard University Press, 1997.

Hurston, Zora Neale. *The Sanctified Church.* Berkeley: Turtle Island, 1981.

Hurt, Douglass R. *African American Life in the Rural South, 1900–1950.* Columbia: University of Missouri Press, 2003.

Jackson, Jerma. *Singing in My Soul: Black Gospel Music in a Secular Age.* Chapel Hill: University of North Carolina Press, 2004.

Jacobs, Sylvia M. *Black Americans and the Missionary Movement in Africa.* Westport, Conn.: Greenwood Press, 1982.

Jaynes, Gerald D. *Branches Without Roots: Genesis of the Black Working Class.* New York: Oxford University Press, 1985.

Jones, Beverly Washington. *Quest for Equality: The Life and Writings of Mary Eliza Church Terrell, 1863–1954.* New York: Carlson Publishing, 1990.

Keith, Jeanette. *Rich Man's War, Poor Man's Fight.* Chapel Hill: University of North Carolina Press, 2004.

Kennedy, David M. *Over Here: The First World War and American Society.* New York: Oxford University Press, 1980.

Kornweibel, Theodore. *"Investigate Everything": Federal Effort to Ensure Black Loyalty during World War I.* Bloomington: University of Indiana Press, 2002.

Lanterari, Vittorio. *The Religion of the Oppressed: A Study of Modern Messianic Cults.* New York: Knopf Publishing, 1963.

Leman, Nicholas. *The Promised Land: The Great Black Migration and How It Changed America.* New York: Alfred A. Knopf Publishing, 1991.

Levine, Lawrence W. *Black Culture and Black Consciousness: Afro-American Folk Thought from Slavery to Freedom.* New York: Oxford University Press, 1977.

Lindner, Eileen W. *Yearbook of American and Canadian Churches.* Nashville: Abingdon Press, 2001.

Little, Arthur W. *From Harlem to the Rhine.* New York: Covici Publishers, 1936.

Litwack, Leon F. *Trouble in the Mind: Black Southerners in the Age of Jim Crow.* New York: Alfred A. Knopf Publishing, 1998.

Maffly-Kipp, Laurie. *An Introduction to the Church in the Southern Black Community.* Chapel Hill: University of North Carolina Press, 2001.

Marsh, Charles. *God's Long Summer: Stories of Faith and Civil Rights.* Princeton, N.J.: Princeton University Press, 1997.

Mathews, Donald G. *Religion in the Old South.* Chicago: University of Chicago Press, 1977.

McMillen, Neil R. *Dark Journeys: Black Mississippians in the Age of Jim Crow.* Urbana: University of Illinois Press, 1989.

Meier, August. *Negro Thought in America, 1880–1915: Racial Ideologies in the Age of Booker T. Washington.* Ann Arbor: University of Michigan Press, 1963.

Mendelsohn, Jack. *The Martyrs: Sixteen Who Gave Their Lives for Racial Justice.* New York: Harper Publishing, 1966.

Miller, William D. *Mr. Crump of Memphis.* Baton Rouge: Louisiana State University Press, 1964.

Montgomery, William E. *Under Their Own Vine and Fig Tree: The African-*

American Church in the South, 1865–1900. Baton Rouge: Louisiana State University Press, 1993.

Mursell, Phillippo J. *Jamaica: Its Past and Present State.* London: Dawson Publishing, 1969.

Ofele, Martin W. *German Speaking Officers and the U.S. Colored Troops, 1863–1867.* Gainesville: University of Florida Press, 2004.

Osborn, George C. *James Kimble Vardaman, a Southern Commoner.* Jackson, Miss.: Hederman Brothers Publishing, 1984.

Painter, Nell Irvin. *Exoduster: Black Migration to Kansas after the Civil War.* Lawrence: University Press of Kansas, 1986.

Parham, Mrs. Charles F. *The Life of Charles F. Parham: Founder of the Apostolic Faith Movement.* Birmingham: Commercial Printing Company, 1930.

Paris, Arthur E. *Black Pentecostalism: Southern Religion in an Urban World.* Amherst: University of Massachusetts Press, 1982.

Parish, Arlyn J. *Kansas Mennonites during World War I.* Fort Hayes: Kansas State College Press, 1968.

Parish, Arlyn J. "Kansas Mennonites During World War I." *Fort Hays Studies* no. 4 (May 1968): 7.

Posner, Gerald. *Killing the Dream: James Earl Ray and the Assassination of Martin Luther King, Jr.* New York: Random House, 1998.

Raboteau, Albert J. *Slave Religion: The Invisible Institution in the Antebellum South.* New York: Oxford University Press, 1978.

Ransom, Roger L., and Richard Sutch. *One Kind of Freedom: The Economic Consequences of Emancipation.* Cambridge, U.K.: Cambridge University Press, 1977.

Redkey, Edwin S. *Black Exodus Black Nationalist and the Back to Africa Movement, 1890–1910.* New Haven, Conn.: Yale University Press, 1969.

Reed, Teresa L. *The Holy Profane: Religion in Black Popular Music.* Lexington: University Press of Kentucky, 2003.

Robinson, Charles F. *Dangerous Liaisons: Sex and Love in the Segregated South.* Fayetteville: University of Arkansas Press, 2003.

Rose, Delbert R. *A Theology of Christian Experience.* Minneapolis: Bethany Fellowship, 1965.

Ross, Stewart H. *Propaganda for War: How the United States Was Conditioned to Fight the Great War of 1914–1918.* Jefferson, N.C.: McFarland & Company, 1996.

Salter, John R. *Jackson, Mississippi: An American Chronicle of Struggle and Schism.* Hicksville, Miss.: Exposition Press, c. 1979.

Sanders, Cheryl J. *Saints in Exile: The Holiness-Pentecostal Experience in African American Religion and Culture.* New York: Oxford University Press, 1996.

Sanders, Cheryl J. *The Holiness-Pentecostal Experience in African American Religion and Tradition.* New York: Oxford University Press, 1996.

Schechter, Patricia A. *Ida B. Wells Barnett and American Reform, 1880–1930.* Chapel Hill: University of North Carolina Press, 2001.

Scott, Emmett J. *Negro Migration during the War.* New York: Oxford University Press, 1920.

Sernett, Milton C. *African American Religious History Documentary.* Durham, N.C.: Duke University Press, 1999.

Sitkoff, Harvard. *The Struggle for Black Equality*. New York: Hill and Wang Publishing, 1993.

Stephens, Randall J. *The Fire Spreads: Holiness and Pentecostalism in the American South*. Cambridge, Mass.: Harvard University Press, 2008.

Stuckey, Sterling. *Slave Culture: Nationalist Theory and the Foundation of Black America*. New York: Oxford University Press, 1987.

Sweeny, William A. *History of the African American Negro in the Great World War*. New York: Johnson Reprinting Company, 1970.

Synan, Harold V. *Aspects of Pentecostal Origins*. Plainfield, N.J.: Logos International, 1975.

Synan, Harold V. *The Holiness-Pentecostal Movement in the United States*. Grand Rapids: William B. Eerdmans, 1971.

Terill, Robert E. *The Cambridge Companion to Malcolm X*. New York: Cambridge University Press, 2010.

Terrell, Mary C. *A Colored Woman in a White World*. Washington, D.C.: Ransdall, 1940.

Thompson, Patrick. *History of the Negro Baptist in Mississippi*. Jackson, Miss.: R. W. Bailey, 1899.

Tindall, George B. *The Emergence of the New South, 1913–1945*. Baton Rouge: Louisiana State University Press, 1967.

Tucker, David M. *Black Pastors and Leaders: Memphis, 1819–1972*. Memphis: Memphis State University Press, 1975.

Tucker, David M. *Since Crump: Bossism, Blacks and Civic Reformers, 1948–1968*. Knoxville: University of Tennessee Press, 1980.

Vollers, Maryanne. *Ghost of Mississippi: The Murder of Medgar Evers, the Trial of Bryon De La Beckwith, and the Haunting of the New South*. Canada: Little, Brown, and Company, 1995.

Wacker, Grant. *Heaven Below: Early Pentecostals and American Culture*. Cambridge, Mass.: Harvard University Press, 2001.

Wailoo, Keith. *Dying in the City of Blues: Sickle Cell Anemia and the Politics of Race and Health*. Chapel Hill: University of North Carolina Press, 2001.

Washington, Booker T. *Up From Slavery: An Autobiography By Booker T. Washington*. New York: Bantam Books, 1901.

Washington, James Melvin. *Frustrated Fellowship: The Black Baptist Quest for Social Power*. Macon, Ga.: Mercer Press, 1986.

Waskow, Arthur I. *From Race Riot to Sit-In*. Garden City, N.Y.: Doubleday and Company, 1965.

Whalan, Mark. *The Great War and the Culture of the New Negro*. Gainesville: University of Florida Press, 2008.

Wharton, Vernon Lane. *The Negro in Mississippi, 1865–1890*. 1947; rpt., New York: Harper Torchbooks, 1965.

Whitfield, Stephen J. *A Death in the Delta: The Story of Emmett Till*. Baltimore: Johns Hopkins University Press, 1991.

Wiley, Bell I. *Slaves No More: Letters from Liberia, 1833–1869*. Lexington: University Press of Kentucky, 1979.

Williams, Michael. *Medgar Evers: Mississippi Martyr*. Fayetteville: University of Arkansas Press, 2011.

Williams, Walter L. *Black America and the Evangelization of Africa, 1877–1900.* Madison: University of Wisconsin Press, 1982.

Wilmore, Gayraud. *Black Religion and Black Radicalism: An Interpretation of the Religious History of Afro-American People.* 2nd ed. Maryknoll: Orbis Press, 1983.

Woodson, Carter G. *A Century of Negro Migration.* Washington, D.C.: Institution for the Study of Negro Life and History, 1918.

Woodson, Carter G. *A History of the Negro Church.* Washington, D.C.: Associated Publishers, 1945.

Wright, Simeon. *Simeon's Story: An Eyewitness Account to the Kidnapping of Emmett Till.* Chicago: Lawrence Hill Books, 2010.

Index

Synan, Vinson, 8

Tabernacle Baptist Church, 102, 104
Tabernacle Missionary Baptist Church, 20
Tallahatchie River, 114
Taylor, Alex, 153n65
Taylor, Amanda, 148n64
Taylor, Elizabeth, 148n64
Taylor, Gardner, 129
Taylor, Mamie, 148n64
Taylor, W. H., 109
Taylor, William J., 26
Temple of Deliverance the Cathedral of
    Bountiful Blessing, 136
Temple University, 131
Tennessee: black Holiness movement, 29,
    44, 47–48; Holiness-Pentecostal move-
    ment, 40–41; slavery, 11, 12. *See also*
    Memphis, Tennessee; *specific place*
tent revival meetings, 36
Terrell, Mary Church, 84
third blessing, 33, 39
Thomas, Julia, 148n64
Thomas, Sara, 148n64
Thompson, George, 148n64
Thompson, William C., 71, 74–75
Thurman, Leticia, 145n77
Thurman, William, 64
Thurmond, Cornelius, 145n77
Thurmond, William, 145n77
Till, Emmett Louis, 8, 114–22, 134
Tillman, Benjamin Ryan, 115
Tingle, Willie, 123
Topeka, Kansas, 32
Townsend, James, 78
Toxoway Tennis Club, 157n28
Trinidad, 92
Tri-State Iron Company, 109, 110
Troop E (black cavalry), 60
Truman, Harry S., 158n62
Truth, 24, 47
Tubake, Liberia, 90
Tucker, David, 103–4
Tulsa, Oklahoma, 92
Turks Islands, 92
Turley, Lavinia, 148n64
Turner, Gilbert, 45

Turner, Henry, 53
Turner, Henry M., 77–78
Turner, Johnnie Roger, 100
Turner, Robert, 148n63
Turner, William A., 53, 149n79
Tuskegee Institute, 102
typhoid outbreaks, 105

uneducated preachers, 3, 22, 24, 25–26
Universal Military Service Act (1903), 58,
    61

Vardaman, James K., 62–63, 151n35
Vineland Camp Meeting Association, 8
Virginia Union University, 150n10
voting rights, 23

Wacker, Grant, 4
WADO (radio station), 125
Wailoo, Keith, 100
Wale, Dicy, 148n64
Walker, J. J., 107–8
Wall, W. J., 116
war bonds, 55–57, 65, 69–70, 74
War Department, 59, 61
Ward, Luke, 118
War Production Board (WPB), 109–10
Warren, Eliza, 148n64
Warren, Mary, 148n64
Warren, Ruben, 148n64
Warrenton, North Carolina, 150n10
Washington, Arthur, 148n64
Washington Bee, 57
Washington, Booker T., 14, 55, 102
Washington, Denzel, 137
Washington, Indiana, 148n64
Washington, John, 148n64
Washington, Lula McCollough, 27, 45,
    145n77, 148n63
Washington, Maud, 45, 148n63
Washington, Minor, 145n77
Weaver, Elton, 5–6, 39
Webb, Easter, 148n64
Webster, Dorothy, 90, 92
Welch, William, 40
Wells, Ida B., 22–23, 43, 99
West Angeles Church of God in Christ,

Calvin White Jr. is assistant professor of history and director of the African and African American Studies Program at the University of Arkansas. He teaches African American and southern history.